A Guide to the EASA IR Flight Test

Jonathan Shooter

Nothing in this manual supersedes any EU legislation, rules or EASA regulations or procedures and any operational documents issued by The Stationery Office, the Civil Aviation Authority, National Aviation Authorities, the manufacturers of aircraft, engines and systems, or by the operators of aircraft throughout the world. Note that as maps and charts are changed regularly, those extracts reproduced in this book must not be used for flight planning or flight operations.

Jeppesen charts and Aerad charts in this book have been reproduced with permission and are copyrighted by Jeppesen & Co GmbH and Thales Avionics.

Copyright © 2017 Pooleys Flight Equipment Limited
ISBN 978-1-184336-190-9

First edition published September 2012
Second edition December 2017

All rights reserved. No part of this book may be reproduced or transmitted in any form by any means, electronic or mechanical, including photocopying, recording or by any information storage and retrieval system, without permission from the publisher in writing.

Published by:

Pooleys Flight Equipment Ltd
Elstree Aerodrome
Elstree, Hertfordshire
United Kingdom WD6 3AW

Tel: **+44(0)20 8953 4870**
Web: **www.pooleys.com**
Email: **sales@pooleys.com**

FOREWARD

Jonathan Shooter

Jonathan had his first trial lesson on his twelfth birthday before going on to gain his PPL with the help of an RAF flying scholarship. He went on to fly with the University Air Squadron before gaining airline sponsorship in conjunction with one of Europe's largest flying schools. He taught the PPL and associated ratings at Elstree aerodrome before gaining an internal promotion to teach the CPL and Instrument Rating at the commercial college at Cranfield aerodrome. In 2004 he was awarded a flying bursary from The Air League. After two years he joined his sponsoring airline and flew the Dash 8 Q400 throughout Europe. In 2005 he joined Europe's largest tour operator and flew the Boeing 757, 767, A320 & A321 both on short and long haul operations. He currently flies the 737NG and has over 7000 hrs with 1500 hrs instructional experience on commercial courses. He holds European, Canadian and American airline transport licences and is an authorised PPL and Class Rating Examiner for numerous piston and turbine aeroplanes. Jonathan is also the Chief Flying Instructor at Oysterair who specialize in training pilots in high performance aeroplanes such as the TBM 700-930, PC12, PA46 and the Cessna Caravan.

Daljeet Gill

Daljeet is Head of Design & Development for Pooleys Flight Equipment and editor of the Air Pilot's Manuals, Pre-flight Briefing series, R/T Communications and Air Presentations titles as well as many others. Daljeet has been involved with the editing, typesetting and designing of all Pooleys publications and products since she joined us in 2001. Graduating in 1999 with a BA(Hons) in Graphic Design, she deals with marketing, advertising & design of our products. She maintains our website and produces our Pooleys Catalogue. Daljeet's design skills and imaginative approach have brought a new level of clarity and readability to the projects she has touched.

Acknowledgments

My thanks go to everyone at Pooleys who has worked on the production of this book. Particular thanks go to Sebastian Pooley, Dorothy Pooley and Daljeet Gill, for their valuable input and support. My gratitude also goes to Capt. John Dale, Head of Training at JD Aviation and a CAA initial Instrument Rating Examiner for his technical input. Finally, thank you to Joanne Shooter for her assistance with proof reading.

A GUIDE TO THE EASA IR FLIGHT TEST

Contents

Chapter 1 Preparation 1 - 8
- Pre-course revision 1
- Choosing an Approved Training Organisation (ATO) 2
- Pre-course experience 3
- Course structure 4
- Aircraft 5
- IRT skill test profile & Examiner briefing 6

Chapter 2 Departure 9 - 56
- **a)** Use of Flight Manual (or equivalent) 9
- **b)** Air Traffic Services documents and weather document 11
- **c)** Preparation of ATC flight plan and IFR flight log 12
- **d)** Pre-flight Inspection 20
- **e)** Weather Minima 26
- **f)** Taxying 31
- **g)** Pre take-off briefing 36
- **h)** Transition to instrument flight 39
- **i)** Instrument departure procedure 40

Chapter 3 En-Route 47 - 62
- **a)** Tracking 47
- **b)** Use of radio aids 51
- **c)** Level flight control 53
- **d)** Altimeter settings 54
- **e)** Timings and ETAs 56
- **f)** Monitoring flight progress 57
- **g)** Ice protection procedures 59
- **h)** ATC Liaison 61

Chapter 4	3D Approach	63 - 92
a)	Navigation Aids	63
b)	Arrival procedures	64
c)	Approach and Landing briefing	71
d)	Holding Procedure	74
e)	Published Approach procedure	74
f)	Approach timing	77
g)	Control of the Aeroplane	77
h)	Go-around	78
i)	Missed approach procedure/landing	80
j)	ATC liaison	81

Chapter 5	General Handling	83 - 114
a & b) Full Panel		83
c & d) Full Panel Recoveries		84
e) Limited Panel including recoveries from unusual attitudes		91

Chapter 6	2D Approach	115 - 152
a)	Navigation Aids	115
b)	Arrival Procedures, descent planning and considerations of MSA	118
c)	Approach and Landing briefing	119
d)	Holding procedure	124
e)	Published approach procedure	136
f)	Approach timing	142
g)	Control of the Aeroplane	143
h)	Go-around	146
i)	Missed approach procedure/landing	146
j)	ATC liaison	146

Chapter 7	Simulated Asymmetric Flight	153 - 162
a)	Engine Failure After Take-Off	153
b)	Asymmetric approach and procedural go-around	154
c)	Asymmetric approach and full stop landing	155
d)	ATC Liaison	156

Chapter 8	Oral Questioning		163 - 168
	- Altimetry		163
	- Flight Planning		164
	- RTF		165
	- Airfield Operating Minima		166
	- Icing		166
	- Test tolerances		167
Answers	To Oral Questioning		169 - 172
Appendix 1	Typical test routes		173
Appendix 2	Airfield contact details & ATIS telephone numbers		177
Appendix 3	Calculation of Aerodrome Operating Minima		179
Appendix 4	Test day checklist		181
Appendix 5	To Part-FCL IR Skill test		183
Appendix 6	Common errors and omissions		187
Appendix 7	Skill test tolerances		189
Appendix 8	Power & Attitude settings table		191
Abbreviations			193 - 200
Index			201 - 203

intentionally blank

CHAPTER ONE

Preparation

The Instrument Rating (IR) course and test is regarded as the one of the hardest parts of a pilot's career. In reality, it is just like any other flying course with a skill test at the end. Many myths have built up over the years regarding the course and the skill test, which are untrue. It is fair to say that it is very demanding, and many pilots believe that once they have gained an IR, the required standard in any subsequent renewal is less than for the initial test; sadly this is not the case.

Most candidates will be aiming to pursue careers as commercial pilots; consequently the IR course aims to lay down solid instrument flying skills which can be built upon as more experienced is gained. A commercial pilot operating for a company which holds an Air Operator's Certificate (AOC), can expect to demonstrate their instrument flying knowledge and skill every six months to a Class Rating Examiner (CRE), or Type Rating Examiner (TRE), who will demand the exact same standards as demonstrated in the initial Instrument Rating Test (IRT).

Be prepared to work hard and expect to have to revise topics for double the amount of time spent in the air. The course, although demanding, is very rewarding with a real sense of achievement when you pass the skill test. The examiner understands the pressure you are under, as they have been in the same position and will put you at ease.

Pre-Course Revision

Before starting the course revise the following topics pertinent to IFR operations:-

- Air Law & Operational Procedures
- Aircraft General Knowledge
- Flight Performance & Planning
- Human Performance & Limitations
- Meteorology
- Radio Navigation
- IFR Communications & Radio Failure Procedures
- Aircraft Flight Manual Procedures & Limitations
- National Procedures (found in the AIP) & ICAO differences

Choosing an Approved Training Organisation (ATO)

All Approved Training Organisations (ATOs) training candidates for the EASA IR have to be approved and inspected annually. The instructors all have to have a minimum of an EASA PPL/CPL, IR, FI, with the no applied instrument restriction removed and 200 hours of instruction, as well as regular standardisation flights. To be able to teach candidates for the multi-engine phase of the IR course the instructor must have the MEP CRI qualification. The CAA publishes Document 31 on their website which lists all approved schools together with their contact details. Candidates training for the Competency Based IR do not have to complete the full course at an ATO, a proportion can be completed with a suitably qualified freelance instructor operating outside of an ATO. Whilst this provides greater convenience it is imperative that the instructor is qualified to teach applied instrument flying and is up to date with the IR course.

The ATOs have to be inspected annually by the CAA; consequently the standards tend to be high at most schools. However, it is crucial that you feel comfortable with your chosen ATO-when deciding upon a school always consider the following:-

- ATO facilities - building, location, internet access, café facilities
- ATO approvals - review approvals
- Manuals and instrument chart providers - included in course price, EU-OPS compliant
- Aircraft - type, glass cockpit, analogue or combination, age, availability
- Instructors - qualifications, experience, turn over, instructor/student ratio, availability
- Reputation - speak to past and current students, internet search, and ownership
- Course structure - simulator/flying ratio
- Training location - commuting time, type of surrounding airspace, approach aids
- Nearest IRT examiner - do you need to ferry the aircraft to the test location? Number of examiners in the area
- Previous and current students - pass rate, airline contacts, and employment statistics
- Maintenance - where and who keeps the aircraft records?
- Personal compatibility
- Additional costs – exactly what is included in the course price?

Before starting any flying course at a training organisation NEVER pay up front for your training; a reputable school will simply ask that you keep your account in credit or pay a small deposit to secure your place on the course.

CAA Document 31

Organisations conducting CAA and EASA Part-FCL Approved Courses of Flight & Ground Training.

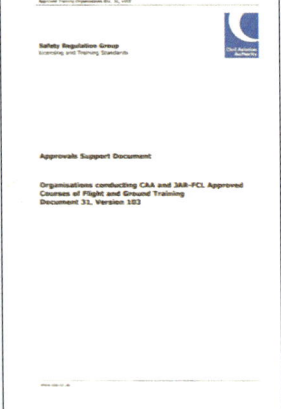

Pre-Course Experience

The pre-course entry requirements are for a modular IR(A) are as follows:

EASA PPL(A) or CPL(A)
EASA Class 1 or 2 medical with audiogram
EASA Night Rating (if IFR privileges are required to be exercised at night)
> 50 hours P1 cross country flight time
Valid class or type rating
ATPL or IR TK exams passed

For candidates wishing to convert an ICAO IR (e.g. FAA IR) the following pre-course entry requirements are required:

EASA PPL(A) or CPL(A)
EASA class 1 or 2 medical with audiogram
EASA Night Rating (if IFR privileges are required to be exercised at night)
Valid ICAO licence & IR(A)
EASA class or type rating
> 50 hours P1 IFR

Applicability

The holder of an EASA IR(A) may exercise the privileges of the rating to fly EASA aeroplanes registered in the EU and non-EASA aeroplanes registered in the UK, that come within the privileges of the licence and the valid ratings included in the licence.

Privileges
FCL.605 IR – Privileges

(a) The privileges of a holder of an IR are to fly aeroplanes under IFR with a minimum decision height of 200 feet (60 m).

(b) In the case of a multi-engine IR, these privileges may be extended to decision heights lower than 200 feet (60 m) when the applicant has undergone specific training at an ATO and has passed section 6 of the skill test prescribed in Appendix 9 to this Part in multi-pilot aeroplanes.

(c) Holders of an IR shall exercise their privileges in accordance with the conditions established in Appendix 8 to Part-FCL.

Course Structure

Extracts from the various applicable appendices to Part-FCL, which describe the IR course requirements and syllabus for fixed-wing aeroplanes are in the appendix section of this book. For the full text and latest copy please refer to CAP 804, found on the UK CAA website.

Validity
FCL.625 IR(A) – Validity, revalidation and renewal:-

(a) Validity. An IR(A) shall be valid for 1 year.

(b) Revalidation:-
  (1) An IR(A) shall be revalidated within the 3 months immediately preceding the expiry date of the rating.
  (2) Applicants who fail to pass the relevant section of an IR(A) proficiency check before the expiry date of the IR(A) shall not exercise the IR(A) privileges until they have passed the proficiency check.

(c) Renewal. If an IR(A) has expired, in order to renew their privileges applicants shall:-
  (1) go through refresher training at an ATO to reach the level of proficiency needed to pass the instrument element of the skill test in accordance with Appendix 9 to Part-FCL; and
  (2) complete a proficiency check in accordance with Appendix 9 to Part-FCL, in an aeroplane.

(d) If the IR(A) has not been revalidated or renewed within the preceding 7 years, the holder will be required to pass again the IR theoretical knowledge examination and skill test.

FCL.625.A IR (A) – Revalidation

(a) Revalidation. Applicants for the revalidation of an IR(A):-
  (1) when combined with the revalidation of a class or type rating, shall pass a proficiency check in accordance with Appendix 9 to Part-FCL;
  (2) when not combined with the revalidation of a class or type rating, shall:-
    (i) for single-pilot aeroplanes, complete section 3b and those parts of section 1 relevant to the intended flight, of the proficiency check prescribed in Appendix 9 to Part-FCL; and
    (ii) for multi-engine aeroplanes, complete section 6 of the proficiency check for single-pilot aeroplanes in accordance with Appendix 9 to Part-FCL by sole reference to instruments.
  (3) An FNPT II or an FFS representing the relevant class or type of aeroplane may be used in the case of paragraph (2), but at least each alternate proficiency check for the revalidation of an IR(A) in these circumstances shall be performed in an aeroplane.
(b) Cross-credit shall be given in accordance with Appendix 8 to Part-FCL.

Aircraft

The type of aircraft used on the skill test will determine the type of instrument rating issued. As the majority of applicants will be aiming to go into professional flying careers and this will be their first IRT, a typical test would be conducted in a MEP aircraft such as a DA42, PA34 or BE76. A PPL holder may wish to attempt the test in a SEP aircraft such as a Cirrus SR22. However, the IR would be restricted to SEP aircraft only. EASA Part-FCL states:-

FCL.620 IR(A) – Skill Test

(a) Applicants for an IR(A) shall pass a skill test in accordance with Appendix 7 to Part-FCL to demonstrate the ability to perform the relevant procedures and manoeuvres with a degree of competency appropriate to the privileges granted.
(b) For a multi-engine IR(A), the skill test shall be taken in a multi-engine aeroplane. For a single-engine IR, the test shall be taken in a single-engine aeroplane. A multi-engine centerline thrust aeroplane shall be considered a single-engine aeroplane for the purposes of this paragraph.

PA34 a typical aircraft
Used on the IR Course

DA42
One of the latest generation of MEP training aircraft

SR22
A high performance SEP aircraft

The EASA requirements for training aeroplanes are detailed at EASA AMC1-OR.ATO.135 Training aircraft and FSTDs. Essentially, the training organisation responsible for the training of the applicant must make sure that the aircraft used for the test meets the requisite specification and is appropriately equipped. More information regarding whether an aircraft is suitable to be used for an IRT can be found in Standards Document 7, found on the CAA website. It is possible for private owners to complete training and test in their own aeroplane, providing it is IFR certified and other airworthiness/insurance requirements are met.

IRT Skill Test Profile & Examiner Briefing

The examiner will meet you at an agreed time and give you a comprehensive brief on the test profile. Standards Document 1 covers this in detail. Ensure that you arrive on time, if not a few minutes early, first impressions count. The IR is a professional rating and you should dress accordingly.

The examiner briefing will usually be split into three parts consisting of the following:-

Initial briefing

- Meet & Greet
- Type of test, experience level, training provider
- Forms
- Proof of payment, relevant CAA correspondence
- Licence, R/T licence, medical check
- Aircraft documents, technical Log
- Confirmation of fuel/oil state
- Test aims
- Operating procedures
- Responsibilities
- Simulated weather conditions
- Outline of flight (including location to carry out section 2)
- Use of on board equipment

1 - PREPARATION

Route briefing

- Approach plates
- Departure
- Radar Vectored approach flown to minima at ___ go-around
- EFATO during go-around, expeditious IFR pre-planned diversion to single needle tracking to facility
- Single engine hold entry and procedural approach (different from the initial approach)
- Single engine go-around
- Visual circling approach to land
- Time check, performance planning data, call sign Exam, 45 to 60 minutes planning time

Pre-flight briefing (after the planning has been completed)

- Planning review
- Speeds
- Aerodrome Operating Minima (AOM)
- Tolerances
- ATC liaison
- Error management
- Handling of Emergencies

NOTE: *Either the 3D or 2D approach can be performed under simulated asymmetric conditions, which one will depend on navigational aid availability; the examiner will inform you in the brief which type to expect.*

The test is made up of 6 sections. Sections 1-5 are common to all IRTs, while section 6 is to assess asymmetric flight which is applicable to multi-engine aircraft. Each section is then subdivided to allow the examiner to assess you accurately.

1 - PREPARATION

Air Pilot's Manual
Volume 5, Radio Navigation & Instrument Flying contains a detailed description of IF techniques

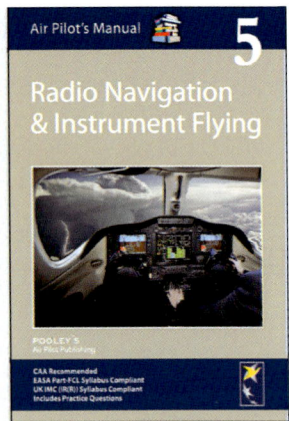

This book follows the test profile, with each chapter broken down into each subsection as reflected on the skill test report form. The examiner may not complete the sections in numerical order, this is done to allow the test to progress more efficiently and this book is written to follow that format.

Additional benefit can be gained by reading Air Pilot's Manual, Volume 5, 'Radio Navigation and Instrument Flying' which has a detailed description of instrument flying and procedures.

This book aims to give a comprehensive description of the test profile and what to expect along with some useful tips to ensure success.

Standards Document 1
Should be thoroughly read before attempting the IRT

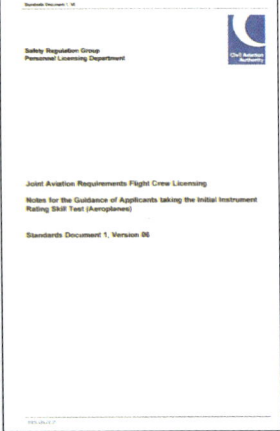

CHAPTER TWO

Departure

A) USE OF FLIGHT MANUAL (OR EQUIVALENT)

The authoritative documents during your IR course and test are your individual ATO's Operations and Training manuals.

Approved Training Organisation required manuals:-

The IRT is merely simulating a public transport flight, therefore, the ATO is not required to hold an AOC and consequently produce the manuals required under EASA OPS. They are required, however, as ATOs to have the following manuals:-

- **Operations Manual**
- **Training Manual**
- **Management Manual**

These follow a similar format to AOC manuals and are essential reading when training candidates for commercial licences and ratings. These are the point of reference for information and instructions on the course and test so make sure that you read them thoroughly as the examiner may ask questions on them. Candidates converting an ICAO IR operating outside of an ATO have to as a minimum, operate to the rules and procedures laid out under Part-NCO.

Operations Manual

Will provide relevant information to particular groups of staff and comprises of the following parts:-

- Part A General
- Part B Technical
- Part C Route
- Part D Staff Training

Training Manual

The Training Manual for each course will state the aim, requirements, training goals and standards for each course, comprising the following parts:-

- Part 1 The Training Plan
- Part 2 Briefing and Air exercises
- Part 3 Synthetic Flight Training
- Part 4 Theoretical Knowledge Instruction

The examiner does not expect you to be able to answer all of his questions from memory. He wants to see that you know where to look in the various manuals for the answers and operating procedures. For the purposes of the test here is a brief review of where to find the information required for the test:-

OPERATIONS MANUAL - Planning and weather minima, IFR, rules of the air, currency and qualifications requirements, required documents, staff details, flight time duty limitations, fuel, performance, mass and balance planning requirements, abnormal weather operations.

AIRCRAFT FLIGHT MANUAL (AFM) - System descriptions, normal and abnormal operating procedures, mass and balance tables and performance charts, checklists, approved flight conditions, abnormal weather procedures, limitations.

TRAINING MANUAL - Training profiles and expanded briefings.

TECHNICAL LOG - Hours left before next check, deferred defects, record of de-icing, previous flight history, valid CRS.

MEL - Allowed defects, operating restrictions and allowable deferred period.

The examiner expects to see performance calculations for departure, destination and any alternates together with a completed mass and balance calculation or load sheet. Please refer to Pooley's 'A Guide to the EASA CPL Flight Test' for more information.

B) **AIR TRAFFIC** SERVICES DOCUMENT AND WEATHER DOCUMENT

Before the briefing collate all the required weather, NOTAMs, NANUs, maps, charts and approach plates. Do not wait until the planning phase. Compiling these in a folder or binder can help. Here are some of the typical required items:-

- **1:500,000 VFR chart** - it is good airmanship to draw the route on the chart, as it helps with situational awareness.

- **En-route airway charts** - valid and applicable to the route of flight. It is acceptable to take a photocopy of the chart and highlight the route on it, to help when you are planning the flight.

- **Airfield instrument approach plates** - collate all taxi, departure, arrival, and approach plates for the departure, destination, en-route and alternate aerodromes. Do not forget to make sure that they are in date, and include the notes at the start of the plates on LVP and radio failure procedures.

- **Blank flight log** - pre-prepared ones are not allowed. Computer derived navigation/flight logs are allowed during the planning period.

- **Blank flight plan** - most flight plans are filed online, however, carry a blank form just in case.

- **Weather documents** - collate and study the weather. You will be expected to give a weather brief. Bring the AIRMET, F214 and F215, together with the TAF/METAR for all possible destinations and alternates. Make sure that the forecasts are valid for a period ± 1 hr of your ETD and ETA at the departure, en-route, destination and destination alternate aerodromes. Note the freezing level.

- **NOTAMs/TRAs** - Make sure that you are aware of any pertinent NOTAMs and make a note of any airspace upgrades or changes. Examiners often comment that this is overlooked.

Instrument Plates

Jeppesen Airway Manual

When collating the instrument plates make sure that you get all of them for each aerodrome, not just the ones you think you will fly based on the prevailing wind or expected routing. If you are using electronic charts ensure that the database is current and has appropriate chart coverage. Also, make sure that the device has sufficient battery power for the flight!

*Make sure you collate **all** of the plates for all the possible instrument approaches*

Pre-prepared flight logs or specially drawn routes shall not be used during the IRT. Only routinely available planning information and documents shall be used. Computer derived flight/navigation plans or aeroplane mass and balance calculations may be used during the allowed planning period. You are responsible for what is produced so make sure that you enter all the information correctly.

C) **PREPARATION** OF ATC FLIGHT PLAN AND IFR FLIGHT LOG

Obtains and assesses all elements of the prevailing and forecast weather conditions for the route.

At this point after collating the weather, you should assess the conditions and make sure that they meet the requirements in the Operations Manual. These cannot be any less restrictive than ATO planning minima. You must then decide whether to attempt the skill test. Typical required test conditions for the examiner to make a fair assessment are:-

- *Visibility*-not less than minimum approach RVR + 200 m
- *Cloud base*-DA/MDA + 100 ft at the final destination
- *Wind*-Max 30 kts, 75% of the aeroplane crosswind limit, maximum 10 kts tailwind component on approach and final landing (all including gusts)

The examiner may override your decision in the interests of making a fair assessment.

2 - DEPARTURE

Complete an appropriate flight navigation log.

A Pilots Log or PLOG must be prepared and the examiner will require a copy; commercially these are kept after the flight for quality audits and if an incident occurred. The PLOG is used to aid navigation and fuel monitoring during the flight so it needs to be updated and kept relatively neat. Post-flight the flight log should reflect what happened in the air as the examiner may use it for debrief or assessment purposes. Your ATO should provide blank ones or use a flight planning tool. If you are going to use an electronic derived plan you are responsible for the information. Sometimes the 'whiz wheel' is the better option! The navigation log should include items such as:-

- ATC call sign and aircraft registration
- Captain's name
- Date of flight
- Space for recording off-block, departure, landing and on-block times
- Route-both for destination and alternate
- ATC flight plan information (or a copy of the filed flight plan)
- Level/Altitude for destination and alternate
- Timings, ETA and ATA
- MSA, MORA, MOCA
- Fuel Plan
- Clearances
- Space for recording weather, expected approach times, and notes

MFA FL	AIRWAY WAYPNT	LAT LONG	WIND TEMP	GS SR	TRM TRT	DST ZT	ETA	TIMES RETA	ATO	DTG TET	FOB MFRQ
	EGKK	N51089 W000114								4774 0958	56230 54790
024 250	DEP DVR EBUR	N51098 E001215	35050 M041	306 02	090 088	0059 012	.....	.....	.....	4715 0012	----
023 298	UL9 KONAN	N51079 E002000	00059 M051	433 03	096 095	0024 003	.....	.....	.....	4691 0015	----
023 330	UL607 TOC		35045 M054	455 04	096 095	0019 002	.....	.....	.....	4672 0017	----
023 330	UL607 KOK	N51057 E002391	35045 M054	461 04	096 095	0006 001	.....	.....	.....	4666 0018	52680 51240
028 330	UL607 FERDI	N50548 E003382	35039 M053	470 03	107 106	0039 005	.....	.....	.....	4627 0023	52230 50790

Electronic Operational Flight Plan

(c) PREPARATION OF ATC FLIGHT PLAN & IFR FLIGHT LOG

Complete the required ATC flight plan(s).

An ATC flight plan is required for all IFR flights. It is usually filed electronically; however, you can still complete and fax your flight plan to ATC who will file it for you. Your ATO should have an AFPEx account which is an internet based flight planning system designed for filing flight plans through the Aeronautical Fixed Telecommunication Network (AFTN). The AFPEx website is www.flightplanningonline.co.uk. A training website is also available for help on filing ATC flight plans found at www.myafpex.co.uk. CAA publication CAP 694 also has a detailed explanation of ATC flight planning.

When you file the flight plan electronically addressing of the plan to the various ATSUs is done automatically, whereas, if you write one manually you will have to ensure that you have addressed it correctly, which is time consuming especially when planning everything else! Here is a brief explanation of what is required in each item:-

Addressees = AFPex will automatically address an IFR flight plan to the 2 IFPS addresses. It will ensure that the FPL is distributed to all ATSUs along the route within the IFPS zone.

Item 7 = Aircraft call sign; each IRE will have their own call sign starting with the prefix EXM.

Item 8 = Flight Rules. Enter I for IFR.

Type of flight = Enter X for other, or G for General.

Item 9 = Number of aircraft only needs to be completed if flying in formation.

Type of Aircraft = Listed in ICAO DOC 8643. A Piper Seneca is entered as PA34.

Wake turbulence = Enter the wake vortex category.

Item 10 = Split into two parts. The first box refers to the radio communication, navigation and approach equipment, enter S for standard. The second box refers to the type of transponder carried. Mode S is now mandatory for flights in controlled airspace, enter S.

Item 13 = Enter departure airfield in ICAO format e.g. EGHH.

Time = Enter the Estimated Off Blocks Time in UTC with four digits e.g.1030.

Item 15 = Enter the cruising speed (TAS) for knots use N e.g. N0160.

Altitude/Level = Enter the planned cruising level for the first or whole of the flight. For Flight Level use F followed by 3 figures e.g. F060. For Altitude which is written in hundreds of feet use A followed by 3 figures e.g. A050 for 5 000 ft.

Routing = Enter the route of the flight. For a flight along the airways enter the first waypoint on the airway, followed by the coded designator and the exit waypoint, e.g. THRED Q41 ORTAC DCT; DCT is used to indicate the next point outside a designated route. For a flight outside the ATS route network waypoints can be defined by Latitude and Longitude and bearing/distance from a navigation aid. Refer to CAP 694 for a more detailed explanation as it is a complex topic.

Item 16 = Enter the destination airfield. This means the airfield you will actually land at, not the one that you may go to complete instrument approaches at, e.g. for a flight from Bournemouth to Alderney, complete an approach; followed by a return to Bournemouth, the destination entered is Bournemouth.

Total EET = Enter the Estimated Elapsed Time to the destination using four figures e.g. 0130.

Alternate = Enter the alternate airfield in ICAO format; use the second box if two alternates are required.

Item 18 = Add information pertinent to the flight. For IFR flights, it is useful to add RMK/IFPS REROUTE ACCEPTED this means that if the flight plan route is rejected an IFPS operator will make changes to the route so that it is accepted. However, if you do this you must check the route on the acknowledgement message, as there will be no other indication that your route has been changed. Some schools enter training requirements in this section, but this information is not printed out on the strip that the air traffic controller receives. Other items that can be included are:-

DOF/YYMMDD = Date of flight if filing more than 24 hours in advance.
REG/ = Aircraft registration. This must be included if EXM call sign used.
OPR/ = Aircraft operator if not clearly visible.

RMK/ = Remarks. Enter CAA IRT if X entered under Type of Flight.

EET/ = Estimated Elapsed Time. State the EET for FIR boundaries along the route.

Item 19 = Endurance as four figures e.g. 0400.

Person on Board = Enter the POB as three figures e.g. 002.

Emergency Radio = Indicate the equipment you DO NOT have.

Survival Equipment = Indicate the survival equipment you DO NOT have. If you are carrying lifejackets you must also have at least one of the following functions on them, Lights, Fluorescein, UHF or VHF radio. If not, then enter JACKETS CARRIED in item 19 Remark filed (Not in item 18).

Dinghies = Enter if any dinghies are carried, if none, cross the D.

Colour and Markings = Enter the aircraft colour and markings.

Remark = Enter any relevant information regarding survival information such as 'JACKETS CARRIED'. If using the AFPex online form you can enter a mobile phone number, this is also useful in the event of a radio failure as ATC will try to make contact with you. ON a CA48 form this information can added here, or on the bottom of the form. Be aware, this is not the same field as item 18, so do not enter information such as date of flight here, as it will not be received.

Pilot-in-command = Enter the name of the Pilot in command. For the IRT this is the examiner's name.

AFPex Online Flight Plan

Screenshot

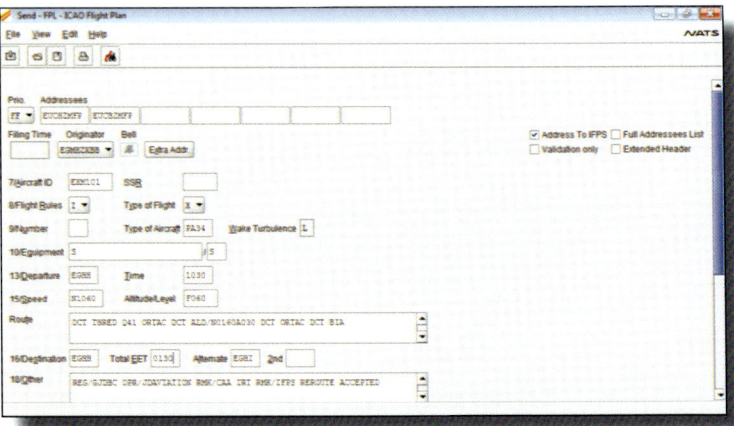

(c) PREPARATION OF ATC FLIGHT PLAN & IFR FLIGHT LOG

2 - DEPARTURE

CA48 ATC Flight Plan

```
3 MESSAGE TYPE          7 AIRCRAFT IDENTIFICATION    8 FLIGHT RULES   TYPE OF FLIGHT
<<≡ (FPL          - E X M 1 0 1                - I              X        <<≡
9 NUMBER          TYPE OF AIRCRAFT    WAKE TURBULENCE CAT    10 EQUIPMENT
-                    P A 3 4              / L             - S   / S        <<≡
13 DEPARTURE AERODROME          TIME
- E G H H                  1 0 3 0  <<≡
15 CRUISING SPEED    LEVEL       ROUTE
- N 0 1 6 0   F 0 6 0   →  DCT THRED Q41 ORTAC DCT ALD/N0160A030
DCT ORTAC DCT BIA
                                                                        <<≡
                         TOTAL EET
16 DESTINATION AERODROME  HR MIN       ALTN AERODROME   2ND ALTN AERODROME
- E G H H              0 1 3 0       → E G H I         →              <<≡
18 OTHER INFORMATION
RMK/IFPS REROUTE ACCEPTED
OPR/JD AVIATION
REG/GJDBC
RMK/CAA IRT                                                      ) <<≡
             SUPPLEMENTARY INFORMATION (NOT TO BE TRANSMITTED IN FPL MESSAGES)
19 ENDURANCE                                              EMERGENCY RADIO
    HR MIN        PERSONS ON BOARD            UHF     VHF       ELT
- E/ 0 4 0 0   → P/ 0 0 2              → R/ X    X         E
SURVIVAL
EQUIPMENT  POLAR  DESERT  MARITIME  JUNGLE   JACKETS   LIGHT   FLUORES  UHF  VHF
→ S    / X      X        M        X     → J    / L      X      X    X
DINGHIES
      NUMBER   CAPACITY   COVER          COLOUR
→ D / 0 1 → 0 0 4 → C →  ORANGE              <<≡
AIRCRAFT COLOUR AND MARKINGS
A /  WHITE WITH RED AND BLUE STRIPES
    REMARKS
→ X /                                                            <<≡
    PILOT IN COMMAND
C /  J.EXAMINER                     ) <<≡
         FILED BY       SPACE RESERVED FOR ADDITIONAL REQUIREMENTS
           Please provide a telephone number so our operators can contact you if needed
           OPERATIONS +441234 123456
```

The flight plan should be filed 60 minutes before the Estimated Off Blocks Time, (EOBT). The examiner will notify you of the destination and give you approximately one hour to plan the route, so this needs to be your first priority. The examiner will want to see a copy of the flight plan. Always make sure that you get an acknowledgment message when you have sent the flight plan. You do not want to call ATC for engine start and find that they have no flight plan. It is always worth ringing ATC to check that they have it in the system.

(c) PREPARATION OF ATC FLIGHT PLAN & IFR FLIGHT LOG

A Typical ATC Flight Plan

For a commercial flight-a little longer than the IRT!

```
(FPL-TOM063-IS
-B763/H-SXEIHRWYZ/S
-EGKK1830
-N0454F330 DVR UL9 KONAN UL607 AMASI UM149 DETEV UL603 OBEDI
 UN739 NEPOS UM19 ETIDA/K0845F330 UM19 ADORU/N0457F330 UL606
 EKI/N0455F350 UL606 KFK UL620 VESAR UB15 BALMA/N0456F350 J222
 BASEM R785 ZELAF UR785 TRF UP559 TOKLU/N0452F370 UP559 KEDAT
 R219 KUSAR UN318 LOXAT B457 TOLDA P570 KITAL R456 LELEM
-VRMM0958 VOTV
-REG/GDBLA SEL/MPHQ DOF/081112 EET/EBUR0015 EDVV0037 EDUU0038
 LOVV0117 LHCC0137 LYBA0153 LBSR0219 LTBB0245 LTAA0313 LCCC0346
 OLBB0358 OSTT0407 OJAC0420 OEJD0429 OBBB0520 OMAE0604 OOMM0624
 VABF0707 VRMF0914 RALT/OMAL VRMM RMK/CALLSIGN TOMSON OPR/TOM
 RVR/75 NAV/RNP10 RMK/TCAS EQUIPPED RMK/ID TOM063 RMK/RTE 43
 RMK/SEQ10003)
-E/1146 P/TBN R/VE S/M J/L D/8 384 SILVER/YELLOW
```

Determine that the aeroplane is correctly fuelled, loaded and legal for the flight

The Operations Manual will have more information on this topic. Below is a simple breakdown of what is needed:

Fuel Required = Taxi fuel + Trip + Contingency (5% of trip) + Diversion to alternate + Final Reserve Fuel (45 minutes holding in a piston engine) + Extra Fuel as required

Make sure that you add extra fuel to take into account the General Handling section of the test. This will last approximately 30 minutes.

Always check the fuel quantity visually and if possible, dip the fuel tanks to confirm the amount is correct.

Confirm any aeroplane performance criteria and limitations applicable

The aeroplane take-off and landing performance has to be calculated for the departure, destination, and any alternate aerodromes taking into account the expected weather and surface conditions for the expected time of landing.

Make sure that you have read any applicable NOTAMs that may affect runway length available. EASA regulations and the ANO specify the rules regarding performance in class B aeroplanes. Here is a brief reminder:-

2 - DEPARTURE

- If there is no Stopway/Clearway then runway length must be TODR × 1.25 (gross TODR)
- If there is a Stopway/Clearway then runway length must be at least the TODR. TODA must be at least TODR ×1.15, and ASDA must be at least TODR ×1.3

With regard to landing performance:-

For all arrival airports, planned landing performance must be checked based on:-
A.   Using the most favourable runway in still air; and
B.   Landing on the runway most likely to be assigned considering the probable windspeed and direction and the ground handling characteristics of the aeroplane and considering other conditions such as landing aids, terrain, and weather.

When calculating the landing distance make sure that from 50 ft above the threshold, you can make a full stop landing within 70% of LDA at the destination and alternate aerodrome.

Remember to factor in the type of surface and the runway state - the CAA publishes Safety Sense Leaflet 7 regarding aeroplane performance which is very useful. You will also have information in the Operations Manual regarding aeroplane performance factors.

Demonstrates sufficient knowledge of the regulatory requirements relating to instrument flight

In the UK the ANO is the authoritative document regarding Instrument Flight Rules. You must know these rules and are likely to get asked questions on them. Your ATO's Operations Manual will also contain information regarding IFR flight.

(c) PREPARATION OF ATC FLIGHT PLAN & IFR FLIGHT LOG

D) PRE-FLIGHT INSPECTION

Perform all elements of the aeroplane pre-flight inspections as detailed and applicable to the actual or simulated weather conditions

The aircraft is to be treated as if it is the first flight of the day and sub zero temperatures exist. It might be difficult to imagine freezing temperatures on a hot summer's day; however, the examiner needs to assess your knowledge of preparing an aircraft for a flight into known icing conditions.

Before you even start the IR course, make sure that you have read the Operations Manual regarding flight in abnormal weather. Read the AFM for any related procedures or configurations for flight in icing conditions. The aircraft may not be approved for flight into known icing conditions and may not have any anti-icing or de-icing equipment. This does not necessarily mean that you can't attempt the test as it maybe a lovely clear autumnal day; however, you must understand what conditions you can legally and safely operate in.

Pre-flight the aircraft before meeting the examiner, ideally in a hangar. Delay getting the aircraft outside as it may preclude the need for de-icing. Most aircraft including airliners are left outside overnight, so if icing conditions do exist you will have to make sure that the aircraft is properly de-iced.

When performing the pre-flight inspection use a checklist, but work efficiently! Pay particular attention to the wing, tail and propeller surfaces as they must be free of any ice, frost or contamination; known as the clean aircraft concept. The inspection of the aircraft must cover the following components and be performed from points offering a clear view of each item:-•

- *Wing surfaces including leading edges*
- *Horizontal stabiliser upper and lower surface*
- *Vertical stabiliser and rudder*
- *Fuselage*
- *Air data probes*

Heavily contaminated wing

This is a heavily contaminated wing, the airframe must be completely clear of all deposits

2 - DEPARTURE

- Static vents
- Angle-of-attack sensors
- Control surface cavities
- Engines
- Intakes and outlets
- Landing gear and wheel bays
- Navigation and communication aerials

When you inspect the aircraft it is very important that you check the serviceability of the ice protection equipment fitted. Always consult the AFM on what to inspect and how the system works. If the aircraft employs a weeping wing ice protection system, during the walk-round, check that the gauze is clean. Debris can block the tiny holes which supply the fluid. Don't forget to check the windscreen de-ice system.

An often overlooked part of the pre-flight inspection is checking that sufficient de-icing fluid is on board. Carry enough of this for the flight including reserves. Include the weight of the fluid in the mass and balance calculation.

If your test aircraft is fitted with a pneumatic boot de-icing system, during the pre-flight inspection check that the rubber is not damaged, or ripped, as it will not properly inflate. If you are unsure, consult an engineer before proceeding with the flight. You may find rubber patches glued over the leading edge on older aircraft; this is where previous holes have been repaired-similar to a puncture repair kit for bicycles.

If you need to de-ice the aircraft on the ground, you are unlikely to have the luxury of a de-icing truck. These are used on larger aircraft and smaller airfields are not equipped with them. Most ATOs will use de-icing fluid, applied through a hand spray gun. The person doing the spraying is usually the candidate i.e. you! However, this will allow you to satisfy yourself that the aircraft is properly de-iced. Always take a note of the amount of fluid used, as well as the start and end time of the de-icing. This allows you to calculate the holdover time.

Check that the weeping gauze is clean

A de-icing truck
Used on larger aircraft

(d) PRE-FLIGHT INSPECTION

The holdover time is the estimated time for which de-icing or anti-icing fluid will prevent the formation of frost, ice or the accumulation of snow on protected surfaces of an aircraft, under certain weather conditions. Tables are produced to help you determine this, usually found in the Operations Manual. With a one step de-icing/anti-icing operation, the holdover time begins at the start of the operation, and with a two step operation at the start of the final (anti-icing) step. Holdover time will have effectively run out when frozen deposits start to form/accumulate on treated aircraft surfaces. Holdover tables should be published in the Operations Manual or flight guides e.g. Jeppesen.

This table below is not for operational use – it is given as an example of what a holdover table looks like

OAT		Approximate holdover times under various weather conditions (hours: minutes)						
°C	°F	Active Frost	Freezing Fog	Snow/ Snow Grains/ Snow Pellets (1)	Freezing Drizzle (2)	Light Freezing Rain	Rain on Cold Soaked Wing	Other (3)
-3 and above	27 and above	(5)	0:09 - 0:16	0:03 - 0:06	0:08 - 0:16	0:02 - 0:05	0:01 - 0:05 [4]	
below -3 to -6	below 27 to 21	(5)	0:06 - 0:08	0:02 - 0:05	0:05 - 0:09	0:02 - 0:05		
below -6 to -10	below 21 to 14	(5)	0:04 - 0:08	0:02 - 0:05	0:04 - 0:07	0:02 - 0:05		
below -10	below 14	(5)	0:04 - 0:07	0:02 - 0:04				

Icing is a very important and complex subject, which is beyond the scope of this book. Always follow the guidance in the Operations Manual, AFM, and any regulatory instructions.

Confirms that the aeroplane is in a serviceable and safe condition for flight

As well as checking the normal items associated with a pre-flight inspection, make sure that the aircraft and windscreens are clean and that sufficient fuel, oil and de-icing fluid (if applicable) are on board. Check that the instrument flight screens are in good working order and that you know how to fit them. Do not forget the limited panel screens! Also check that all safety and emergency equipment is in date and serviceable.

Checks and completes all necessary documentation

The required documents to be carried are listed in the Operations Manual. Further guidance is also in Pooley's 'A Guide to the EASA CPL Flight Test'.

Before the day of the test, check that the aircraft is serviceable and all the required equipment for IFR flight is in good working order. This may seem overly cautious, however, it allows defects to be fixed and ensures that the test can proceed.

On the day of the test, review the aircraft technical log. Specific items for the IRT are:-

- The last sector has been signed by the previous Captain post-flight
- Check any deferred defects against the MEL
- Any fuel or oil uplift is recorded
- Any de-icing is recorded along with the fluid type, amount and start time
- That you have signed the pre-flight section of the technical log

The examiner should complete the authorisation sheets, and will ultimately sign the technical log, as he is legally the commander of the aeroplane.

Make sure that you have with you the following for the briefing:-

- Identification
- Medical certificate
- Logbook
- Licence and evidence of a valid rating
- Course Completion Certificate (not required for candidates converting an ICAO IR)
- 2 compatible headsets
- 2 copies of the approved checklist
- Proof of payment for the test

(d) PRE-FLIGHT INSPECTION

Takes appropriate action with respect to any identified unsatisfactory conditions

If there are any deferred defects, or any item that you have found to be unserviceable, you must check these against the company approved Minimum Equipment List (MEL). This document will tell you whether the aircraft can depart legally with the defect, together with any operational restrictions and the time period allowed before maintenance action is required. If the defect is not listed in the MEL then you cannot depart without maintenance action. The defect must be entered into the technical log and signed/stamped by an engineer with the MEL reference before you can depart. The MEL is applicable before dispatch. Candidates completing training in their own aircraft without an MEL must refer to the list of required equipment in the AFM and ANO to asses whether they can dispatch.

Here are some definitions regarding the MEL which you may be asked:

- **AUTHORITY:** For aircraft registered in the UK this is the Civil Aviation Authority

- **COMMENCEMENT OF FLIGHT:** The point when an aircraft begins to move under its own power for the purpose of preparing for flight

- **DAY OF DISCOVERY:** The date (UTC) that a defect is recorded in the aircraft Technical Log

- **DAY OF OPERATION:** Any flight conducted from the point of take-off to landing between 30 minutes before sunrise and 30 minutes after sunset

- **DISPATCH:** The point at which an aircraft first moves under its own power for the purpose of commencing a flight

- **FLIGHT:** For the purpose of the MEL, a flight is the period of time between the moment when an aeroplane begins to move by its own means, for the purpose of preparing for take-off, until the moment the aeroplane comes to a complete stop on its parking area, after the subsequent landing (and no subsequent takeoff)

2 - DEPARTURE

- **FLIGHT DAY:** A 24 hour period (from 0001 UTC until 2359 UTC) during which at least one flight is scheduled for the affected aircraft, excluding the Day of Discovery

- **(M):** Maintenance Procedure must be established, published and utilised prior to the first flight undertaken following discovery of the defect, and if necessary repeated

- **(O):** Operational Procedure

- **NUMBER INSTALLED:** The number of specified items normally installed in the aircraft. Where the number installed varies, a dash will appear as the entry in this column

- **NUMBER REQUIRED FOR DISPATCH:** The minimum number of the specified items required for operation provided the conditions defined are met. Where the number required for dispatch is variable, a dash will appear as the entry in this column

- **RECTIFICATION INTERVAL:** Inoperative items or components, deferred in accordance with the MEL, must be rectified at or prior to the rectification intervals established by the following letter designators given in the 'Rectification Interval' column

Flight in accordance with IFR requires more equipment to be fully serviceable than flight under VFR. Take a note of any restrictions and inform operations as they might be able to get the item fixed or give you a replacement aircraft. If you accept the defect, then always inform the examiner. He may override your decision if he isn't happy to accept the defect as he is the aeroplane commander.

DA42 MEL	ATA Chapter: 22 Autoflight				
(1) System & Sequence Numbers ITEM		(2) Rectification Interval			
		(3) Number installed			
			(4) Number required for dispatch		
ATA				(5) Remarks or Exceptions	
22-10	Autopilot	D	1	0	(O) May be inoperative provided single pilot AOC operations are conducted under VFR.
22-10	Autopilot disconnect button	D	1	0	One may be INOP provided the autopilot is not utilized at less than initial approach altitude
22-71	Navigation database	C	2	0	(O)IFR B-RNAV operations and GPS approaches not authorised without current database in at least one unit

A typical page from an MEL

(d) PRE-FLIGHT INSPECTION

E) WEATHER MINIMA

The examiner needs to assess how you have decided that the weather conditions are suitable for the flight. Consult the ATO Operations Manual for company planning minima.

Aerodrome Operating Minima

The Aerodrome Operating Minima are the minimum conditions of cloud ceiling and Runway Visual Range for take-off and of Decision Height/Minimum Descent Height, Runway Visual Range and Visual Reference for landing. Planning and operating minima will be stipulated in the ATO Operations Manual (for candidates on an approved course) or in EASA Part NCO or NCC as applicable to the aircraft type (for ICAO IR conversions).

Most initial IRT will be attempted in a Performance Class B aeroplane. Aeroplanes such as the Diamond DA-42 or Piper PA-34, are popular choices due to the economics involved. The UK AIP AD 1.1.2 is very useful for UK IFR operations and is compliant with EASA regulations. It is essential reading if undertaking an IRT in UK airspace.

The AIP will specify each aerodrome's take-off minima. Aerad and Jeppesen also publish these on their aerodrome charts. The ATO's Operations Manual will state the minimum visibility for take-off. This may well be more restrictive than the legal minimum to allow for training.

Take-off Minima
Is specified for each aerodrome. ATO's may specify higher values.

EU OPS	TAKE OFF MINIMA		RVR	
RWY	Facilities		A B C	D
28	HRCLL + HREDL + Multiple RVR + HUD Ap.O LVTO		75 m	75 m
	HRCLL + HREDL + Multiple RVR Ap.O LVTO		125 m	150 m
10/28	RCLL + REDL + Multiple RVR LVTO		150 m	200 m
	RCLL + REDL LVTO		200 m	250 m
	RCL (day only) or RCL + REDL LVTO		250 m	300 m
ALL	RCL (day only) or RCL + REDL		400 m	400 m
	NIL (day only)		500 m	500 m

Take off alternate

The examiner may ask:

'When is a take-off alternate required?'

ANSWER: A take-off alternate is required when it would not be possible to return to the departure aerodrome for meteorological or performance reasons. The take-off alternate must be located within 1 hours flight time at the one engine inoperative cruising speed.

100 nm is a typical distance to use for a class B performance aeroplane when considering take-off alternate. It will be specified in the Operations Manual.

The examiner may then also ask:-

'What weather conditions need to exist for an aerodrome to be nominated as a take-off alternate?'

ANSWER: TAKE-OFF alternate planning minima will be stated in the ATO Operations Manual, or Part NCO/NCC regulations (as applicable). Essentially the weather must be equal or better than the applicable procedure minima.

Destination Minima

Essentially, the forecast weather conditions at the destination, affects the number of alternates required at the planning stage, which is discussed later. You may depart if the weather at the destination is marginal. However, once airborne the AOM is to be strictly adhered to. For the IRT you must assume that both the 3D and 2D approaches are to be flow in minimum weather conditions (even if it is a CAVOK day!).

During the briefing you must inform the examiner of the minima you are using for the approaches including any circling approaches. This is found on the approach charts.

One addition that you may need to add to the precision approach DA (H) is for Precision Error Correction (PEC). The PEC error is found in the AFM and is typically 50 ft. However, not all light aircraft need to apply it as the aircraft's altimeter may be sufficiently accurate. Below is an extract from the UK AIP Aerodrome section 1.1.8 regarding altimeter error:-

When calculating DH, account must be taken of the errors of indicated height which occur when the aircraft is in the approach configuration. Details of the Pressure Error Correction (PEC) should be available from the aircraft flight manual or handbook. In the absence of this information a PEC of +50 ft has been found to be suitable for a wide range of light aircraft and should be used. This addition of 50 ft need only be applied to DH. The required RVR should be calculated prior to applying the PEC.

A 2D Approach flown using the Constant Descent Final Approach (CDFA) technique needs a correction for altitude lost in the go-around, unless a specific exemption has been given to the operator by the CAA.

Visibility is the key element when deciding whether you can legally fly the approach. Consequently the examiner is highly likely to ask:-

'What is the approach ban?'

Answer from UK AIP AD 1.1:-

10   Approach Ban - All Aircraft

10.1   *The requirements for the commencement and continuation of an approach (approach ban) applicable to all EU-OPS AOC operations is given in EU OPS 1.405. The UK CAA has obtained a derogation to allow all UK EU OPS AOC operations to apply the approach ban method outlined in this section.*

10.2   *The approach ban requirements for public transport operations, aerial work and private operations are defined in Articles 107, 108 and 109 of the Air Navigation Order 2009.*

2 - DEPARTURE

10.3   An aircraft may commence an instrument approach regardless of the reported RVR/Visibility but the approach shall not be continued below 1000 ft above the aerodrome if the relevant RVR/Visibility for that runway is at the time less than the specified minimum for landing.

10.4   If, after passing 1000 ft in accordance with paragraph 10.3, the reported RVR/Visibility falls below the applicable minimum, the approach may be continued to DA/H or MDA/H.

10.5   The approach may be continued below DA/H or MDA/H and the landing may be completed provided that the required visual reference is established at the DA/H or MDA/H and is maintained.

EASA Part OPS requires that unless either a suitable autopilot or Head Up Display is used than the lowest allowable RVR is 800 m.

Unfortunately, you are not allowed to use an autopilot for any of the approaches, so the single pilot operation restriction of 800 m is often the most restrictive visibility for the approaches you will face on the IRT. Be aware, some approaches do have a higher published visibility minimum than 800 m, e.g. EGNH RNAV Rwy 28 GNSS Cat A is 1400 m.

Some approaches have a higher required RVR than 800 m

Destination alternate and En-Route planning minima

Consult the ATO Operations Manual for destination and en-route planning minima.

EASA regulations provide a table on the applicability of aerodrome forecasts to pre-flight planning, an extract is shown below:-

Application of Aerodrome Forecasts

(e) WEATHER MINIMA

Where a TAF or METAR with landing forecast (TREND) is used as forecast, the following criteria should be used:-

1. *From the start of a TAF validity period up to the time of applicability of the first subsequent 'FM...' or 'BECMG' or, if no 'FM' or BECMG is given, up to the end of the validity period of the TAF, the prevailing weather conditions forecast in the initial part of the TAF should be applied.*

2. *From the time of observation of a METAR up to the time of applicability of the first subsequent 'FM...' or 'BECMG' or, if no 'FM' or BECMG is given, up to the end of the validity period of the TREND, the prevailing weather conditions forecast in the METAR should be applied.*

3. *Following FM (alone) or BECMG AT, any specified change should be applied from the time of the change.*

4. *Following BECMG (alone), BECMG FM, BECMG TL, BECMG FM TL:-*
   a) *In the case of deterioration, any specified change should be applied from the start of the change; and*
   b) *In the case of improvement, any specified change should be applied from the end of the change.*

5. *In a period indicated by TEMPO (alone), TEMPO FM, TEMPO TL, TEMPO FM TL, PROB30/40 (alone):-*
   a) *Deteriorations associated with persistent conditions in connection with e.g. haze, mist, fog, dust/sandstorm, continuous precipitation should be applied;*
   b) *Deteriorations associated with transient/showery conditions in connection with short-lived weather phenomena, e.g. thunderstorms, showers may be ignored; and*
   c) *Improvements should in all cases be disregarded.*

6. *In a period indicated by PROB30/40 TEMPO:-*
   a) *Deteriorations may be disregarded; and*
   b) *Improvements should be disregarded.*

Summary

It must be emphasised that planning minima is a complex topic and EASA regulations are is designed for all types of commercial operations, consequently it has a lot of different rules and requirements depending on the type of operation and class of aeroplane used. It is revised regularly so always follow what is in your ATO's Operations Manual.

The IRT also has manoeuvres which require VMC, which may preclude attempting section 2 of the test. It is the responsibility of the examiner to decide if the weather conditions are suitable to complete all sections of the test.

F) TAXYING

Completes all departure checks and drills including engine operations

When calculating what time to walk out to the aeroplane, you should remember to work back from the Estimated Off Blocks Time (EOBT) which you stipulated on the flight plan. Remember that you will only have 1 hr to plan, file the flight plan, complete the pre-flight inspection (ideally you should do this before the briefing) and start the engines. A suggested time line would be as follows:-

- EOBT-60mins, file flight plan
- EOBT-50mins complete planning
- EOBT-20mins check tech log and documents and walk to the aircraft
- EOBT-15mins, exterior inspection
- EOBT-10mins, request IFR clearance and engine start, complete after start checklist
- EOBT-request taxi

When you request start, ATC may inform you that you have a Calculated Take Off Time (CTOT), more commonly known as a 'slot'. These are issued from EUROCONTROL in Brussels, who look at the amount of traffic in the airways and issue take off times to keep the traffic flowing steadily. They are also issued in the event of industrial action or airspace restrictions. You could see them as traffic calming!

(f) TAXYING

Eurocontrol

May issue a CTOT

A CTOT has a take-off time tolerance of -5/+10 mins. Do NOT miss the CTOT because of inadequate time planning. You may fail the departure section as a result. These 'slots' will become an irritation when you start commercial flying because if you miss your CTOT, operations will request another one, however it may be a long time off!

If you are given a CTOT which will give you a long delay you can ask ATC to submit a '**Ready Message**'. This will inform EUROCONTROL that you are ready to depart and can accept an improved CTOT. For more information consult the Air Traffic Flow Management User Manual found on EUROCONTROL's website, **www.eurocontrol.init**.

When you set the altimeters make sure that they read within 60 feet of the datum and each other, or as specified in the Operations Manual.

Set the radio aids in accordance with the expected instrument departure. Take your time doing this and make sure you set the correct tracks. If you have an IFR approved GPS, such as a Garmin 530, complete a A RAIM check is not required for a SBAS equipped GPS unit. Insert the flight plan route into the GPS/FMS; this is especially useful for giving ETAs. Make sure that you check each waypoint flows sequentially and the total

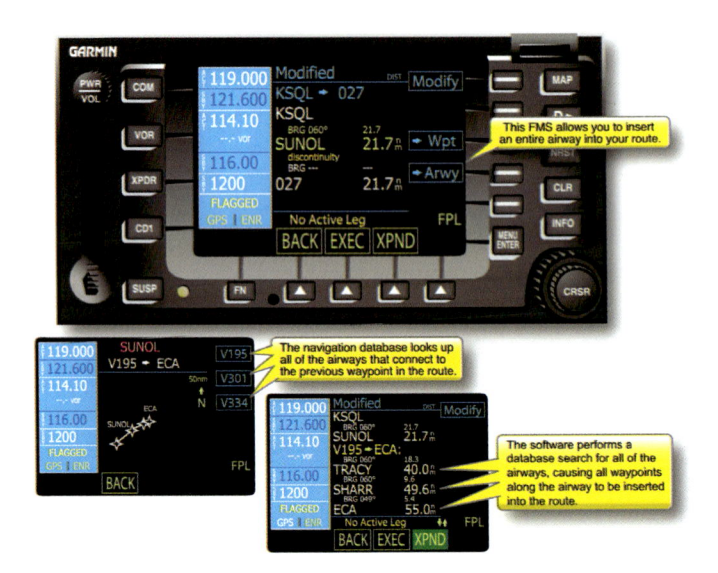

GPS/FMS

Insert the route into the GPS/FMS

distance is accurate.

(f) TAXYING

… Check the sequence of waypoints.

Check the distances and desired tracks between the waypoints.

Engage cursor mode on the flight plan page. Use the outer knob to scroll between the waypoints in the route.

GPS/FMS

Always check the track and distances entered into the GPS or FMS

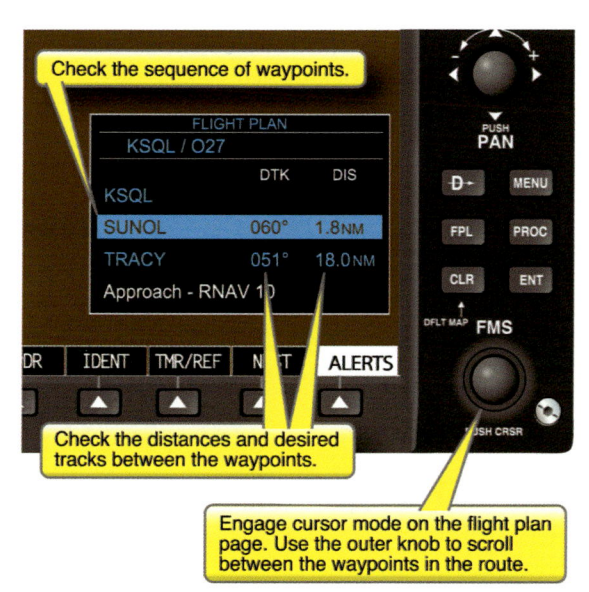

Information regarding testing the aids is found in Pooley's 'A Guide to the EASA CPL Flight Test' and your ATO's Training Manual. Note the Off Blocks Time on the navigation log before you taxi.

Complies with airport marking and signals

Before requesting taxi have an airfield taxi chart to hand. It may well be possible that if the visibility is low (typically <1500 m) the aerodrome will be in Low Visibility Procedures (LVPs). Each aerodrome's limit will be in the AIP (AD specific) and aerodrome briefing plate supplied by Jeppesen or Aerad.

```
1.3. LOW VISIBILITY PROCEDURES
1.3.1. GENERAL
     During CAT II/III operations, special ATC procedures (Low Visibility Procedures)
     will be applied.
     Pilots will be informed when these procedures are in operation via RTF and ATIS.

     CAT II/III holding positions are B, C, D1, D3 and N1 only, amber/green coded TWY
     centerline lights are switched for routing guidance.
     ACFT on stands 7 thru 18 will normally taxi through holding positions C and D3.
     Pilots must request marshaller assistance, wingtip guidance or Follow-me car if it is
     considered necessary, prior to start-up or after landing before entering the apron.

     Holding points F3 and L2 are used as the CAT II/III holding point for ACFT taxiing
     from the South side facility.
```

Always review the LVPs before starting taxying

(f) TAXYING

2 - DEPARTURE

The UK AIP AD section
Gives guidance on when LVPs should be applied

> 2.12 **Low Visibility Procedure (LVP).** Procedures applied at an aerodrome for the purpose of ensuring safe operation during Category 2 and 3 approaches and Low Visibility Take-off. (LVPs are initiated when the cloudbase lowers to 300 ft and is expected to lower further or the RVR falls to 1200 m and is expected to deteriorate further. They should be fully in place by the time the cloudbase reaches 200 ft or the RVR falls to 600 m).
>
> 2.13 **Low Visibility Take-off.** A take-off where the runway visual range is less than 400 m.

Even if LVPs are not in force, it is good airmanship to have a taxi chart to hand, especially if you are at an unfamiliar airfield. Make sure that you write down the clearance limit and follow the centreline. Never cross a red stop bar, stop and contact ATC if unsure. Runway incursion hotspots are marked on large aerodrome taxi charts.

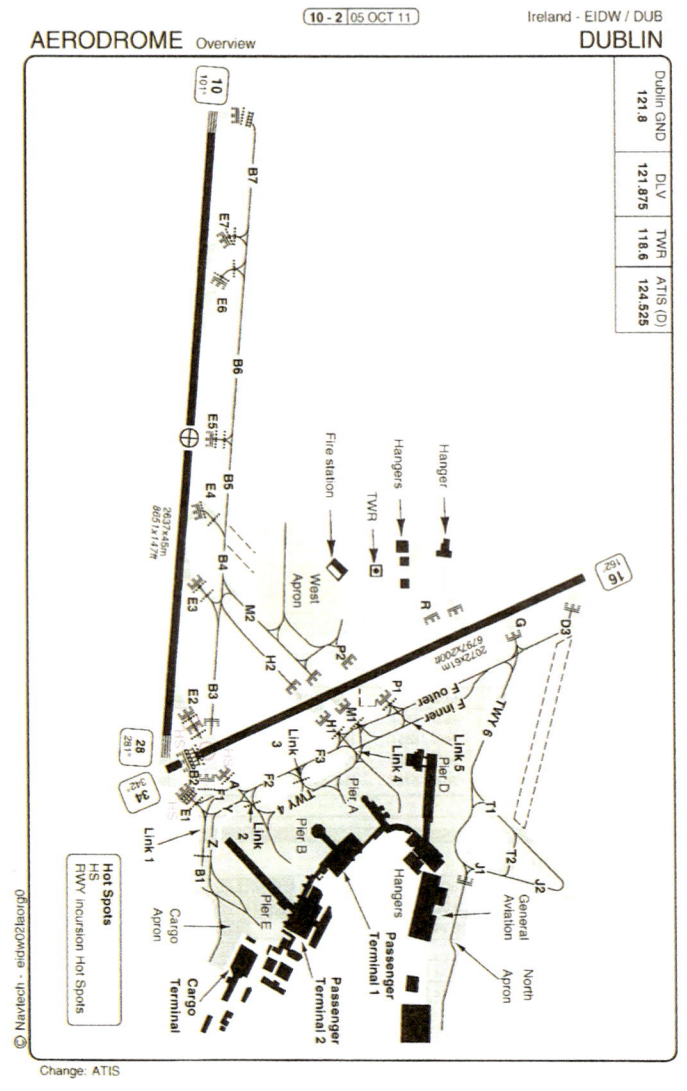

Aerodrome taxi chart
Always have a taxi chart to hand and note the clearance limit

(f) TAXYING

2 - DEPARTURE

As you taxi out to the runway check the instruments on natural turns and do not 'ride' the brakes. It is uncomfortable and it reduces braking effectiveness.

Obtains ATC clearance

You are most likely to start the IRT with an instrument departure from an aerodrome and join controlled airspace. Consequently, you must request the clearance from ATC. In the future, however, you may have to join controlled airspace from uncontrolled airspace which is a little more involved. Air Pilot's Manual volume 7 and CAP 413 have more information. Here is an example of requesting an IFR departure clearance from Bournemouth:-

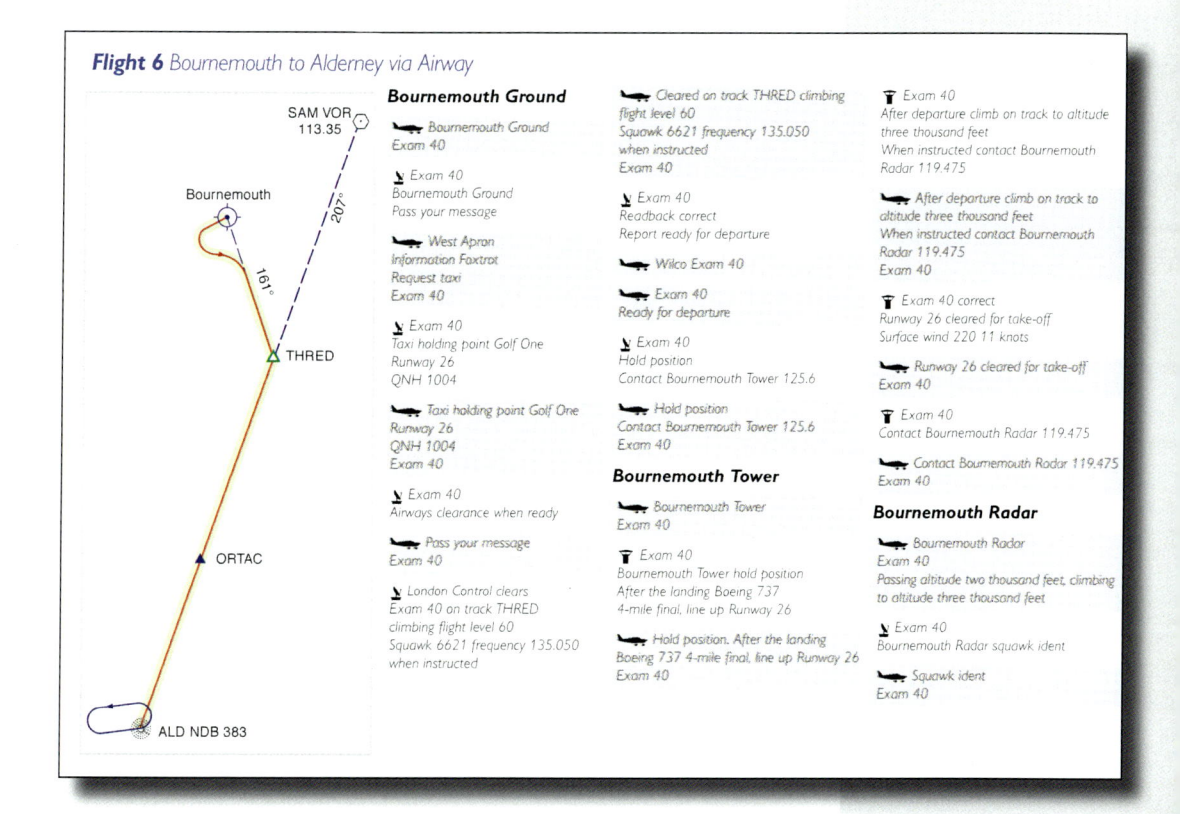

Flight 6 *Bournemouth to Alderney via Airway*

SAM VOR 113.35
Bournemouth
207°
161°
THRED
ORTAC
ALD NDB 383

Bournemouth Ground

↗ Bournemouth Ground
Exam 40

↘ Exam 40
Bournemouth Ground
Pass your message

↗ West Apron
Information Foxtrot
Request taxi
Exam 40

↘ Exam 40
Taxi holding point Golf One
Runway 26
QNH 1004

↗ Taxi holding point Golf One
Runway 26
QNH 1004
Exam 40

↘ Exam 40
Airways clearance when ready

↗ Pass your message
Exam 40

↘ London Control clears
Exam 40 on track THRED
climbing flight level 60
Squawk 6621 frequency 135.050
when instructed

↗ Cleared on track THRED climbing
flight level 60
Squawk 6621 frequency 135.050
when instructed
Exam 40

↘ Exam 40
Readback correct
Report ready for departure

↗ Wilco Exam 40

↗ Exam 40
Ready for departure

↘ Exam 40
Hold position
Contact Bournemouth Tower 125.6

↗ Hold position
Contact Bournemouth Tower 125.6
Exam 40

Bournemouth Tower

↗ Bournemouth Tower
Exam 40

↘ Exam 40
Bournemouth Tower hold position
After the landing Boeing 737
4-mile final, line up Runway 26

↗ Hold position. After the landing
Boeing 737 4-mile final, line up Runway 26
Exam 40

↘ Exam 40
After departure climb on track to altitude
three thousand feet
When instructed contact Bournemouth
Radar 119.475

↗ After departure climb on track to
altitude three thousand feet
When instructed contact Bournemouth
Radar 119.475
Exam 40

↘ Exam 40 correct
Runway 26 cleared for take-off
Surface wind 220 11 knots

↗ Runway 26 cleared for take-off
Exam 40

↘ Exam 40
Contact Bournemouth Radar 119.475

↗ Contact Bournemouth Radar 119.475
Exam 40

Bournemouth Radar

↗ Bournemouth Radar
Exam 40
Passing altitude two thousand feet, climbing
to altitude three thousand feet

↘ Exam 40
Bournemouth Radar squawk ident

↗ Squawk ident
Exam 40

(f) TAXYING

G) PRE TAKE-OFF BRIEFING

Completes an appropriate passenger briefing

You are expected to give a suitable brief to the passenger describing both normal and non-normal procedures and location of emergency equipment. Keep it clear, simple and concise. If your aircraft has printed emergency cards, these are acceptable, but the examiner is entitled to ask questions. Below is an example, however, always follow your ATO's training guidance:-

> '**THE FIRE** extinguisher is located here, your life jacket is under your seat, and the first aid kit is located on the parcel shelf at the rear of the aircraft. Your seat belt is locked and adjusted like this, to release, pull the latch through 90° (highlight that it is different from a car style locking mechanism). In the event that I tell you to brace, assume this position. The emergency exits are located here; to exit first undo the top latch and then the bottom. Having vacated the aircraft follow me to an upwind location, any questions?'

A Captain's emergency brief is not required for single crew operations. The examiner will discuss how actual emergencies will be handled in the main briefing. However, it is always good airmanship to review engine failure procedures but tailor it to the actual conditions.

Confirms any performance criteria including crosswind

Make sure that your performance figures reflect where you depart from and take into account any reduction in distance available and weather conditions. It is always sensible to calculate the take-off performance from any likely intersection.

Before entering the runway, confirm to the examiner the crosswind component and check that it doesn't exceed the aircraft's maximum demonstrated limit. You could do this by using a flight computer. However, this is not the time to have your head inside the cockpit searching for your 'whiz wheel'! There are various methods of calculating both the crosswind and headwind components. Here is one such method:-

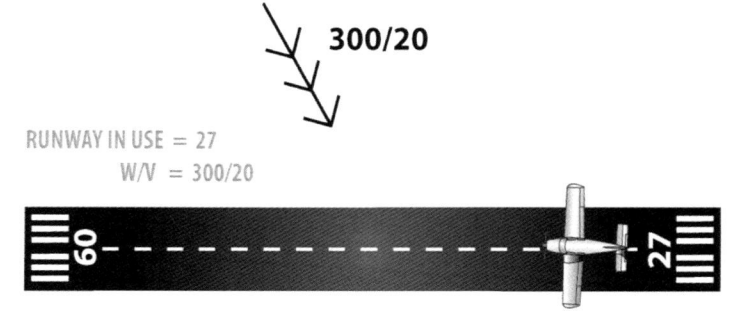

300/20

RUNWAY IN USE = 27
W/V = 300/20

(1) Calculate the angle between the runway and w/v eg. 300°−270° = 30°.
(2) Set this into the clock code to find proportion of wind velocity that is a crosswind.

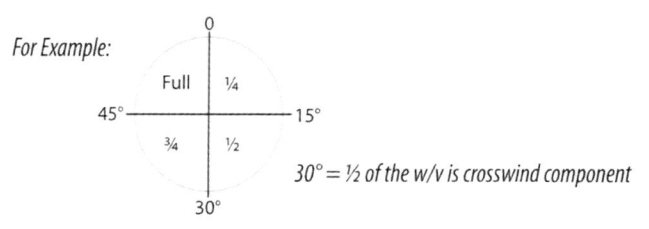

For Example:

	0	
Full	¼	
45°		15°
¾	½	
	30°	

30° = ½ of the w/v is crosswind component

(3) ½ of 20 kts = 10kts
The crosswind component is 10kts.

Actions any anti-icing procedures

Icing conditions exist when OAT (on the ground) or TAT (in flight) is 10°C or below and any of the following exist:-

- Visible moisture (clouds, fog with visibility of one statute mile (1600m) or less, rain, snow, sleet, ice crystals, and so on) is present; or
- Ice, snow, slush or standing water is present on the ramps, taxiways, or runways.

The AFM and aircraft checklist will have information and procedures to be followed for flight into known icing, and obviously you have to tailor it to the actual conditions. However, the test assumes icing conditions exist,

(g) PRE TAKE-OFF BRIEFING

so the examiner may expect to see the touch drills demonstrated, which for a MEP aircraft will typically include:-

- Pitot heaters on
- Propeller anti ice on
- Cabin heaters as required

Here is an extract from the DA-42 AFM, which uses a 'weeping wing' system of de-icing for flight into icing conditions immediately before take-off:-

---

4A.6.6 BEFORE TAKE-OFF

If icing conditions are anticipated immediately after take-off:

1. DE-ICE . . . . NORM
2. Pitot heating . . . . ON
3. ICE LIGHT . . . . ON, as required
4. Cabin heat & defrost . . . . ON

Positions the aeroplane correctly for take-off and advances the throttles to take off power with the appropriate checks

Before departure you are expected to fit the instrument flying screens. The examiner will probably taxi the aircraft onto the departure runway as your view will be limited. You should still, however, complete standard checks when entering a runway. Make sure that you align the heading bug, and review your cleared altitude or flight level. Note the take off time on the navigation log.

The examiner will hand over controls to you when the aircraft is safely lined up on the runway. Advance the throttles and confirm symmetrical power. Track the centreline and confirm that ASI is increasing. Confirm take-off power is set.

Conforms to the correct take-off technique using the recommended speeds for rotation (Vr) and initial climb

Follow the take off technique as described in your ATO's Training Manual and AFM. At Vr rotate to the climbing attitude, once airborne dab the toe brakes to stop the wheels spinning. Check Vlr and when a positive rate of climb is indicated on both the VSI and Altimeter retract the landing gear. Check that the landing gear is safely retracted and transfer your scan to the instruments. Do not look for visual references again.

Irrespective of the actual weather conditions, the examiner will simulate a low cloud base of about 200 ft by fitting the final screen blanking your outside references. You will not see the outside world again until the final approach for landing!

Instrument Flying
Screens are fitted to shield your view of the outside world

Ensures a safe climb and departure, adjusts power and aeroplane configuration as appropriate

Reduce to climb power in accordance with the AFM and synchronise the propellers-you do not want to be distracted by any unwanted noise or vibrations!

Completes all necessary after take-off checks

Complete these once you are settled in the climb, by memory.

H)   TRANSITION TO INSTRUMENT FLIGHT

You will naturally be nervous so soon after departure, so give yourself time to settle into an effective instrument scan. Remember the climb speed you nominated to the examiner and stick to it. Trim the aircraft accurately.

| i) | **INSTRUMENT DEPARTURE** PROCEDURE |

Maintains directional control and drift corrections within acceptable limits of speed, heading height and track

Follow the instrument departure as depicted on the departure plate, allowing for drift as appropriate. It is not uncommon for ATC to issue you with a different instrument departure from the one you were expecting, consequently make sure that you review all possible routings before the test and have all of the departure plates to hand. The holding point is not the time to start rooting through bags attempting to find the correct departure plate!

2 - DEPARTURE

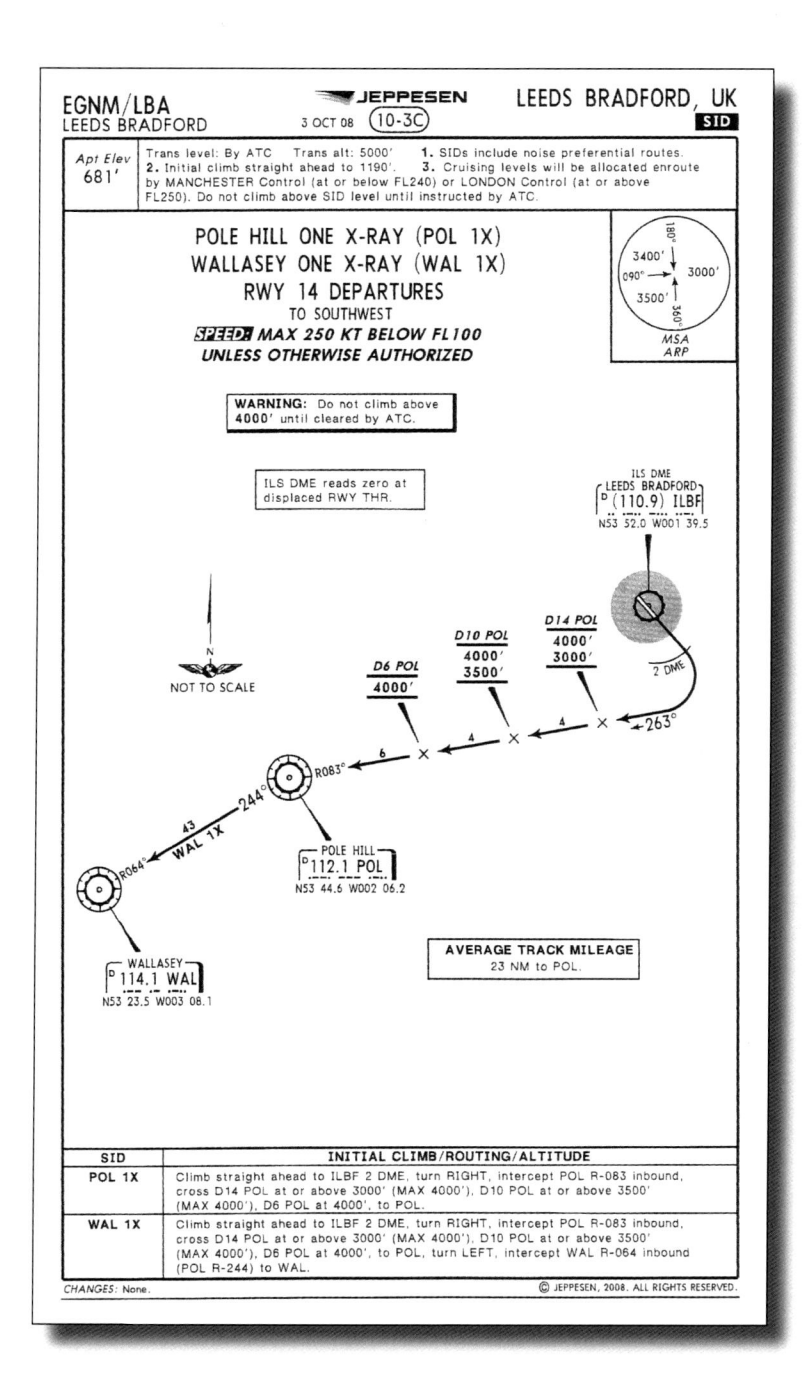

EGNM/LBA LEEDS BRADFORD
JEPPESEN 3 OCT 08 (10-3C) LEEDS BRADFORD, UK — SID

Apt Elev 681'

Trans level: By ATC   Trans alt: 5000'   1. SIDs include noise preferential routes.
2. Initial climb straight ahead to 1190'.   3. Cruising levels will be allocated enroute by MANCHESTER Control (at or below FL240) or LONDON Control (at or above FL250). Do not climb above SID level until instructed by ATC.

POLE HILL ONE X-RAY (POL 1X)
WALLASEY ONE X-RAY (WAL 1X)
RWY 14 DEPARTURES
TO SOUTHWEST
SPEED: MAX 250 KT BELOW FL100 UNLESS OTHERWISE AUTHORIZED

MSA ARP: 180° 3400', 090° 3000', 360° 3500'

WARNING: Do not climb above 4000' until cleared by ATC.

ILS DME reads zero at displaced RWY THR.

ILS DME LEEDS BRADFORD
D (110.9) ILBF
N53 52.0 W001 39.5

D14 POL 4000' 3000'
D10 POL 4000' 3500'
D6 POL 4000'
2 DME
263°
R083°
6
244°
43
WAL 1X
R064°

POLE HILL
D 112.1 POL
N53 44.6 W002 06.2

WALLASEY
D 114.1 WAL
N53 23.5 W003 08.1

NOT TO SCALE

AVERAGE TRACK MILEAGE
23 NM to POL.

SID	INITIAL CLIMB/ROUTING/ALTITUDE
POL 1X	Climb straight ahead to ILBF 2 DME, turn RIGHT, intercept POL R-083 inbound, cross D14 POL at or above 3000' (MAX 4000'), D10 POL at or above 3500' (MAX 4000'), D6 POL at 4000', to POL.
WAL 1X	Climb straight ahead to ILBF 2 DME, turn RIGHT, intercept POL R-083 inbound, cross D14 POL at or above 3000' (MAX 4000'), D10 POL at or above 3500' (MAX 4000'), D6 POL at 4000', to POL, turn LEFT, intercept WAL R-064 inbound (POL R-244) to WAL.

CHANGES: None.   © JEPPESEN, 2008. ALL RIGHTS RESERVED.

Departure Plates
Have all the possible departure plates to hand

(i) INSTRUMENT DEPARTURE PROCEDURE

The skill test tolerances are to be used as a guide. If you exceed them it does not necessarily mean that you will fail. The examiner expects you to make sensible corrections and will assess how the whole flight was flown, including factors affecting the flight beyond your control e.g. turbulence. Here are the IRT tolerances for this part of the test:-

- Altitude +/- 100 ft
- Heading +/- 5°
- Tracking +/- 5° (half scale deflection on a HSI)
- Speed (all engines operating) Vr and climb +/-5 kts

Identifies any navigation aids used

If you have not identified the radio aids required for the instrument departure on the ground, you must identify them before using them. The Morse code identification for the appropriate beacons required for the departure is displayed on the departure plate.

For Performance Based Navigation departures ensure that you have loaded the correct procedure from the database & have the required ANP.

Follows any noise routing or departure procedures and ATC clearances

Joining an airway from controlled airspace via a SID:-

Fly the departure as depicted on the plate. The noise abatement procedure will be built into the design of the SID. Each airfield will have its own Noise Abatement Procedure (NAP) which will affect the departure; review these procedures on the appropriate plate. Most NAPs will only apply to aircraft over a certain weight or jet aircraft so are unlikely to affect you. With a view to standardise thrust reduction and acceleration altitudes, ICAO have published two types of noise abatement techniques, NADP 1 and NADP 2; you will learn more on these when you progress to larger aircraft.

During the SID, ATC may issue you a radar vector to expedite the flow of traffic. Expect ATC to clear you direct to a waypoint on the airway once clear; this is where entering the route in the GPS/FMS is sensible.

2 - DEPARTURE

Pay particular attention to the vertical profile of the SID and any altitude restrictions. If in any doubt, confirm your cleared level or altitude with ATC.

The standard RTF when departing on a SID is as follows:

a)   Call sign;
b)   SID or Standard Departure Route Designator (where appropriate);
c)   Current or passing level; PLUS
d)   Initial climb level (i.e. the first level at which the aircraft will level off unless otherwise cleared).

FOR EXAMPLE: (PILOT) Scottish Control, Exam 01, WAL 5D, Passing Altitude 2300 feet climbing 5000 feet

(ATC) Exam 01, Scottish, Roger

NB *Most instrument departures will stop at the transition altitude and further clearance will be issued by ATC*

Joining an airway from uncontrolled airspace:-

If you depart from an airfield that lies outside controlled airspace, or one which does not have any published instrument departures, you will have to obtain an airborne airways joining clearance. This is not an ideal scenario as it increases your workload and you may have to hold whilst waiting for the clearance. The UK AIP ENR 4.1.4 has the following information on it:-

4.1.4   Flights Joining Airways

4.1.4.1   Pilots wishing to join an Airway are required to file a flight plan either before departure or when airborne, and to request joining clearance when at least 10 minutes flying time from the intended joining point. If the destination or any part of the route is subject to Air Traffic Flow Management, pilots must have received the required authorisation/approval from the appropriate Air Traffic Flow Management Unit (ENR 1.9).

(i) INSTRUMENT DEPARTURE PROCEDURE

4.1.4.2 Joining clearance should be obtained as follows:
Initial call - '....... (identification) request joining clearance .... (Airway) at....... (position)'. When instructed by ATC the following flight details should be passed:
      (a)   *Identification;*
      (b)   *Aircraft type;*
      (c)   *Position and heading;*
      (d)   *Level and flight conditions;*
      (e)   *Departure aerodrome;*
      (f)   *Estimated time at entry point;*
      (g)   *Route and point of first intended landing;*
      (h)   *True Airspeed;*
      (i)   *Desired level on Airway (if different from the above).*

4.1.4.3 Requests for joining clearance of Airways for which the Controlling Authorities are London or Scottish Control should be obtained as follows:-
      (a)   *From the ATSU with which the aircraft is already in communication; or*
      (b)   *from the appropriate FIR Controller (if different from (a));or, if it is not possible to obtain any form of clearance using (a) or (b), then*
      (c)   *on the published frequency of the Airway Controlling Authority.*

4.1.4.4 In order to prevent confliction with other Airways traffic, pilots should ensure that they are at the cleared flight level when they cross the Airway boundary, unless specific permission to do otherwise has been given by ATC.

If the aircraft is fitted with weather radar, turn it on as you enter the runway. If you need to manoeuvre to avoid weather during the flight, request a suitable heading from ATC. If not equipped with weather radar, the examiner may inform you of weather ahead and suggest a suitable heading. In either case, once you are clear of the weather inform ATC.

2 - DEPARTURE

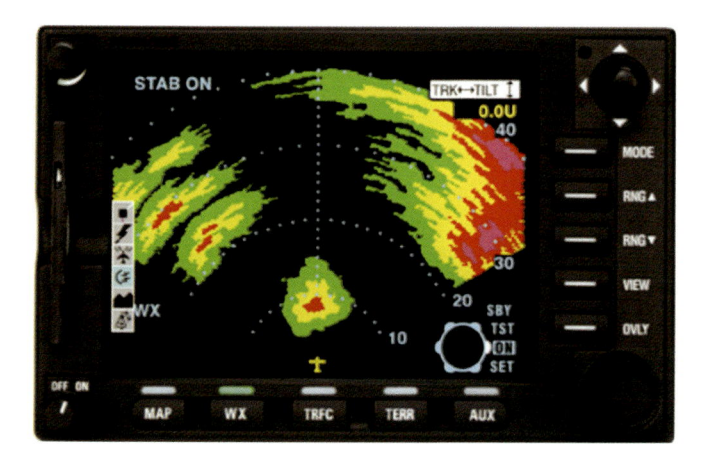

Bendix/King weather radar

Have the weather radar turned on throughout the flight to avoid flying through bad weather as shown on this Bendix/King unit

Completes all necessary climb checks including altimeter setting procedures and ice precautions

Complete the climb checks once established in the climb and on track. Resist the temptation to do any checks whilst completing a complex departure and whilst below MSA.

Set the altimeters in accordance with your ATO's Operations Manual and of course, as required by the SID. Once you are cleared to climb to a flight level, set the Standard Pressure Setting (SPS) on the primary altimeter. Leave the aerodrome QNH on the secondary altimeter to monitor terrain separation.

Complete an ice check with reference to the OAT, for example:-

'The OAT is -3 °C, check for ice please'.

The examiner will look at the wings and tail and assess for ice (ironically the first place ice often accumulates is the OAT probe). He may respond with either:-

'There is no ice' or 'Ice is forming on the XX sections of the aeroplane'.

(i) INSTRUMENT DEPARTURE PROCEDURE

You must then carry out the appropriate actions to remove the ice, as stated in the AFM. These may be touch drills if the examiner is simulating ice accretion. Ask for ice checks at sensible intervals, every 1000 ft is usually adequate.

If you conduct the test at night the aircraft will have ice inspection lights so make sure that you turn them on when conducting an ice check. It is also sensible to have a small and powerful torch to hand to inspect unlit parts of the airframe, such as the windscreen.

CHAPTER THREE

En-Route

The examiner will complete the En-Route section before the General Handling, to allow the flight to follow a typical commercial profile. The General Handling section is usually completed during the transit back to the point of departure in uncontrolled airspace.

A)   TRACKING

Follows the flight planned route or any other ATC route requirements within the operating limits specified

The examiner needs to assess that you can track to and from a primary radio beacon, e.g. VOR. He will brief you on any single needle tracking. Make sure that you have correctly selected and identified the radio aid. If you are using a conventional RMI or digital display on an EFIS equipped aircraft make sure that you track using the correct needle as it can get confusing!

Single Needle Tracking
Make sure that you look at the correct needle when demonstrating single needle tracking

(a) TRACKING

Due to the large amount of IFR traffic in the European airway system, standard routings have been established to simplify flight planning between two airfields. In the UK, these are published in the Standard Route Document found in the UK AIP. Although it is not mandatory to put these routes on the flight plan it makes it easier for ATC, and there is more chance that the flight plan will be accepted by EUROCONTROL. A standard routing from Bournemouth (EGHH) to Jersey (EGJJ) would be as follows:-

EGHH DCT THRED Q41 ORTAC JSY 1A EGJJ

Minimum and maximum altitudes are published to help you decide upon an appropriate level to fly at.

UK SRD
An extract from the UK SRD

ADEP/Entry	SID	Min	Max	Route-Segment	STAR	ADES/Exit	Remarks
EGHH		195	245	DCT SAM Q41 WCO DCT DTY Y250 GASKO P18 ADN DCT		EGPD	Notes: 225 - 226
EGHH		245	660	DCT SAM Q41 WCO DCT DTY DCT SAPCO UN57 POL UN601 TLA DCT GRICE P600 ADN DCT		EGPD	Notes: 303
EGHH		245	660	DCT SAM Q41 WCO DCT DTY UY250 GASKO UP18 NEXUS P18 ADN DCT		EGPD	Notes: 225 - 226

When joining the airway, correctly set the centreline radial of the airway on the HSI; this is on your navigation log and depicted on the airway chart. The tolerances are in accordance with the departure. It is acceptable to have a photocopy of a current airways chart on which you can then highlight your intended route. It can be difficult to distinguish between different airways on a chart with lots of routes e.g. London TMA. However, you must also carry a current airways chart if you are going to do this.

Try not to mark on an original chart, unless it is your own. Most ATOs do not have an endless supply and the next person who may need the chart may not be flying the same route. Electronic planning software will allow the user to print the route, which is of great benefit.

3 - EN-ROUTE

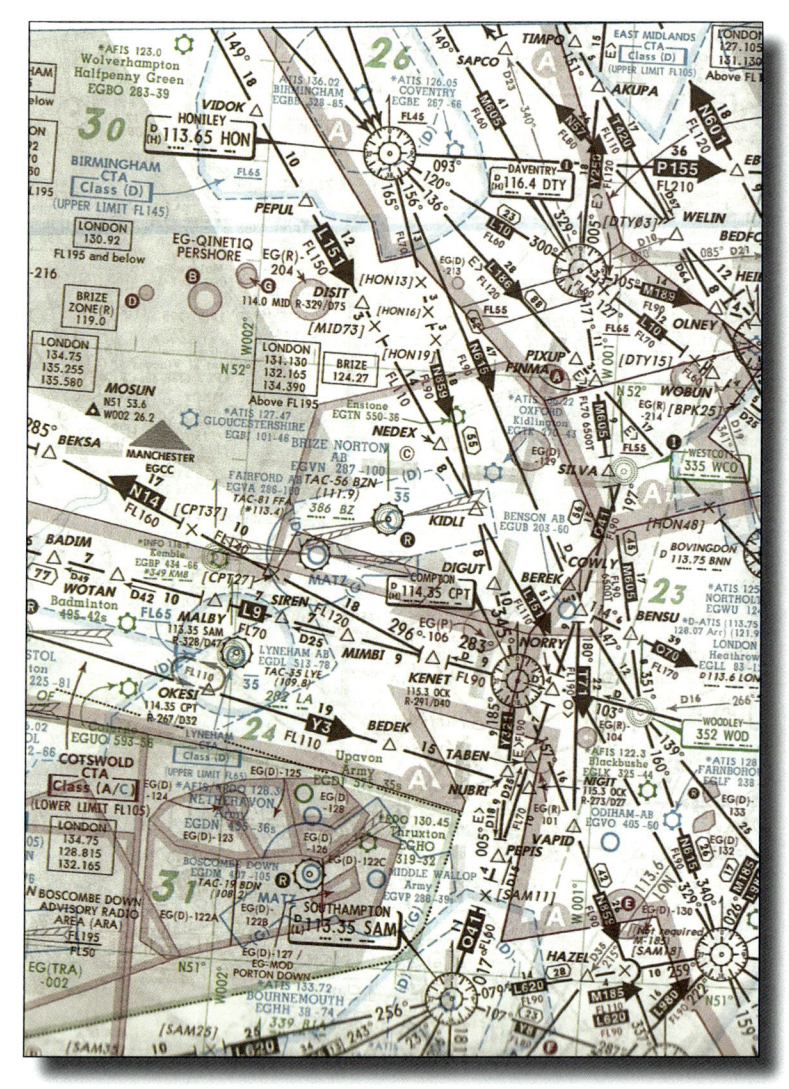

Airways Chart

Always carry an airways chart

Airways Chart

Highlight the intended route on a photocopied chart

(a) TRACKING

The carriage of Basic Area Navigation (B-RNAV) equipment is mandatory on the entire ATS Route Network in the European Civil Aviation Conference (ECAC) area including designated feeder routes (SIDs and STARs) in/out of designated TMAs. RNAV 5 (B-RNAV) requires a track-keeping accuracy of ± 5 nm for 95% of the flight time. Most modern GPS units will meet B-RNAV requirements, however, always consult the appropriate flight supplement.

One major benefit of RNAV is direct routings. If ATC give you a direct routing to a waypoint, then initially turn onto a dead reckoned heading. You are allowed to use the GPS 'GOTO' function as long as the GPS is IFR certified and has a valid database. However, make sure that you have entered the correct waypoint and always gross error check the result. If you are confused, ask ATC for a vector and request them to spell the waypoint. Again, inputting the route in the GPS or FMS on the ground pays dividends!

'GOTO' Function

You are allowed to use the 'GOTO' function of a GPS

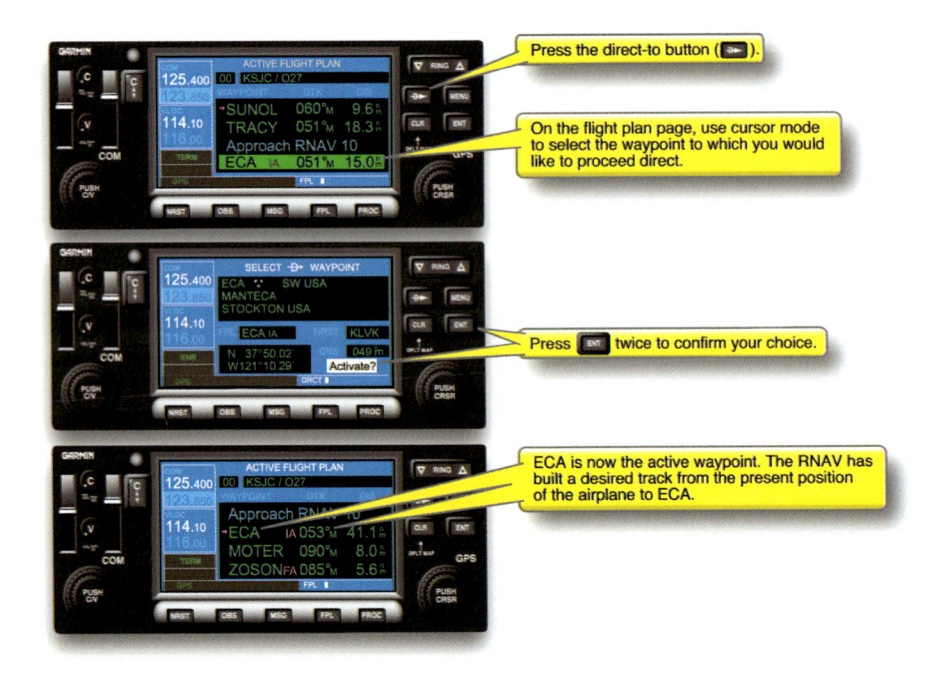

Press the direct-to button.

On the flight plan page, use cursor mode to select the waypoint to which you would like to proceed direct.

Press ENT twice to confirm your choice.

ECA is now the active waypoint. The RNAV has built a desired track from the present position of the airplane to ECA.

(a) TRACKING

If you are given a direct routing, this will reduce your track miles to the destination and consequently the time available to prepare for the arrival, so keep ahead of the aircraft.

As most of the IRT routes are short, you will probably find that the departure and arrival charts will cover the entire route and that you do not need to refer to the airways en-route one at all. However, ATC may instruct you to route to a waypoint not depicted on either of the departure or arrival charts so you must have it to hand.

B) **USE OF** RADIO AIDS

Identifies and uses navigation systems correctly

By now you should know that you need to identify a radio aid before use. However, do not forget to check that you are within the Designated Operational Coverage (DOC), or promulgated range, as appropriate, found in the AIP. It is handy to have this marked on the navigation log. If you are outside the range, you can use the GPS or use dead reckoning towards the beacon until you become within the range. Identify the aid again before using it.

ENR 4.1

Cross check the DOC or promulgated range as appropriate in the UK AIP

ENR 4-1-1-6 (9 Feb 12)						UK AIP
ENR 4.1 — RADIO NAVIGATION AIDS — EN-ROUTE						
Name of Station MAG Var VOR Declination	IDENT	Frequency (Channel)	Hours of Operation (Winter/Summer)	Co-ordinates	DME Aerial Elevation	Remarks
1	2	3	4	5	6	7
Southampton VOR/DME Var 2.17°W - 2009 VOR 1.4°W - 2010	SAM	113.35 MHz (Ch 80Y)	H24	AD Purpose: 505718.90N 0012042.20W ENR Purpose: 505719N 0012042W	66 ft amsl	APCH Aid to Southampton. VOR/DME DOC: 100 nm/50000 ft (150 nm/50000 ft in Sector RDL 226°-316°). On RDL 204° VOR flag alarms and DME unlocks may be experienced at ranges exceeding 30 nm below 8000 ft.

(b) USE OF RADIO AIDS

3 - EN-ROUTE

If the aircraft is equipped with navigation equipment which has an auto-tune facility, check with the examiner in the briefing that he will allow you to use it. If you are using this function, then when selecting a radio aid cross check the alphabetic decode with the correct one annotated on the chart/approach plate. When checking a co-located station, such as a VOR/DME, make sure that both components are identified. If small letters are displayed, depending on the equipment, this could mean that only the DME has been identified and NOT the VOR, e.g. MCT 113.55 should be displayed digitally as **MCT**, not **mct**. Always check the user manual to confirm what should be displayed.

As soon as you are established in the cruise, ideally with the autopilot engaged, obtain the destination weather. Most airfields will have an ATIS, be aware, some only have a departure or arrival one. The ATIS frequency is found on the plate and in a flight guide supplement.

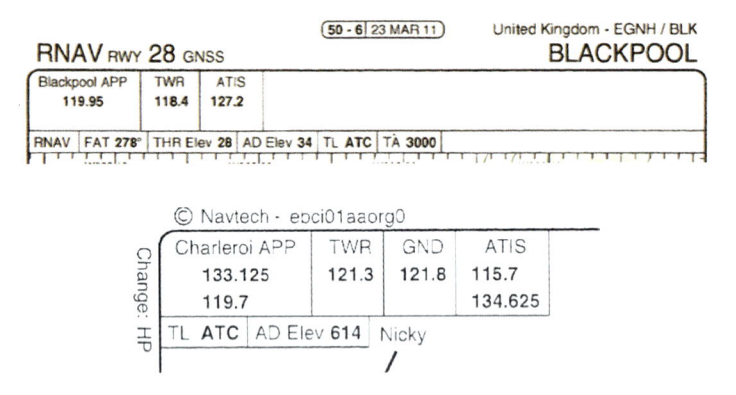

ATIS Frequencies

Blackpool APP	TWR	ATIS
119.95	118.4	127.2

RNAV RWY 28 GNSS — 50-6 23 MAR 11 — United Kingdom - EGNH / BLK — BLACKPOOL

RNAV | FAT 278° | THR Elev 28 | AD Elev 34 | TL ATC | TA 3000

© Navtech · epci01aaorg0

Charleroi APP	TWR	GND	ATIS
133.125	121.3	121.8	115.7
119.7			134.625

TL ATC | AD Elev 614 | Nicky

Change: HP

To get the ATIS always use the second box. Do not let it drown out ATC on box 1; you may fail this section if missed calls result. A typical ATIS will be as follows:-

London Stansted information A, time 0830, runway in use 22, pilots should expect an ILS approach, surface wind 280/08kt, visibility 10km or more, Few 2000 ft, temperature +15, dew point +10, QNH 1015. Report a/c type and information A received on initial contact with Stansted approach.

(b) USE OF RADIO AIDS

If there is no ATIS and ATC are quiet, ask them for the destination weather. However, if ATC are busy, you may have to wait until you are in contact with destination aerodrome controller. You could also listen to the VOLMET if it is included on it. You may also get the weather via a satellite link if you are lucky enough to have it!

As the pilot-in-command, you are required to check that the weather conditions are suitable to make a safe approach and landing.

C)   **LEVEL FLIGHT** CONTROL

Once the examiner is satisfied that you can track a primary beacon and can achieve straight and level flight in trim he may allow you to engage a serviceable autopilot (if fitted). This is the easiest way to ensure that level flight is accurately maintained.

The use of the autopilot has only recently been allowed in IRTs, the examiner will brief you on which parts of the test you can use it. Expect that it will only be allowed to be used during the cruise portions of the test.

The examiner will brief you on when you can use the autopilot

This is the time to complete the cruise/approach checks, obtain the weather and prepare for the first approach. Set up as much as you can at this point and review the minima. Inform the examiner. The tolerances are as follows:-

- Altitude +/- 100 ft
- Heading +/- 5°
- Tracking +/- 5° (half scale deflection on a HSI)
- Speed (all engine operating) cruise +/-5 kts

If you are hand flying the aircraft, do things very slowly and pay particular attention to maintaining your cleared level. A deviation of more than 300 ft is classed as a level bust. The examiner will almost certainly take control and will have no choice but to award a fail on this section. ATC would also have to file a Mandatory Occurrence Report (MOR). There is only 1000 ft vertical separation between aircraft in an airway, so what seems a relatively small deviation could have serious consequences.

ATC will expect a minimum rate of climb/descent of 500 ft per minute when changing altitude. If you are unable to achieve this then you must inform ATC. This requirement applies to both the en-route phase and holding whilst above the transition altitude. However, for operational reasons you can use less than 500 ft per minute.

Whilst operating within London or Scottish controlled airspace ATC will expect higher performance aircraft to reduce the rate of climb to a maximum of 1500 ft per minute within 1500 ft of the cleared level. Between 500 ft and 1000 ft per minute is ideal. This avoids unnecessary TCAS events in busy airspace.

D)   **ALTIMETER SETTING** PROCEDURES

Uses the correct altimeter setting procedures and shows awareness of MSA

A candidate's poor understanding of altimeter setting procedures is often a cause of failure. AIP ENR 1.7 Altimeter Setting Procedures has information regarding altimetry in UK airspace. Your ATO will have their own guidance on procedures contained in the checklist and Training Manual. When operating IFR it is essential that you have a good grasp of what to set on the altimeter subscale and when, as it helps to stop you colliding with the ground and other aircraft!

3 - EN-ROUTE

En-route in an airway above the transition altitude, you would have SPS set on the primary altitude and either RPS or aerodrome QNH set on the secondary altimeter, to monitor terrain separation. Typical altimeter setting procedures are shown in the following table:-

Phase of flight	Primary Altimeter	Secondary Altimeter
T/O and Departure	Aerodrome QNH	Aerodrome QNH
En-Route (above TA)	SPS	RPS or suitable Aerodrome QNH
Arrival	SPS then aerodrome QNH when cleared to an altitude	Aerodrome QNH
Approach	Aerodrome QNH	Aerodrome QNH
Missed approach	Aerodrome QNH	Aerodrome QNH

The examiner will expect you to know the MORA or MSA at any point in the flight. During the En-Route section this is shown by the grid MORA depicted on the airway chart. At the planning stage you should have noted this on your navigation log. Depending on the chart design, MORA appears similar to this:-

$$3_5 \quad \text{or} \quad 3_5$$

The examiner may question you on the definition of the following:-

MEA-The Minimum En-route Altitude (MEA) is the altitude for an en-route segment that provides adequate reception of relevant navigation facilities and ATS communications complies with the airspace structure and provides the required obstacle clearance

MOCA - Minimum Obstacle Clearance Altitude (MOCA) is the minimum altitude for a defined segment that provides the required obstacle clearance. A MOCA is determined and published for each segment of the route. 1000 ft is the standard clearance between the highest fixed obstacles, 2000 ft in mountainous terrain

MORA- Minimum Off Route Altitude (MORA) similar to MOCA, provides terrain clearance within the section outlined by latitude and longitude. It does not provide for radio navigation or communication signal coverage

(d) ALTIMETER SETTING PROCEDURES

3 - EN-ROUTE

> **MSA** - The Minimum Sector Altitude (MSA) is the lowest altitude which may be used which will provide a minimum clearance of 1000 ft above all objects located in the area contained within a sector of a circle of 25 nm radius centred on a radio aid to navigation, or, airfield reference point

E) TIMINGS AND ETAs

Once established in the cruise, update the navigation log and calculate the ETA for the waypoints along the route, including destination. You can cross check these with the GPS/FMS ETA to give accurate estimates. Notify the examiner, aim to achieve the times ± 3 minutes. You can update them if required.

Calculate the ETAs

And inform the examiner, update them as required to achieve ETA±3 minutes

EGHH	AWY	MC	DIST	TAS	TIME	ETA	ATA	MSA	FOB
THRED		161	17	160	00:07	10 47	10 47	24	365
ORTAC	Q41	206	33	160	00:13	11 00	11 00	24	340
ALD		206	19	160	00:08	11 08		20	
APPROACH					00:10	11 18		20	
ORTAC		026	19	160	00:08	11 26		24	
BIA		011	47	160	00:18	11 44		24	

ETAs

Can also be cross checked with the GPS or FMS

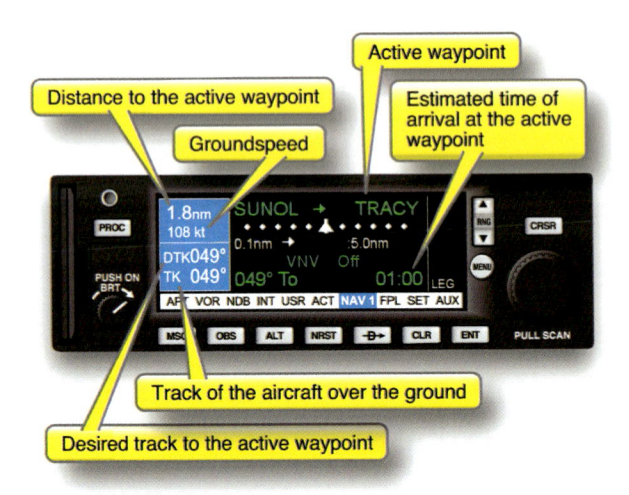

Labels on GPS/FMS display:
- Active waypoint
- Distance to the active waypoint
- Estimated time of arrival at the active waypoint
- Groundspeed
- Track of the aircraft over the ground
- Desired track to the active waypoint

3 - EN-ROUTE

If ATC instruct you to hold en-route (usually when waiting to enter controlled airspace) you will be assessed on the hold. Unfortunately you will still have to do another one. Holding is discussed in Chapter 6.

F) **MONITORING FLIGHT** PROGRESS

Maintains the flight log for navigation, RTF and fuel use, sufficient to give position reports and to confirm acceptable minimum fuel states.

Update the flight/navigation log at regular intervals. Complete a fuel check at a convenient point in the cruise, top of climb is usually appropriate. Commercially, you will need to complete a fuel check every 30 minutes. Compare the actual fuel on board against the planned, and confirm whether there is a surplus or deficit. If the fuel quantity is less than you thought, it could be due to strong headwinds, or a longer routing. However, you may have a fuel leak.

```
LFFF
022 UN615   N50123   00065 474 148   0062         0403 4090   4400/
350 XAMAB   E000159  M063  06  146   008 1108 ... 1107 0031 3890   +0500
    350
022 UL612   N49514   01061 470 148   0025              0378 3960
350 VEULE   E000372  M062  04  147   003 1111  ...     0034 3760  134x900
027 UL612   N48341   01058 461 142   0100              0278 3450
350 RESMI   E002115  M061  06  141   013 1124  ...     0047 3250  sq 1234
024 UM975   N48165   02055 445 125   0031              0247 3280
350 PEKIM   E002495  M058  07  125   004 1128  ...     0051 3080
039 UM975   N48050   02053 456 143   0015              0232 3210
350 PILUL   E003029  M058  07  143   002 1130  ...     0053 3010
039 UM975   N47324   02050 466 157   0035              0197 3130   3500/
350 PIMUP   E003233  M057  06  157   005 1135 ... 1134 0058 2930  +0500
    350
053 UM975   N46564   03072 430 157   0039              0158 2920
270 PIXIS   E003452  M049  01  157   005 .... .... ... 0103 2720
```

Fuel Check

Complete a fuel check at regular intervals

Never trust the fuel gauges on light aircraft, as they are notoriously inaccurate. This is why a pre-flight inspection is critical especially if carrying less than full fuel.

When approaching a turning point such as a VOR, it is expected that you anticipate the change of course and turn early at a suitable distance or radial. Use the navigation log to confirm the next course. If using the RNAV function of the GPS you will get a flashing navigation message highlighting the next course.

(f) MONITORING FLIGHT PROGRESS

Anticipate the change of course

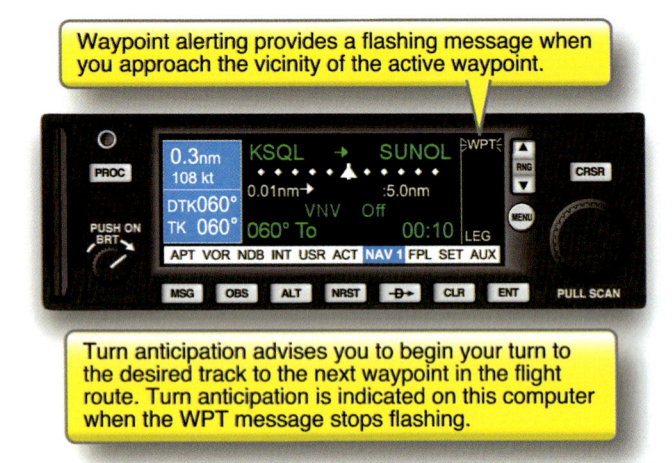

> Waypoint alerting provides a flashing message when you approach the vicinity of the active waypoint.

> Turn anticipation advises you to begin your turn to the desired track to the next waypoint in the flight route. Turn anticipation is indicated on this computer when the WPT message stops flashing.

Position reports are no longer required in a radar environment. However, you will need to know how to transmit a position report when flying in non radar airspace, e.g. flying across the Atlantic Ocean or operating under a Procedural Service. The examiner will expect you to give him a position report but not to ATC, unless requested. Use the standard format:-

a) **Aircraft identification**
b) **Position**
c) **Time**
d) **Level**
e) **Next position and ETA**

FOR EXAMPLE:-
(PILOT) Exam 01, THRED at 1025, FL 80, estimate position ORTAC at 1040, ALD next
(ATC) Exam 01, Roger, report at ORTAC
(PILOT) Exam 01, Wilco

(f) MONITORING FLIGHT PROGRESS

3 - EN-ROUTE

G)   ICE PROTECTION PROCEDURES

Monitoring of OAT and ice accretion rate (simulated if necessary); use of anti-icing and de-icing procedures

Throughout the whole flight you must monitor for ice accretion unless the examiner has told you that no further checks are required. When you are checking for ice, always look at the OAT probe first and confirm if you are indeed in icing conditions. If ice is forming follow the AFM procedures. Even if you are conducting the test when the OAT is +30°C, the examiner will still ask you to perform the touch drill procedures for de-icing the airframe.

You must not enter icing conditions unless the aircraft is certified and serviceable to do so. Here is an extract from the DA-42 AFM regarding icing procedures in the cruise:-

---

4A.6.9 CRUISE

if icing conditions do exist:

1. DE-ICE .... NORM, monitor ice build-up
   HIGH, if no shedding, or to prevent excessive ice build up
2. MAX .... press push button if no sheddin in HIGH mode.
   Repeat as required.

NOTE

The MAX push button activates the maximum possible system flow rate for 120 seconds.

WARNING

If ice fails to shed, proceed with Section 3.10.2 FAILURE OF THE ICE PROTECTION SYSTEM.

whilst in icing conditions:

3. Pitot heating .... check ON
4. ICE LIGHT .... ON, as required
5. Cabin heat & defrost .... check ON
6. WINDSHIELD .... press push button, as required
7. De-icing fluid level .... check periodically
8. Airspeed .... maintain 121 to 160 KIAS

Icing procedures in the cruise

Airframe Ice

Check regularly for ice on all parts of the airframe

It is unlikely that you will have experienced much exposure to icing conditions so far in your flying career. Treat it with a lot of caution as it affects all types of aircraft. Unfortunately, piston engine aircraft are particularly badly affected and do not have much excess performance. The UK AIC 106/2004 is a good source of information. Canadian and American Aviation Authorities' websites have some excellent information on the subject. Symptoms of airframe and engine icing include:-

- *Visual detection of ice forming on the OAT probe and windshield*
- *Engine vibration (ice forming on the propellers)*
- *Visual detection of ice on the leading edge of the wing and empennage*
- *Poor radio reception and transmissions (ice forming on the aerials)*
- *Higher power settings required to maintain flight (ice is increasing the weight of the aircraft)*
- *Rough running engines (carburettor icing)*
- *Erroneous instrument indications (ice blocking pitot or static probes)*

Once you have carried out the AFM procedures, you have to decide whether to continue at the same altitude or change to avoid the icing conditions. Before you decide, ask ATC if they have had any reports of the cloud tops, as you may be able to climb into VMC rather than having to descend. You need to request a change in level with ATC within controlled airspace. Always check the MSA before descending!

You should also inform ATC of the type and intensity of the icing, once you are in a safe position. An AIRMET should be produced to warn other aircraft. The UK AIP GEN section states:-

6.3.3   Airframe Icing

6.3.3.1   All pilots encountering unforecast icing are requested to report time, location, level, intensity, icing type and aircraft type to the ATS Unit with whom they are in radio contact. It should be noted that the following icing intensity criteria are reporting definitions; they are not necessarily the same as forecasting definitions because reporting definitions are related to aircraft type and to the ice protection equipment installed, and do not involve cloud characteristics. For similar reasons, aircraft icing certification criteria might differ from reporting and/or forecasting criteria.

(g) ICE PROTECTION PROCEDURES

Icing Intensity Definitions

For use in pilot reports

Intensity	Ice accumulation
Trace	Ice becomes perceptible. Rate of accumulation slightly greater than rate of sublimation. It is not hazardous even though de-icing/anti-icing equipment is not utilised, unless encountered for more than one hour.
Light	The rate of accumulation might create a problem if flight in this environment exceeds one hour. Occasional use of de-icing/ anti-icing equipment removes/prevents accumulation. It does not present a problem if de-icing/anti-icing equipment is used.
Moderate	The rate of accumulation is such that even short encounters become potentially hazardous and use of de-icing/anti-icing equipment, or diversion, is necessary.
Severe	The rate of accumulation is such that de-icing/anti-icing equipment fails to reduce or control the hazard. Immediate diversion is necessary.
Rime	Rough, milky, opaque ice formed by the instantaneous freezing of small super cooled water droplets.
Clear Ice	A glossy, clear, or translucent ice formed by the relatively slow freezing of large super cooled water droplets.

H)   ATC LIAISON

Uses the correct RTF procedures and phraseology

Before starting the Instrument Rating course, review CAP 413 and Air Pilot's Manual, Volume 7. Radio failure procedures are detailed in AIP ENR 1-1-3-2 and are discussed in Chapter 7. National differences from ICAO are also detailed in a suitable flight information supplement.

intentionally blank

CHAPTER FOUR

3D Approach

'Three-dimensional (3D) instrument approach operation' means an instrument approach operation using both lateral and vertical navigation guidance

A Standard Instrument Arrival (STAR) should link the airways section into the approach. Be aware that not all airfields have a published arrival procedure. In which case you will route direct to the IAF. This book assumes that the first instrument approach following the airways section is a radar vectored ILS approach, however, some examiners complete the procedural hold and NPA first, followed by a radar vectored SE ILS approach at the home airfield.

Following the missed approach on the first instrument procedure, expect a simulated engine failure. Once you have secured the engine the examiner will reset power and you will execute a planned IFR diversion to the aerodrome of departure. The profile of the test will be comprehensively briefed on the ground by the examiner.

A) **NAVIGATION AIDS**

Confirms the serviceability and monitors the correct operation of selected navigation equipment

Once under radar vectors set up the radio aids for the approach. It is wise to select the ILS frequency on both ILS receivers, unless one is required for the missed approach procedure. Always identify both the ILS and co-located DME, if installed. Check that you are within the designated operational coverage. The Morse identifier is on the approach plate.

ILS Frequency & Morse Identifier

Is printed on the approach plate

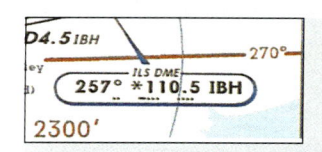

(a) NAVIGATION AIDS

Make sure that you correctly set the inbound course on the HSI or equivalent. Check for correct indications once on an intercept heading. You should have full scale deflection on the localiser and be below the glideslope. Make sure that the indications are not GPS derived. This can happen when leaving the airway on course to the aerodrome using GPS data, and not selecting back to raw data signals.

B)	ARRIVAL PROCEDURES

Completes the necessary aeroplane checks and drills

Follow the STAR until under radar vectors. Always note the clearance limit at the end of the STAR. You cannot proceed past this point without ATC clearance, always be prepared to enter the hold.

4 - PRECISION APPROACH

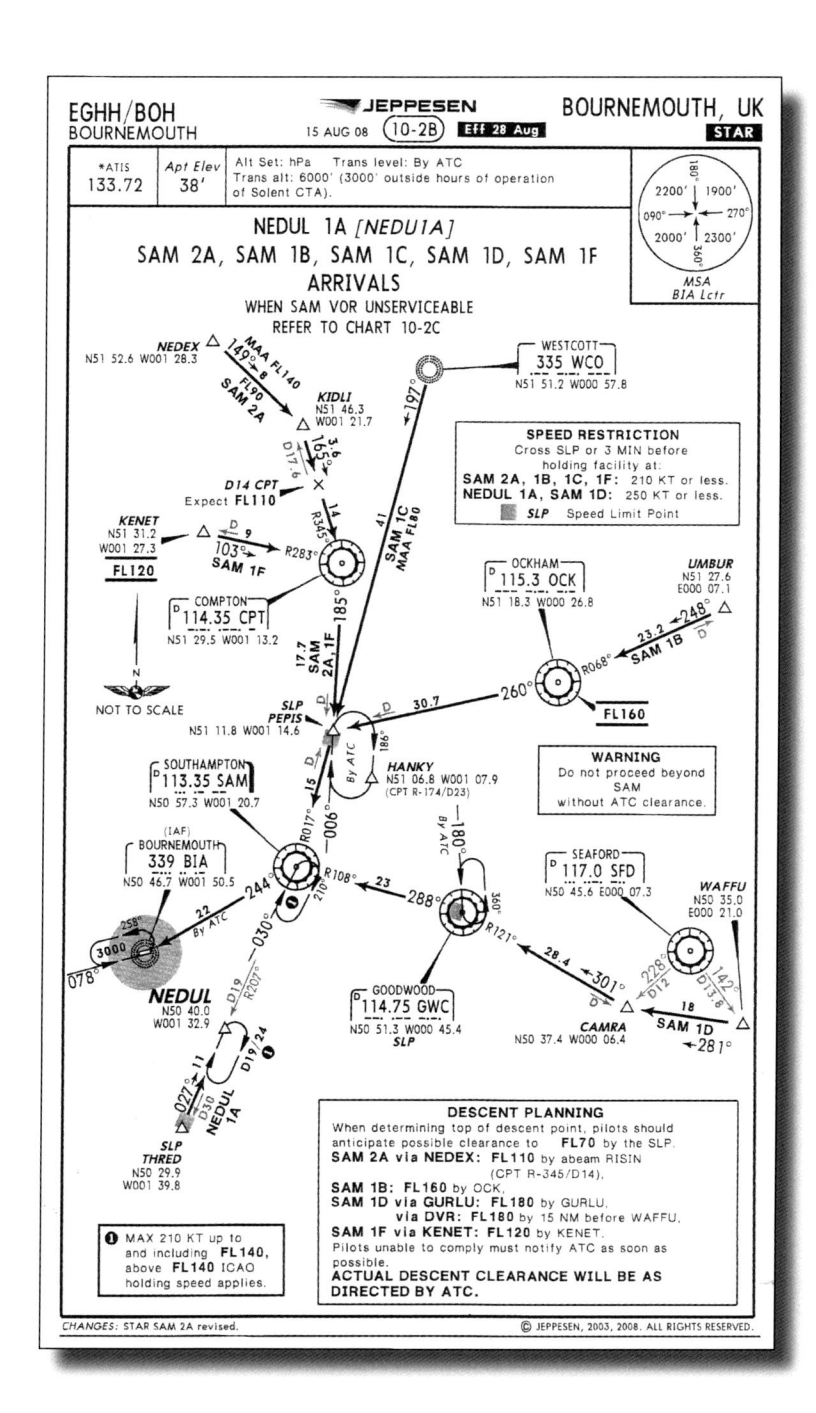

A STAR

For Bournemouth Airport

(b) ARRIVAL PROCEDURES

If the destination does not have any published instrument arrivals then the airway ATSU will co-ordinate the arrival with the airfield. Usually from the last waypoint on the airway you will route to an appropriate IAF or beacon at the airfield. You will be given a new transponder code and once identified, descent clearance. This will depend on the traffic at the airfield. Use the RNAV equipment to navigate a waypoint. If the examiner instructs you to track towards to the beacon using raw data information (rather than using the RNAV equipment), make sure that you are within the promulgated range.

Once outside controlled airspace you must request an appropriate service from ATC. The examiner will expect you to demonstrate knowledge on air traffic services outside controlled airspace.

ATC Service Principles Outside Controlled Airspace

Pilots are reminded that in uncontrolled airspace the pilot is ultimately responsible for terrain and obstacle avoidance although ATC may assist them. A core element of the new procedures is the principle of Pilot/Controller agreement which may restrict aircraft to a particular level or band or heading or area. Once a pilot has acknowledged a particular type of service there is assumed to be an 'accord' between pilot and controller. If a pilot subsequently requires a different service a new 'accord' shall be negotiated. Controllers will not provide elements of a higher level of service unless a new 'accord' is agreed. Although controllers will endeavour to pass timely traffic information there may be occasions due to workload or equipment limitations when this is not possible. In this case the controller will inform the pilot of the downgrade to the ATC service.

Basic Service

This provides the pilot with maximum autonomy. Avoidance of other traffic and terrain is solely the pilot's responsibility. This service is not appropriate for flight in IMC.

> **NOTE:** An ATC radar is not required to provide this service and it may be provided by a lower grade of controller (FISO).

RADIO PROCEDURE: **'REQUEST BASIC SERVICE'.**

Traffic Service

Pilots will be passed traffic information on conflicting aircraft. No deconfliction advice will be offered however, and the pilot remains responsible for collision and terrain avoidance. ATC may however offer headings or levels for positioning/sequencing/navigation. Again this service is not appropriate for flight in IMC. If given a heading or level a pilot should not alter course or change level without first advising and obtaining a response from the controller.

RADIO PROCEDURE: **'REQUEST TRAFFIC SERVICE'.**

Deconfliction Service

This provides the pilot with traffic information and deconfliction advice on conflicting aircraft. Headings and levels may be issued by the controller for deconfliction but avoidance of other aircraft remains the pilot's ultimate responsibility. ATC will expect the pilot to accept headings and levels that may require flight in IMC and they may request turns or squawk changes to identify a particular aircraft. Controllers will pass traffic information on conflicting traffic and advice to avoid. A pilot may elect to ignore such deconfliction advice but he MUST inform ATC and then accept responsibility for avoiding action. When under a Deconfliction Service pilots must not change heading or level without first obtaining a response from the controller, unless safety is likely to be compromised. A Deconfliction Service is only provided above an ATC unit's safe terrain level (above MFA) unless an aircraft is departing an aerodrome (and climbing to a safe level) or following an instrument approach procedure.

RADIO PROCEDURE: **'REQUEST DECONFLICTION SERVICE'.**

(b) ARRIVAL PROCEDURES

Procedural Service

This is a NON RADAR Service in which separation is provided between those IFR aircraft that are participating in an ATC Service and traffic information may be provided on known VFR aircraft. ATC will pass instructions which if followed will achieve deconfliction against other aircraft in receipt of a service from the same controller. Avoidance of traffic remains the pilot's responsibility. Deconfliction or traffic information will NOT be passed on aircraft that are not in receipt of an ATC Service. Controllers will expect pilots to accept instructions (tracks/radials or levels/level bands) that may require flight in IMC. Pilot's shall not change a level or track without obtaining approval from the controller as other aircraft may be coordinated by ATC. The pilot remains responsible for terrain avoidance.

RADIO PROCEDURE: **'REQUEST PROCEDURAL SERVICE'.**

A Deconfliction Service is often the most appropriate service to request if the ATSU is equipped with radar. The examiner may downgrade to a Traffic Service during the General Handling section to accommodate the manoeuvres required.

Once under radar vectors, ATC are responsible for terrain and traffic separation. However, it is good airmanship to cross check altitudes given against the radar vectoring chart.

4 - 3D APPROACH

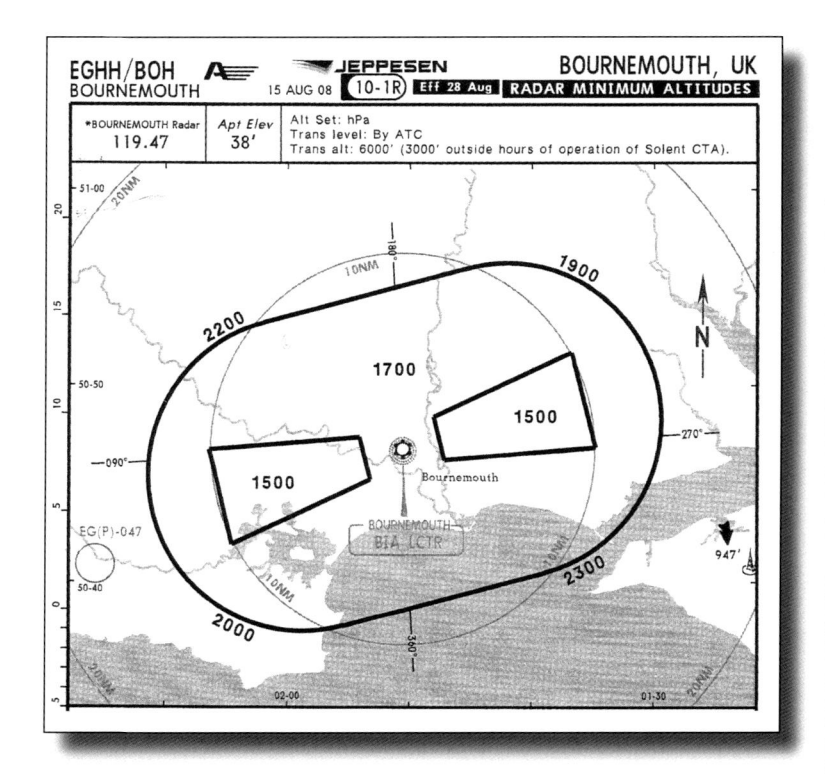

A Typical Radar Vectoring Chart

Complete the approach checks once cleared to an altitude and cross check the indications on both altimeters. Most civilian operators conduct approaches using the QNH. Complete the approach checks once this has been done. Complete the landing checklist once at an equivalent downwind position. Delay extending the landing gear and selecting final flap until intercepting the glide slope.

ATC may give you the number of track miles to be flown to touchdown. This allows you to calculate whether you are on the correct vertical profile to achieve a **Continuous Descent Approach (CDA)**. A CDA is the continuous descent from 6000 ft aal to interception of the glideslope with no level segment longer than 2 nm. A CDA reduces the fuel required for the approach and the noise pattern on the ground. They are really intended for higher performance aircraft, although it is useful to be aware of them for future use. During your IRT you are not required to fly one, however, if you have the spare capacity to do one then the examiner will be impressed. To calculate the correct track miles required multiply your height by 5 and compare this with the track miles given.

(b) ARRIVAL PROCEDURES

E.g. At 5000 ft, ATC inform you that you have 25 track miles until touchdown. (5 x 5 = 25 nm) so in this case you are on the correct descent profile. However, if you were only given 15 track miles you would be high on the profile and would have to increase the rate of descent to regain it.

You can also use any other piece of range information such as DME distance and checking whether you are on the correct profile and adjust the rate of descent as required.

Another useful tool which most modern GPS/FMS units with a moving map have is the ability to display an extended centreline from the FAF. This **'Vectors to Final'** function is most effectively used when under radar vectors, or self positioning onto the final approach course of either a 3D, or 2D approach. It aids in situational awareness and displays total track miles to touchdown. If vertical navigation guidance is available, this will give an accurate indication on whether the aircraft will achieve the FAF altitude stored in the database, based upon the aircrafts present position routing directly to the FAF.

The 'Vectors Final'

Function is very useful once under radar vectors or when self positioning onto final approach course

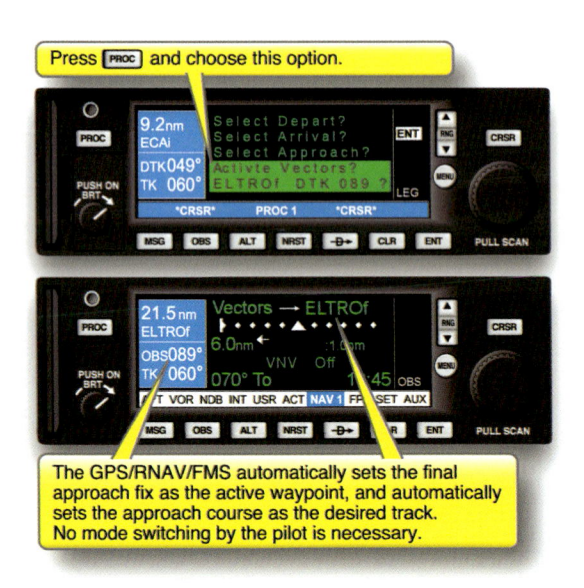

Uses correct RTF for ILS reporting procedure

Review CAP 413 and CAP 413 supplement before starting the course. Full route radiotelephony examples are given later. Use the following to report established:

(ATC) EXAM 01, 12 miles from touchdown turn right heading 240 degrees closing localiser from the right. When established on localiser, descend on glide path QNH 1011

(PILOT) Right heading 240 degrees when established on localiser, descend on the glide path QNH 1011, EXAM 01

C) **APPROACH AND** LANDING BRIEFING

Keep the approach briefing clear, concise, and pertinent to the conditions of the day. The briefing is more for your benefit. It should keep the process of events and associated actions during the approach clear in your mind. It also allows you to check the instrumentation as you brief and avoid setting incorrect radio aid frequencies.

Confirm that no approach ban is in force. Advise the examiner of your minima for the approach. Confirm that you have added **PEC** to the minima and that no cold weather temperature corrections are required.

Cold weather altimeter corrections

Whenever atmospheric conditions differ from ISA, barometric altimeter errors will result due to non-standard air density. When the temperature is colder than ISA, aircraft actual altitude will be lower than indicated altitude. Extremely low temperatures create significant altimeter errors and greater potential for reduced terrain clearance.

Altitude Lost

When flying into an area where the air is colder (more dense) than standard

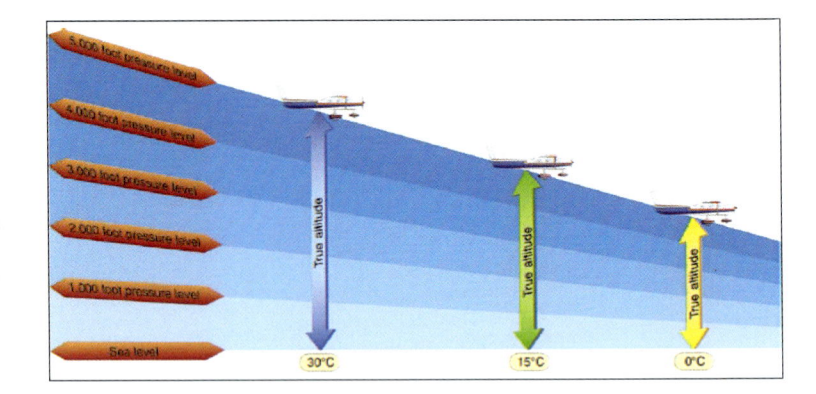

When surface temperatures are unusually cold, it is particularly important to make altitude adjustments on initial, intermediate, final approach, missed approach, MSA and hold altitudes. ATC should be informed of any corrections to the stated platform altitudes. Cold weather altimeter corrections should be found in the Operations Manual and checklist. The following important points should be remembered when applying cold weather corrections:-

- No corrections are required for reported temperatures above 0 °C
- Corrections apply to QNH and QFE operations
- Pilots should not correct altimeter barometric reference settings
- Apply corrections to all published minimum departure, en-route and approach altitudes including missed approach altitudes, according to the table shown overleaf
- Advise ATC of the corrections
- MDA/DA settings should be set at the corrected minimum altitudes for the approach

When calculating the appropriate altimeter corrections follow these steps:-

1. Subtract the elevation of the altimeter barometric reference setting source (normally the departure or destination airport elevation) from the published minimum altitude to be flown to determine "Height Above the elevation of the altimeter setting source (ft)".

2. Enter the table with "Aerodrome Temperature" and with "Height Above the elevation of the altimeter setting source (ft)." Read the correction where these two entries intersect.

4 - 3D APPROACH

3. Add the correction to the published minimum altitude to be flown to determine the corrected indicated altitude to be flown. To correct an altitude above the altitude in the last column, use linear extrapolation (e.g. to correct 6 000 ft use twice the correction for 3 000 ft).

Aerodrome Temperature	Height Above the elevation of the altimeter setting source (feet)												
°C	200	300	400	500	600	700	800	900	1000	1500	2000	3000	4000	5000
0	20	20	30	30	40	40	50	50	60	90	120	170	230	280
-10	20	30	40	50	60	70	80	90	100	150	200	290	390	490
-20	30	50	60	70	90	100	120	130	140	210	280	420	570	710
-30	40	60	80	100	120	140	150	170	190	280	380	570	760	950
-40	50	80	100	120	150	170	190	220	240	360	480	720	970	1210
-50	60	90	120	150	180	210	240	270	300	450	590	890	1190	1500
Values to be added by the pilot to minimum promulgated heights/altitudes (ft)														

Altitude Correction Table

Make sure that the minima you use are for public transport operations, and then add any further corrections as described.

52 - 2 | 16 JUN 10   United Kingdom - EGMH / MSE

JAR-OPS Landing Minima   MANSTON

The following Minima is for Public Transport aircraft and conforms to JAR-OPS1 regulations.

EU-OPS

Make sure that the landing minima is calculated with EU-OPS

STRAIGHT-IN APPROACH		A				B			
R/W	Procedure	DA/ MDA QNH ft	DH/ MDH QFE ft	RVR m	RVR No ALS m	DA/ MDA QNH ft	DH/ MDH QFE ft	RVR m	RVR No ALS m
10	LOC/DME	460	290	800	1500	460	290	800	1500
10	SRA 2nm	530	360	900	1500	530	360	1000	1500
10	NDB/DME Z	490	320	900	1500	490	320	1000	1500
10	NDB/DME Y	490	320	900	1500	490	320	1000	1500
10	NDB Y	530	360	900	1500	530	360	1000	1500
28	ILS	380	200	550	1000	380	200	550	1000
28	LOC/DME	500	330	900	1500	500	330	1000	1500
28	SRA 2nm	650	480	1000	1500	650	480	1200	1500
28	NDB/DME Z	560	390	900	1500	560	390	1000	1500
28	NDB/DME Y	560	390	900	1500	560	390	1000	1500
28	NDB Y	610	440	900	1500	610	440	1000	1500

Notes:

(c) APPROACH AND LANDING BRIEFING

A typical approach brief should include:-

a) Applicable weather and NOTAM information
b) Approach plate and date
c) MSA
d) Approach aid and frequency
e) Platform altitude and FAF
f) Minima (single crew RVR of 800 m; or the AOM whichever is the higher)
g) Missed approach procedure and altitude
h) Alternate, route and minimum fuel required
i) Runway conditions

D) HOLDING PROCEDURES

The hold is normally assessed just before completing the final approach, which is discussed in Chapter 6.

E) PUBLISHED APPROACH PROCEDURE

Completes the manoeuvring pattern as required to establish the final approach segment within the specified tolerances

The tolerances for the 3D approach are as follows:-

- Starting go-around from DA +50 ft/-0 ft (single engine +100 ft/-0 ft)
- Heading +/- 5 kts
- Tracking on 3D approach half scale deflection azimuth and glide path
- Vat or VREF +5 kts/-0 kts

Establishes the final approach segment and maintains the approach path in horizontal and vertical profile to decision altitude

Once you have established on the localiser, keep heading changes within the heading bug and establish a drift corrected heading early on. This will change slightly as you descend, due to surface friction affecting the wind.

When the glide slope reaches half scale deflection, extend the landing gear and select approach flap. Aim to fly a fully stabilised approach, confirm indications and complete the landing checks. Use the following when extending landing gear and flaps:-

LIMITATION – OPERATION – INDICATION

E.G.   *CHECK VLE – SELECT LANDING GEAR DOWN – CHECK FOR SAFE INDICATION.*

Just before you begin the descent on the glide slope, check the groundspeed. Use the following to calculate the appropriate ROD to maintain the glide slope:

ROD required for a 3° glide slope = Groundspeed x 5

Once fully established, maintain the ILS by applying small inputs. Do not chase the needles! Remember:-

- Control the airspeed with power
- Control the ROD with small pitch corrections
- Maintain the LLZ with small heading corrections

(e) PUBLISHED APPROACH PROCEDURE

3D Approach Profile

AIRMANSHIP: Checklist, AOM, Approach Ban, V_{FE}, V_{LE}, V_{LR}, V_{LO}, Approach Plates.

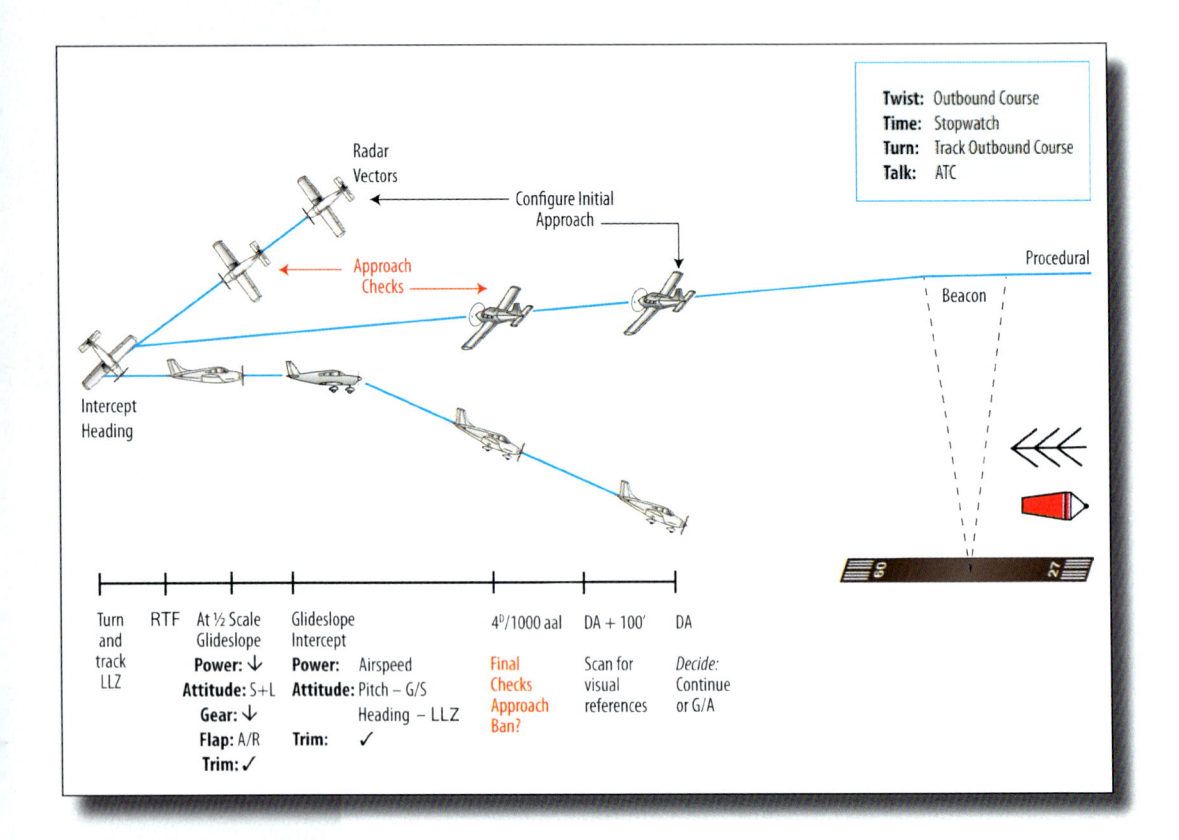

Twist: Outbound Course
Time: Stopwatch
Turn: Track Outbound Course
Talk: ATC

Radar Vectors

Configure Initial Approach

Approach Checks

Procedural Beacon

Intercept Heading

Turn and track LLZ	RTF	At ½ Scale Glideslope	Glideslope Intercept		4^D/1000 aal	DA + 100'	DA
		Power: ↓	**Power:** Airspeed		Final Checks Approach Ban?	Scan for visual references	*Decide:* Continue or G/A
		Attitude: S+L	**Attitude:** Pitch – G/S				
		Gear: ↓	Heading – LLZ				
		Flap: A/R	**Trim:** ✓				
		Trim: ✓					

NOTES:
- SE = Delay landing configuration until just before glideslope capture
- ROD required for a 3° glideslope = Groundspeed x 5
- When using landing gear or flap remember:
   LIMITATION OPERATION INDICATION

CHAPTER FOUR   (e) PUBLISHED APPROACH PROCEDURE

F) APPROACH TIMING

Reset the stopwatch after passing the appropriate fix. Timing is only really required for approaches that do not have DME information to define the missed approach point. It is good airmanship during a ILS approach to begin timing at the appropriate point in the event you lose the glide slope signal. You may be able to continue a LLZ only approach, if the procedure allows you to do so.

G) CONTROL OF THE AEROPLANE

Controls the aircraft as necessary to make adjustment and achieve a stable and trimmed final approach path

A stable approach is an approach which is flown in a controlled and appropriate manner in terms of configuration, energy and control of the flight path from a pre-determined point or altitude/height down to a point where the flare manoeuvre is initiated.

The Operations Manual will have specific information regarding stable approaches, typically operators follow similar guidelines. All approaches should be stabilised by 1000 feet **Above Runway Threshold Elevation (ARTE)** and **must** be stabilised by 500 feet **ARTE**: An approach is considered stabilised when all of the following criteria are met:

A. *The aircraft is on the correct flight path (on an ILS Approach, the aircraft must be within one dot of the localiser and the glide slope)*

B. *Only small changes in pitch and heading are required to maintain the correct flight path (except that on a Circling Approach, the aircraft must be 'wings level' on final by 300 ft ARTE)*

C. *IAS is not more than command airspeed plus 15 kts and not less than VREF (in gusty / turbulent conditions, momentary excursions are permitted)*

D. Sink rate is no greater than 1200 fpm; if an approach requires a rate of descent greater than 1200 fpm it must be briefed

E. The aircraft is in the correct landing configuration

F. The power is appropriate for the aircraft configuration

At a busy airfield you may be asked to maintain a higher than normal approach speed to accommodate traffic e.g. 160 kts until 4 miles from the threshold. If you cannot comply, inform ATC. You are expected to fit into the traffic as efficiently as you can, and still make a stable approach and landing. A common mistake on the IRT is not adjusting the ROD when reducing speed. The glide slope may then exceed test tolerances. Conversely, if ATC ask you to reduce to minimum approach speed on finals, it is generally accepted that in a light twin engine aircraft, this is Vyse + 5 kts.

ATC speed restrictions do not apply within 4 nm from the runway. Adjust speed as appropriate and confirm that the aircraft is configured for landing/go-around i.e. landing gear down, propellers max, mixture rich, flap set.

| H) | GO-AROUND |

Initiates the missed approach procedure upon reaching Decision Height/Altitude if required visual references for landing runway are not obtained

As you reach 100 ft above the DA start to look up and scan for visual references, (you won't see any as the screens will be up!). You must have initiated the go-around by DA; consequently it is wise to start to pitch up just before. The tolerance is:-

- Starting go-around from DA +50ft/-0ft (single engine +100ft/-0ft), or as directed by ATC

4 - 3D APPROACH

The examiner may ask you during the briefing:-

'What visual references are required to continue the approach and landing?'

You must be able to see at least one visual element of the intended runway, such as the threshold lights, elements of the approach lighting system, runway edge lights, etc.

Establishes the aeroplane in a safe climb out and initiates aeroplane configuration changes as required to achieve at least the performance climb gradients

Once you have made the decision to go-around it should not be revoked. Do not rush to reconfigure the aircraft, concentrate on accurate control of the aircraft.

Pay particular attention to the speed control. When retracting the flaps and landing gear, obey any speed limitations. Use the following:-

LIMITATION – OPERATION – INDICATION

Although procedures differ, go-around actions in light aircraft are broadly similar. They consist of:-

- Simultaneously set pitch to the go-around attitude and apply full power
- Hold the go-around attitude and retract landing flap (if appropriate)
- Once a positive rate of climb is indicated on both the VSI and Altimeter retract the landing gear
- Retract the flap in stages
- Accelerate to Vy and trim the aircraft

Approach and Runway Lighting

Do not continue below DA/MDA unless you have suitable visual references

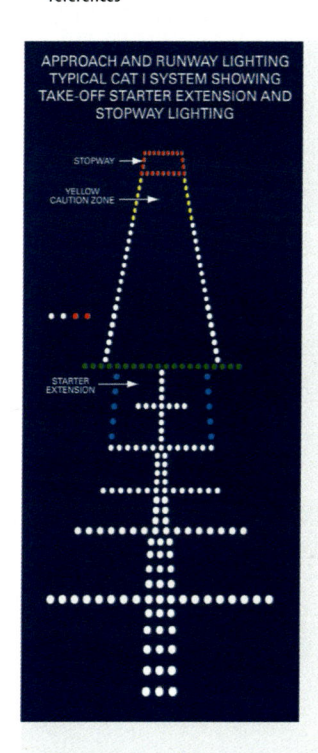

APPROACH AND RUNWAY LIGHTING TYPICAL CAT I SYSTEM SHOWING TAKE-OFF STARTER EXTENSION AND STOPWAY LIGHTING

(h) GO-AROUND

| I) | **MISSED APPROACH** PROCEDURE/LANDING |

Demonstrates knowledge of missed approach procedure.

Follows designated missed approach procedure or as required by ATC

Once you are established in the go-around, review the missed approach procedure and follow it as depicted on the chart. At a busy airfield ATC may give you different instructions. These override the published procedure. Pay particular attention to tracking and the missed approach altitude

Once the aircraft is at a safe altitude, the examiner will shield the throttle quadrant and simulate an engine failure. Carry out standard drills and maintain Vyse. When you have identified the failed engine, the examiner will uncover the throttles and set zero thrust once feathering touch drills are completed. Continue with the missed approach. Once you have 'secured' the failed engine back up your actions with the appropriate checklist. Once this has been completed the examiner will restore the engine.

4 - 3D APPROACH

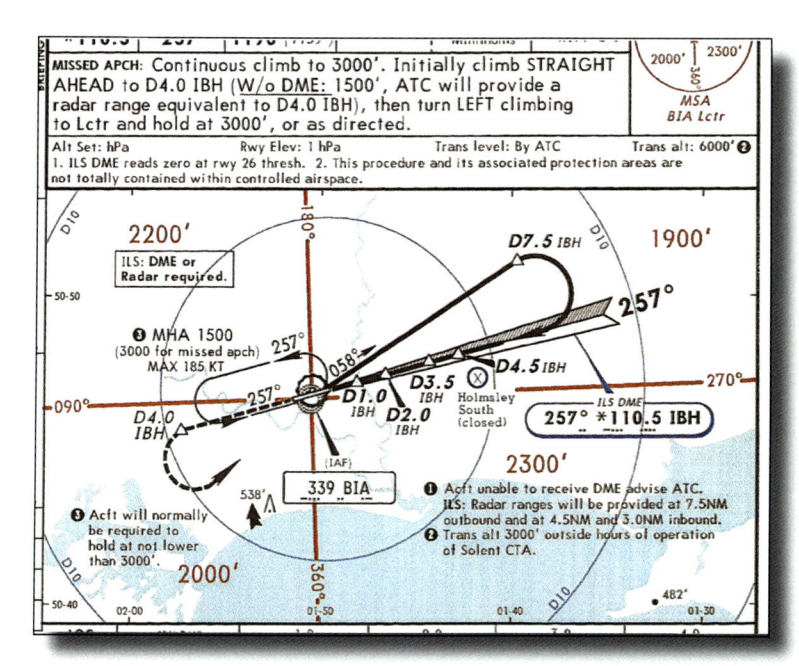

Missed Approach
Always review the missed approach procedure

Do not rush the missed approach and EFATO drills-it is a very busy time. You are very close to the ground and reducing the aircraft's climb performance. It is very easy to get everything done at the expense of controlling the flight path. Use the following as an aide memoir:-

AVIATE − NAVIGATE − COMMUNICATE − CHECKS

J)   ATC LIAISON

Once established in the missed approach, inform ATC:-

(PILOT) EXAM 01, going around

(ATC) EXAM 01, Roger
ATC may also instruct you to go-around at any time;
(ATC) EXAM 01, go-around, I say again go-around acknowledge

(PILOT) Going around EXAM 01

If ATC instruct you to go-around, the examiner will decide and inform you whether another approach is required to fulfil the test criteria.

(j) ATC LIAISON

intentionally blank

CHAPTER FIVE

General Handling

Following the missed approach, you will carry out a pre-planned diversion under IFR, usually in uncontrolled airspace. If you are cruising at an altitude above the transition altitude, fly at an appropriate flight level in accordance with the Quadrantal Rule. If you are below the transition altitude make sure that you are above MSA. Request a Deconfliction service from an appropriate ATSU. Plotting the complete flight, including the return, on a 1:500,000 chart can help situational awareness and help you avoid restricted airspace.

1:500 000 Chart
Can help situational awareness

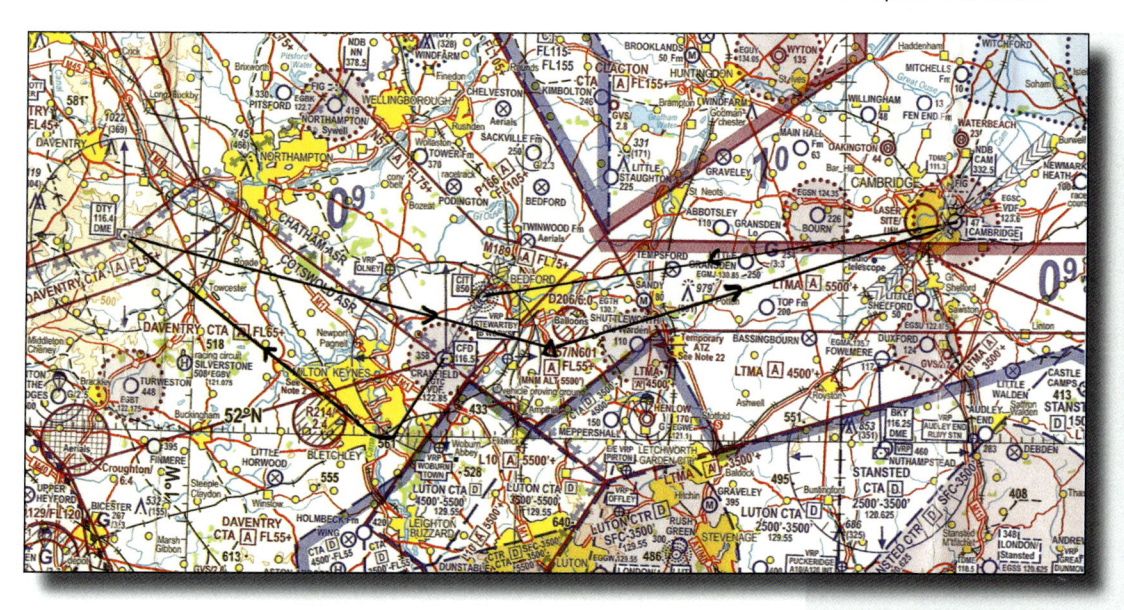

Once the examiner is happy that you are in a suitable position and in VMC, the General Handling section will begin. The examiner is now responsible for R/T, navigation and lookout. He will remind you of his responsibilities before beginning the manoeuvres.

A) & B)	FULL PANEL

(a) & (b) FULL PANEL

5 - GENERAL HANDLING

Controls the aeroplane by sole reference to instruments within the nominated limits (due consideration will be given for turbulence)

Controls flight in straight and level, and climbing and descending, at required speeds. Turns flown at rate 1 onto nominated headings, using the correct technique and demonstrating correct instrument scan and interpretation

These will be assessed throughout the flight rather than asking for specific manoeuvres.

C) & D)   FULL PANEL-RECOVERIES

Recovers from unusual attitudes including sustained 45° bank turns and steep descending turns using the correct technique to minimise height lost

Stall speed increases by 40% in a 60° banked turn.

Maintain airspeed with added power

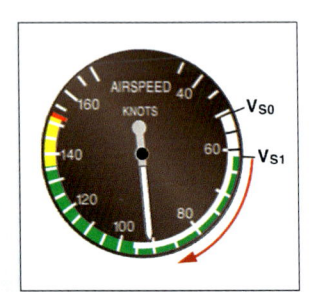

PRIOR TO ENTERING A STEEP LEVEL TURN

Achieve straight and level flight at the desired height and airspeed, and be in trim. Note the heading on the direction indicator, and decide which way you will turn and onto what heading. Ask the safety pilot to check outside for other aircraft.

Rolling into a Steep Level Turn

Roll into the steep turn with coordinated aileron and rudder, the same as you would for a medium turn, except that, as the bank angle increases through 30°:

- progressively increase back pressure to raise the pitch attitude on the AI to maintain height;
- progressively add power to maintain airspeed.

CHAPTER FIVE   (c) & (d) FULL PANEL RECOVERIES

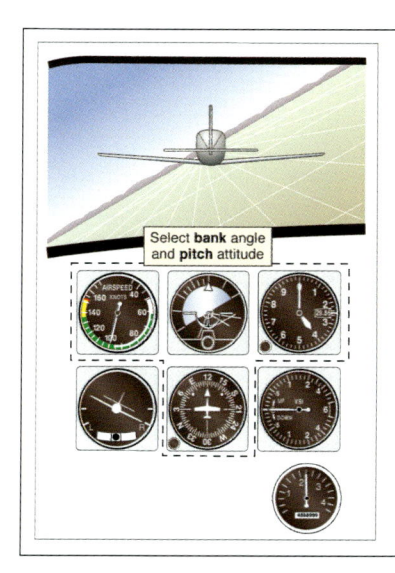

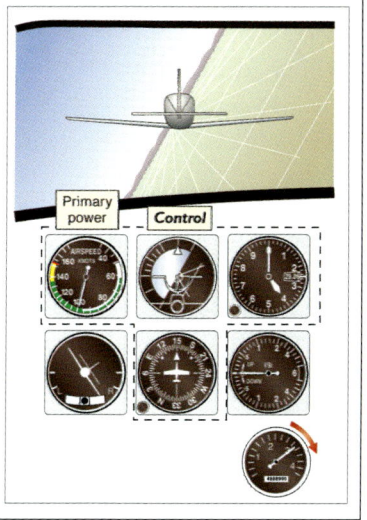

5 - GENERAL HANDLING

Entering and maintaining a steep turn

A steep left turn
As indicated on EFIS

Maintaining a Steep Level Turn

Increase your instrument scan rate as the turn steepens, to cope with all of the variables. The secret of an accurate steep level turn on instruments is to:

- Have a good scan;
- Hold the correct bank angle and pitch attitude on the attitude indicator; and
- Maintain airspeed with power.

BANK ANGLE AND BALANCE

Control of the bank angle and balance is achieved with coordinated use of aileron and rudder, with reference to the attitude indicator and the balance ball. The turn coordinator is of little use, since the steep turn will be well in excess of rate 1, but it is still useful as an indication of the direction of the turn, left or right. The desired bank angle is held on the AI.

HOLD BANK ANGLE ON THE ATTITUDE INDICATOR

PITCH CONTROL

Pitch control is more difficult to achieve than bank control, because of the considerably increased back pressure required (and also, for some people, the slightly unpleasant g-forces that increase as back pressure is applied). The pitch attitude is higher in the steep turn than in level flight. Vertical performance can be monitored on the VSI and altimeter to ensure that height is being maintained. The primary performance indicator that the pitch attitude held on the AI is correct is the altimeter, supported by the VSI.

THE ALTIMETER IS THE PRIMARY PERFORMANCE INDICATOR FOR PITCH ATTITUDE

(c) & (d) FULL PANEL RECOVERIES

THE ASI IS THE PRIMARY PERFORMANCE INDICATOR FOR POWER IN LEVEL FLIGHT

AIRSPEED

Airspeed control is achieved with the throttle. If insufficient additional power is applied, then airspeed can diminish quite rapidly. The power should be increased progressively as the bank angle steepens during the roll-in, and you should imagine that there is a direct link from the airspeed indicator to your hand on the throttle – any hint of an airspeed loss requiring an immediate increase in power. The primary performance indicator for power in level flight (including turns) is the ASI. There is no need to monitor the power indicator directly unless there is a possibility of exceeding limitations.

ALTITUDE

Loss of height will result if insufficient back pressure is applied as the steep turn is entered, the nose will drop, the VSI and altimeter will indicate a rapid loss of altitude, and the ASI will indicate an increasing airspeed. Simply increasing back pressure at a steep bank angle when the nose has dropped will only tighten the turn without raising the nose.

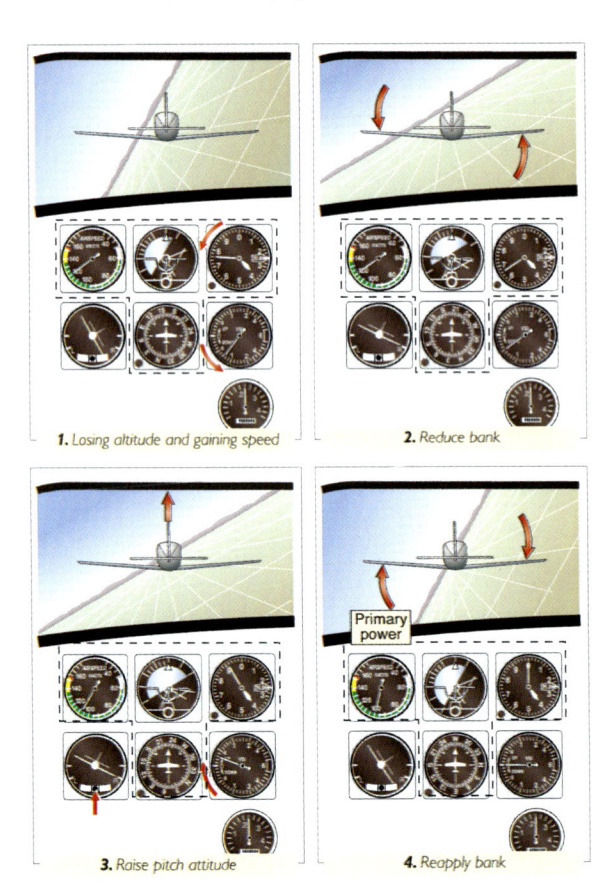

Regaining a height loss in a steep turn

1. Losing altitude and gaining speed
2. Reduce bank
3. Raise pitch attitude
4. Reapply bank

(c) & (d) FULL PANEL RECOVERIES

The recommended technique if **altitude is lost** is:
- reduce bank angle with aileron;
- raise pitch attitude with elevator (back pressure); and
- re-apply bank

If altitude is being gained:
- relax some of the back pressure, and lower the pitch attitude slightly; and/or
- steepen the bank angle slightly.

Extreme cases of nose-high or nose-low attitudes are considered later. They can result from a poorly flown steep turn, especially under instrument conditions, and especially when you have a slow scan rate or are not prepared to exert your authority over the aeroplane and make it do exactly what you want.

Rolling Out of the Steep Level Turn

If the aim is to roll out onto a particular heading, then approximately 30° lead should be allowed because of the high rate of turn. Roll out of the steep turn using coordinated aileron and rudder. Gradually release the back pressure on the control column and lower the pitch attitude on the AI to maintain altitude (as monitored on the VSI and altimeter). Gradually reduce power to maintain the desired airspeed (as monitored on the ASI).

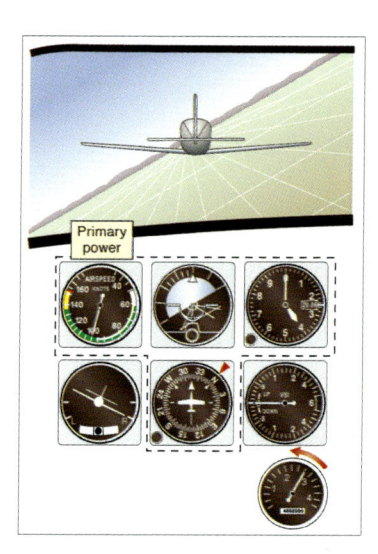

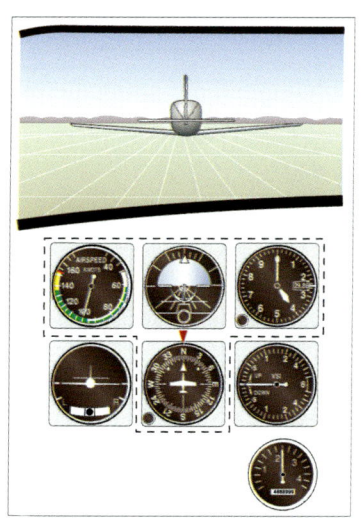

Rolling out of a steep level turn

(c) & (d) FULL PANEL RECOVERIES

Steep Descending Turns

The steep descending turn is never flown in normal instrument flight operations, but it may be used during your training (with your flying instructor on board as safety pilot) as a practice manoeuvre to improve coordination. Note that there is no steep climbing turn, since this is beyond the performance capability of most training aircraft, and a useful rate of climb could not be maintained.

It is usual to allow airspeed to increase in a steep descending turn in order to maintain an adequate safety margin over the stalling speed (which increases during a turn). Typical speed increases, controlled by use of the elevator, are:

- 10 kt for a 45° bank in a steep descending turn; and
- 20 kt for a 60° bank in a steep descending turn.

Rolling into a Steep Descending Turn

From a steady descent, roll on bank with coordinated aileron and rudder. Keep the balance ball centred with whatever rudder pressure is required; in a gliding turn, there will be more rudder pressure required one way compared to the other because of the lack of a slipstream.

Lower the pitch attitude slightly on the AI, using elevator to maintain the desired nose position to achieve the higher airspeed. The nose will tend to drop in a descending turn and so, even though the pitch attitude on the attitude indicator will be lower to achieve a higher airspeed, some back pressure on the control column will be needed to stop the nose dropping too far.

Maintaining a Steep Descending Turn

Increase your scan rate as the turn steepens to cope with all the variables. Hold the desired pitch attitude and bank angle with reference to the AI, and monitor the ASI closely. Control bank angle with coordinated use of aileron and rudder. Control pitch attitude on the AI with elevator to achieve the desired airspeed. The ASI is the primary indicator that pitch attitude is correct.

(c) & (d) FULL PANEL RECOVERIES

If the pitch attitude is too low and the airspeed becomes excessive:
- reduce the bank angle on the AI using ailerons;
- raise the pitch attitude on the AI with elevator to reduce airspeed on the ASI; and
- re-apply the bank.

If the bank angle is not reduced, then simply applying back pressure may only serve to tighten the turn without decreasing airspeed, and the g-loading may increase beyond acceptable limits. A spiral dive can result if pitch attitude, bank angle and airspeed are not kept within acceptable limits.

The rate of descent in a steep descending turn will increase significantly, not only because of the lower pitch attitude for the higher airspeed, but also because the tilting of the lift force reduces its vertical component. If desired, the rate of descent can be controlled with power, and monitored on the VSI and altimeter. Increasing power, and raising the pitch attitude to maintain airspeed, will result in a reduced rate of descent.

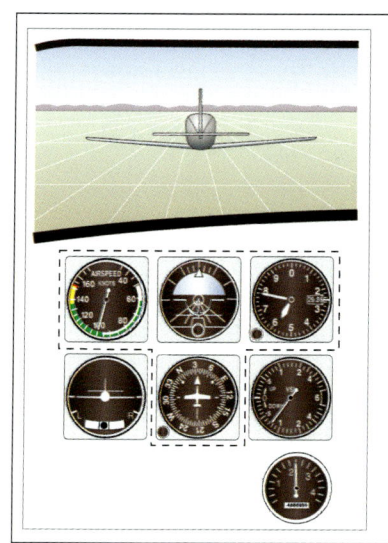

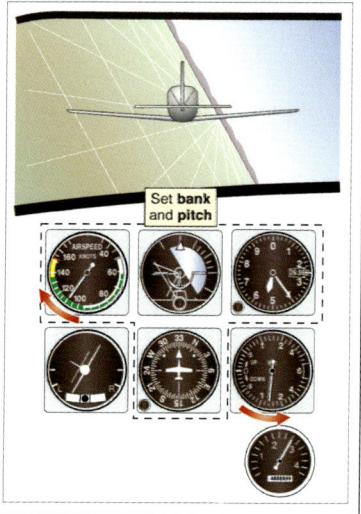

Maintaining a steep descending turn

Rolling out of a Steep Descending Turn

With reference to the attitude indicator, roll off bank with coordinated aileron and rudder, and select the slightly higher pitch attitude with elevator required for the straight descent. Monitor the ASI and adjust pitch attitude on the AI to achieve the desired airspeed. The ASI is the

(c) & (d) FULL PANEL RECOVERIES

primary guide to a correct pitch attitude. If the aim is to roll out onto a particular heading, then approximately 30° lead should be allowed because of the rapid rate of turn.

A steep descending turn that is not monitored carefully can result in a spiral dive, an unusual attitude best avoided.

Recovers from an approach to the stall in level flight, climbing/descending turns and in the landing configuration, with minimum height loss

The examiner will expect you to demonstrate a recovery at the incipient stage in both the approach configuration whilst turning and in the landing configuration whilst in straight flight. The examiner will brief you on exactly how he expects you to configure the aircraft for each stall manoeuvre, below is basic description:-

Approach configuration: Intermediate approach flap, landing gear down, approach power, descending turning at rate 1

Landing configuration: Full flap, landing gear down, approach power, straight flight

Complete a **HASELL** check before starting the first manoeuvre then a **HELL** during any subsequent ones. He will remind you of each manoeuvre before asking you to demonstrate it, but will not tell you how to configure or set it up. He will also remind you of his responsibilities.

A review of the incipient symptoms:-
- Higher than normal attitude
- Low, decreasing airspeed
- Sloppy ineffective controls
- Reduced noise
- Light buffet
- Any stall warning operation

CHAPTER FIVE   (c) & (d) FULL PANEL RECOVERIES

5 - GENERAL HANDLING

Recovery:-
- Apply full power, simultaneously lower the nose
- Prevent Yaw with rudder and level wings on the turn coordinator with coordinated aileron and rudder; and
- Once established in the climb at Vy with a positive rate of climb shown on the Altimeter and VSI, retract the landing gear and retract the flaps in stages. Maintain the aircraft in trim

NB. *The examiner expects to see the standard stall recovery applied*

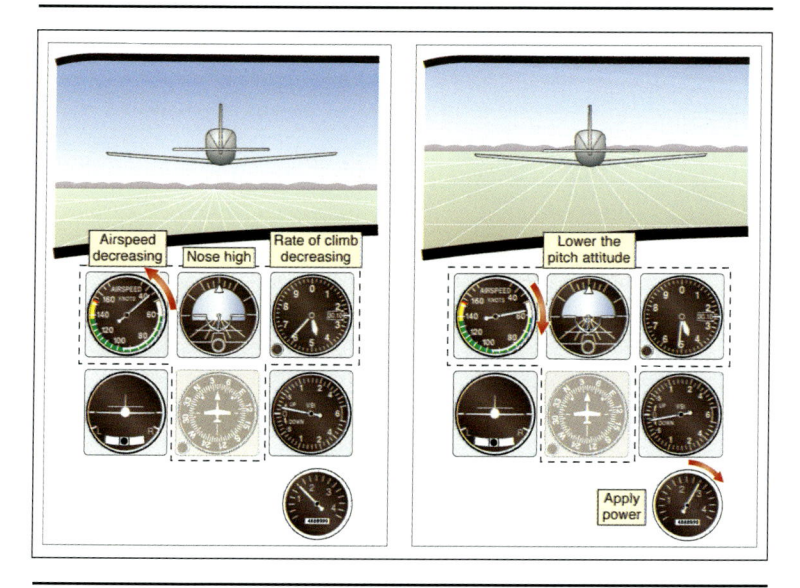

Recovering from the incipient stall

(E) LIMITED PANEL

Completes limited panel straight and level flight, climbing/descending flight and turns at rate 1 onto given headings in level flight. Recovers from unusual attitudes

The examiner will simulate limited panel by applying a small screen which shields the AI, HSI & RMI. Candidates who attempt the test in an aircraft equipped with full EFIS will have to demonstrate limited panel and unusual attitude recoveries with a nominated examiner during training, in an aircraft equipped with analogue instrumentation.

(e) LIMITED PANEL

They will also have to demonstrate during the test, recoveries using the standby conventional instruments fitted in EFIS equipped aircraft.

Determining bank attitude on a limited panel

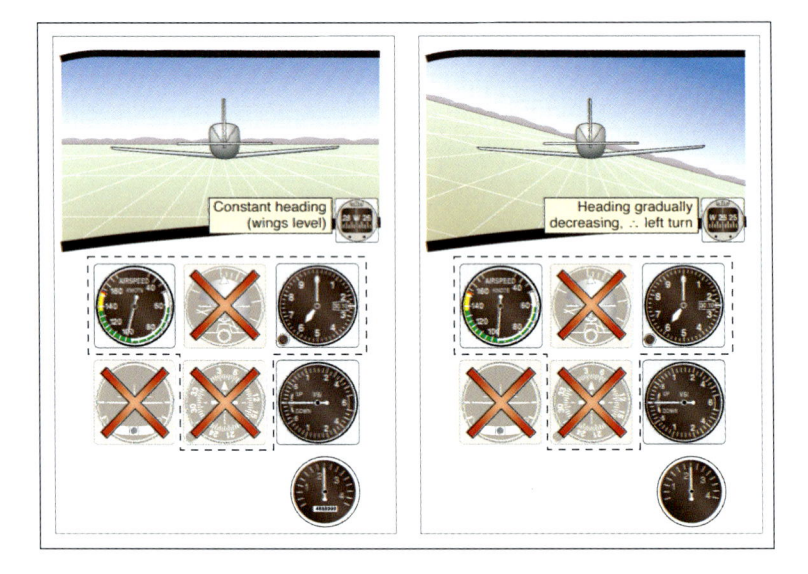

Straight and Level Flight on a Limited Panel

Setting cruise power and placing the aeroplane in the cruise attitude will provide cruise performance, with the aeroplane in straight and level flight.

To achieve straight and level flight at a particular altitude on a limited panel without the use of the AI:

- **set cruise power** on the power indicator;
- **hold the wings level** with reference to the turn coordinator, with the balance ball centred; and
- **adjust the pitch attitude** with reference to the altimeter and VSI; and then
- **trim**.

To maintain straight and level flight at the chosen altitude, once it has been achieved:

HEADING

Maintain heading by keeping the wings level using the turn coordinator, and the ball centred. Heading can be checked on the direction indicator if it is working, otherwise on the magnetic compass.

(e) LIMITED PANEL

5 - GENERAL HANDLING

Any corrections to heading should be made with gentle coordinated turns (rate ½ on the turn coordinator, which is 1.5°/ sec, should be more than adequate). The direction indicator, if usable, will indicate heading directly but, if the magnetic compass is used, then some allowance will be needed to undershoot on northerly headings and overshoot on southerly headings.

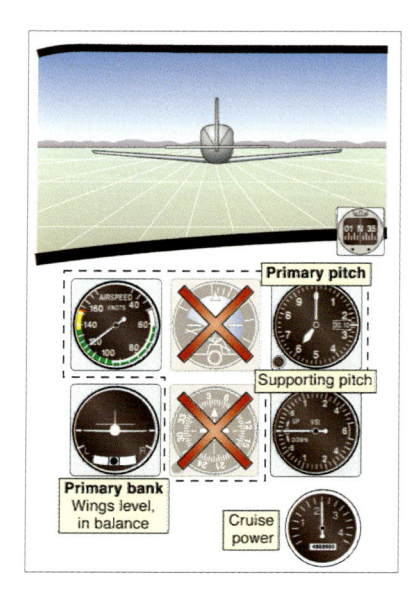

Achieving straight and level flight on a limited panel

ALTITUDE

Any tendency to drift off altitude due to a slightly incorrect pitch attitude will first be shown on the VSI, and minor adjustments with the elevator can be made almost before any change is registered on the altimeter. In turbulent conditions, however, the VSI will tend to fluctuate, in which case the altimeter will be the more useful instrument. Aim to stay right on altitude. Minor deviations of less than 100 ft can generally be corrected with very small pitch alterations; any deviation in excess of 100 ft may also require a small power change as well as an attitude change. Keep in trim to make the task easier.

(e) LIMITED PANEL

Maintaining heading and altitude

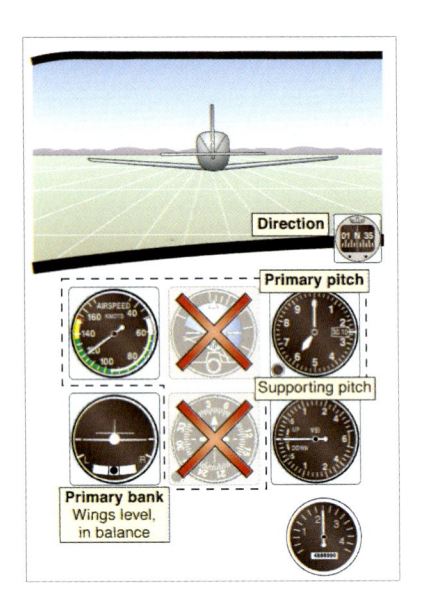

AIRSPEED

Airspeed is normally just accepted in the cruise, once cruise power has been set. If, however, precise airspeed control is desired, then this can be achieved with power. Once cruise speed is achieved, ensure that the aeroplane is in trim.

To change airspeed in straight and level flight, a coordinated change of both power and pitch attitude will be required. Greater precision using only a limited panel of instruments can be achieved if these changes are gradual and smooth.

---

*HIGHER AIRSPEED A higher speed will require more power and a lower pitch attitude. Remember that a power increase will cause a **pitch up/yaw left** tendency in most aircraft, and this should be resisted with gentle control pressures. Therefore, as power is slowly increased with the throttle to achieve a speed increase, monitor the VSI (backed up by the altimeter) to determine the small increases in forward pressure required on the control column to maintain altitude, and keep the ball centred with a slight increase in (right) rudder pressure.*

Refer to the turn coordinator to ensure that the wings are kept level, so that heading is maintained. Power adjustment may be required to maintain the desired airspeed. Once stabilised at the desired speed, retrim the aircraft. The direction indicator (if available) or the magnetic compass (once it has settled down) can be checked to verify heading.

(e) LIMITED PANEL

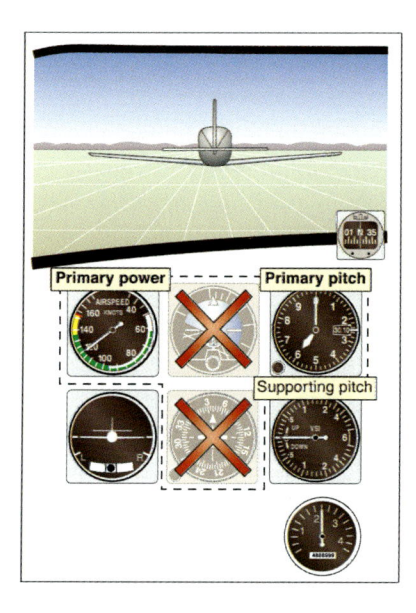

Changing airspeed on a limited panel

LOWER AIRSPEED *A lower airspeed will require less power and a higher pitch attitude. The power reduction will cause a pitch down/yaw right tendency, which the pilot should be ready to counteract. Any tendency to lose altitude can be monitored on the VSI, and corrected with elevator. The turn coordinator and balance ball can be used to monitor any tendency to drift off heading. Once the desired lower airspeed is achieved, minor power adjustments with the throttle may be required. The aeroplane should then be retrimmed.*

Climbing on a Limited Panel

Entering a Climb

The procedure to enter a climb using only a partial instrument panel is the same as with a full panel: **P-A-T, power-attitude-trim**. Smoothly apply climb power (mixture rich if necessary), keeping the wings level on the turn coordinator and the ball centred to maintain heading, and raise the pitch attitude slightly. There will be a pitch-up tendency as power is applied, so probably only a slight back pressure on the control column will be required.

(e) LIMITED PANEL

Hold the new pitch attitude until the airspeed indicator stabilises. The VSI will show a climb and, once you are familiar with the particular aeroplane, this will provide useful backup information to the ASI regarding correct pitch attitude. An initial trim adjustment will assist in maintaining the new attitude. Once the airspeed has settled, minor adjustments can be made with the elevator to fine tune the airspeed, and then the aeroplane can be trimmed precisely to maintain the desired climbing speed.

Entering a climb on a limited panel

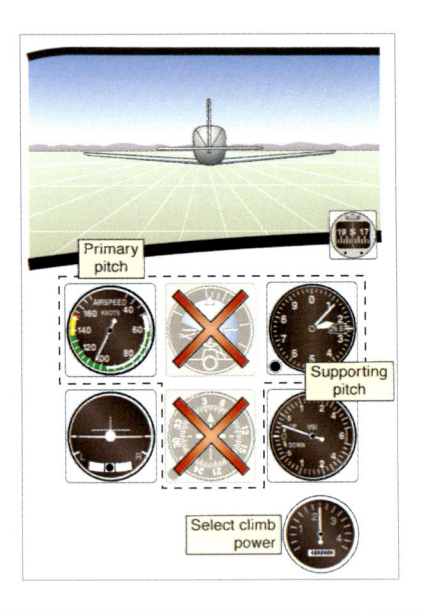

Maintaining a Climb

To maintain a straight climb on a limited panel, hold the pitch attitude with reference to the ASI, which is the primary indicator of correct pitch attitude during the climb. Maintain heading by keeping the wings level on the turn coordinator and the balance ball centred. Heading can be checked on the direction indicator or magnetic compass.

(e) LIMITED PANEL

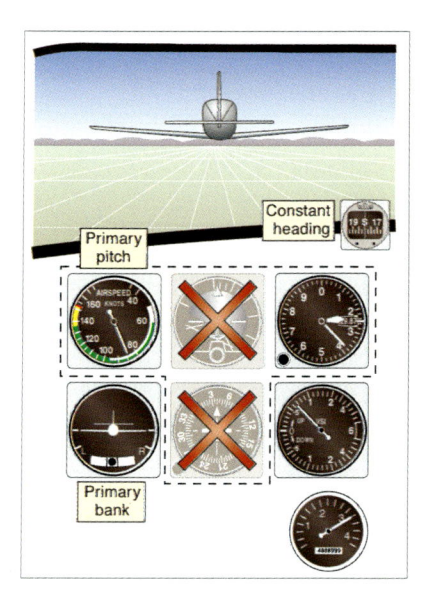

Maintaining the climb on a limited panel

It is good airmanship to check engine temperatures and pressures periodically during the climb, since the engine is working hard and the cooling airflow is less, but this should not take more than one or two seconds and should not distract you from your main scan of the flight instruments. Being in trim will make life easier.

Levelling Off from a Climb

To level off at a particular altitude, it is important that the altimeter has the correct setting in its subscale (Regional Pressure Setting, 1013, or Aerodrome QNH or QFE, as the case may be). The altimeter should increasingly be brought into the scan as the desired altitude is approached, and the focus for pitch control shifted to it from the ASI. Levelling off should be commenced smoothly before the desired altitude is actually reached, a suitable lead-in being 10% of the rate of climb (say 40 ft before the altitude for a rate of climb of 400 ft/min).

(e) LIMITED PANEL

Levelling off from a climb on a limited panel

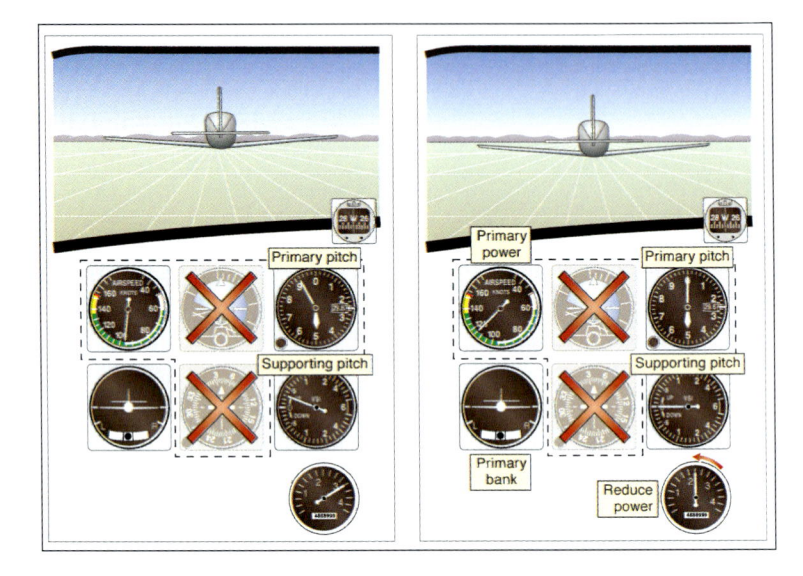

The procedure to level off is A-P-T, attitude-power-trim. Gradually lower the pitch attitude towards the level flight position, noting a decreasing climb rate on the VSI, and capture the desired altitude with reference to the altimeter. Keep the wings level and the ball centred to maintain heading. Once the airspeed has increased to the desired cruising value on the ASI, smoothly reduce power, and then trim the aircraft.

Once the aeroplane is stabilised, the scan becomes that for normal straight and level flight, although particular attention should be paid to the ASI in the early stages to ensure that adequate power is set to maintain the desired airspeed.

Descending on a Limited Panel

Entering a Descent

A descent will require less power and a lower pitch attitude than for level flight. To enter a descent, the procedure is **P-A-T**, power- attitude-trim. Smoothly reduce the power (mixture control rich, carburettor heat hot if necessary) with the throttle. Hold the wings level and the ball centred to maintain heading, and hold the pitch attitude with slight back pressure until the desired descent airspeed on the ASI is almost reached in level flight, at which time the nose can be gently lowered slightly to maintain airspeed.

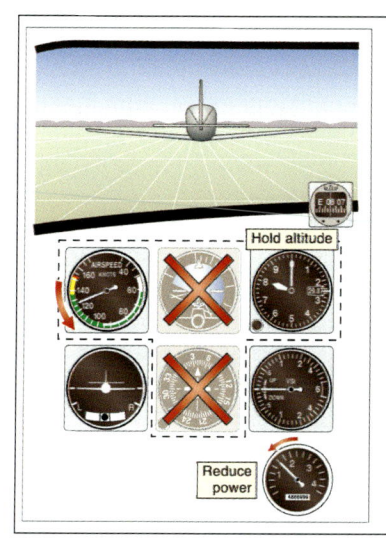

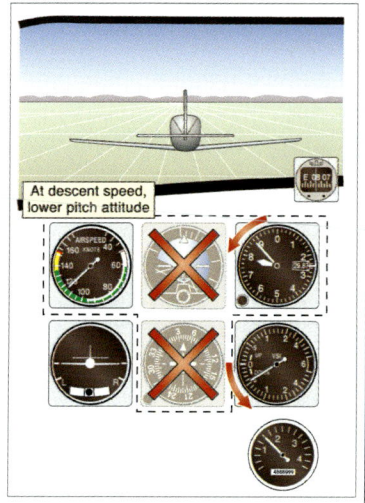

Entering a Descent

If the descent airspeed is to be the same as the level airspeed, then the pitch attitude should be lowered simultaneously with the power reduction. Remember that there will be a natural tendency for the nose to drop and yaw as power is reduced.

The VSI can be used to monitor any vertical tendencies. An initial coarse trim adjustment as soon as the descent attitude is adopted is acceptable to remove most steady control pressures, followed by fine adjustments to the pitch attitude to maintain the desired airspeed and a final fine trim adjustment.

Maintaining a Descent

To maintain the descent on a limited panel:

- **maintain heading** with wings level on the turn coordinator and the balance ball centred, checking heading against the direction indicator or the magnetic compass;
- **maintain airspeed** with gentle changes in pitch attitude, using the ASI and VSI – if a particular rate of descent is required, then coordinated use of power and attitude can be used to achieve it, with the airspeed being monitored on the ASI, and the rate of descent being monitored on the VSI.

(e) LIMITED PANEL

Maintaining a descent on a limited panel

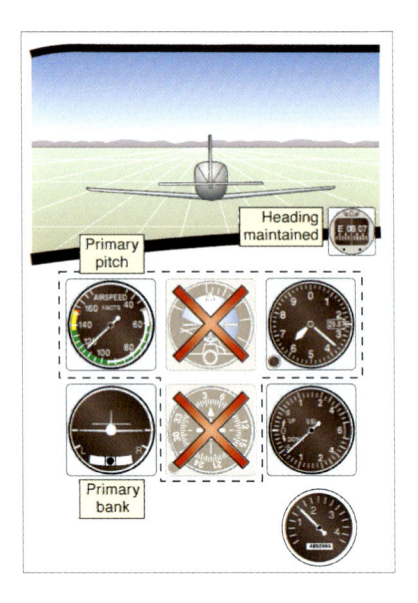

In a prolonged descent with low power, consider clearing the engine every 1,000 ft or so by applying 50% power for a few seconds to keep the engine and oil warm, to avoid carbon fouling of the spark plugs and to keep warm air available for carburettor heat.

Applying the extra power, and then removing it, should not distract you from scanning the flight instruments for more than a few seconds. Be prepared to counteract pitch/yaw tendencies as the power is changed.

Levelling off from a Descent

To level off from a descent at a particular altitude, it is important that the altimeter has the correct setting in its subscale. As the desired altitude is approached, the focus for pitch attitude control should shift from the ASI to the altimeter, and the levelling off manoeuvre commenced before the altitude is actually reached (a suitable lead-in being 10% of the rate of descent).

The procedure to level off from a descent is P-A-T, power- attitude-trim. Smoothly increase power to the cruise setting and raise the pitch attitude, noting that the VSI shows a reducing rate of descent, and aim to capture the desired altitude precisely on the altimeter. Trim the aeroplane. Revert to the normal straight and level scan, checking the altimeter for altitude, and initially checking the ASI to ensure that the desired airspeed is being maintained.

(e) LIMITED PANEL

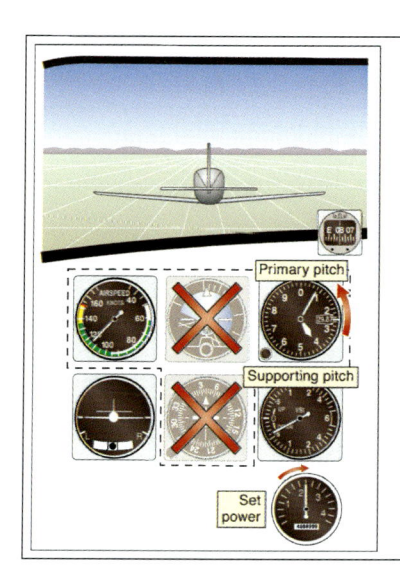

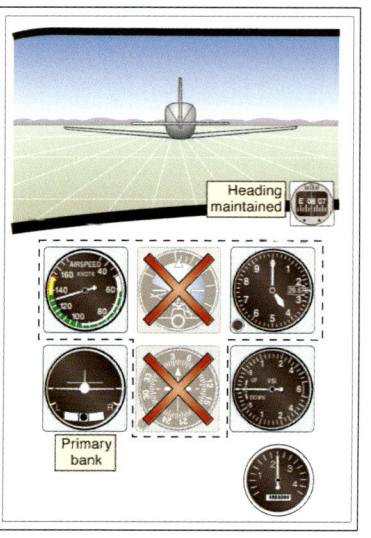

Levelling off from a descent on a limited panel

Entering a Climb from a Descent

Entering a climb from a descent, such as in a go-around, is a more demanding manoeuvre on a limited panel than on a full panel, since a large and fairly rapid power increase, accompanied by a higher pitch attitude, will be required. The large pitch attitude change may cause the VSI to give a reversed reading initially, so it must be disregarded until its reading has stabilised. Practising a go-around on a limited panel is, perhaps, an exercise for the more advanced student.

Turning on a Limited Panel

To turn onto a specific heading, the best instruments to use for directional guidance are (in order):

- **the direction indicator**;
- **the clock** (for timed turns – rate 1 being 3°/sec); or
- **the magnetic compass** (with its turning and acceleration errors).

If the direction indicator is used, then it must first have been aligned with the magnetic compass while in steady straight and level flight.

If the DI is not usable, then a timed turn with **clock** and **turn coordinator** is the preferred method. This method can be quite accurate. Once established in straight flight on the new heading, the magnetic compass will settle down and allow the heading to be checked.

(e) LIMITED PANEL

If, however, the magnetic compass has to be used during the turn, then the roll-out should occur before any desired northerly heading is indicated on the compass (by about 30° in a rate 1 turn) and after any desired southerly heading is indicated. No allowances need be made when using the magnetic compass to turn onto easterly or westerly headings, and lesser corrections are required for intermediate headings.

Prior to commencing a turn, ensure that you are comfortable in straight and level flight, exactly on height, on speed, and in trim. Check the direction indicator (if available) or the magnetic compass for the present heading, establish which way to turn, left or right, to take up the new heading, and what rate of turn, will be used. Rate 1 is suitable for significant heading changes, but just a few degrees of heading change can be achieved satisfactorily at rate ½. Calculating time to turn, even if using the DI or compass, provides a very convenient backup. The ASI, altimeter and VSI should all be fairly steady before rolling into a level turn using a limited panel.

> THE VOR OR ADF **'ROSE'** CAN BE SCANNED TO CONFIRM THE REQUIRED DIRECTION OF TURN. ALSO, AS THESE INSTRUMENTS ARE GRADUATED IN 10° AND 30° SEGMENTS, THEY MAY BE USED TO CALCULATE THE REQUIRED TIME OF THE TURN, E.G. 30° = 10 SECONDS

Entering a Level Turn

To enter a level turn, note the time in seconds on the clock (or start the stopwatch), roll on bank in the desired direction using coordinated aileron and rudder until the turn coordinator shows rate 1, at which point the ailerons should be neutralised to stop further banking, and the balance ball kept centred with rudder pressure. Altitude can be maintained by counteracting any trend on the VSI with elevator, which will probably require a slight back pressure. In turbulent conditions, the altimeter may be more useful than the VSI which could be fluctuating. Neutralising the ailerons will hold the bank angle fairly constant, but minor corrections will have to be made continually to maintain rate 1 on the turn coordinator.

5 - GENERAL HANDLING

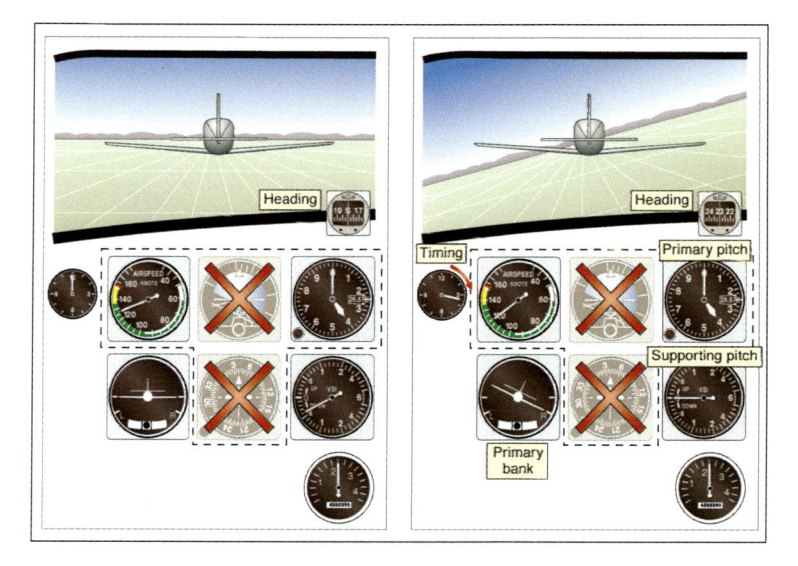

Entering and maintaining a level turn on a limited panel

Maintaining a Level Turn

To maintain a level turn, hold rate 1 on the **turn coordinator** using the ailerons, and keep the ball centred with rudder pressure. Hold altitude on the altimeter, by noticing trends on the VSI and counteracting with elevator. The **altimeter** will confirm that the precise altitude is being maintained. The ASI will show the expected loss of several knots, which is acceptable, unless a constant airspeed is desired, in which case the addition of some power is required. It is not usual to trim in the turn, since it is a transient manoeuvre and straight flight will soon be resumed. As the desired heading is approached, bring the direction indicator (DI, clock or compass) increasingly into the scan.

Rolling Out of a Level Turn

To roll out of a level turn, anticipate the desired heading by some degrees and roll off bank with coordinated aileron and rudder until the **turn coordinator** shows wings level. Hold altitude using the VSI and **altimeter**, smoothly relaxing any back pressure held during the turn. Allow the magnetic compass to settle down in steady straight flight, then check it for heading and make any necessary adjustments with small coordinated turns.

(e) LIMITED PANEL

Climbing Turn on a Limited Panel

The climbing turn is normally entered from a straight climb, and is more easily achieved if the aeroplane is first well established and trimmed in the straight climb. Climb airspeed should be maintained in the climbing turn, therefore the primary performance guide to pitch attitude is the ASI.

To enter a climbing turn, roll on bank with coordinated aileron and rudder until the desired rate of turn is indicated on the **turn coordinator**. Adjust the pitch attitude with reference to the **ASI**. It will be slightly lower than in the straight climb.

Entering and maintaining a climbing turn

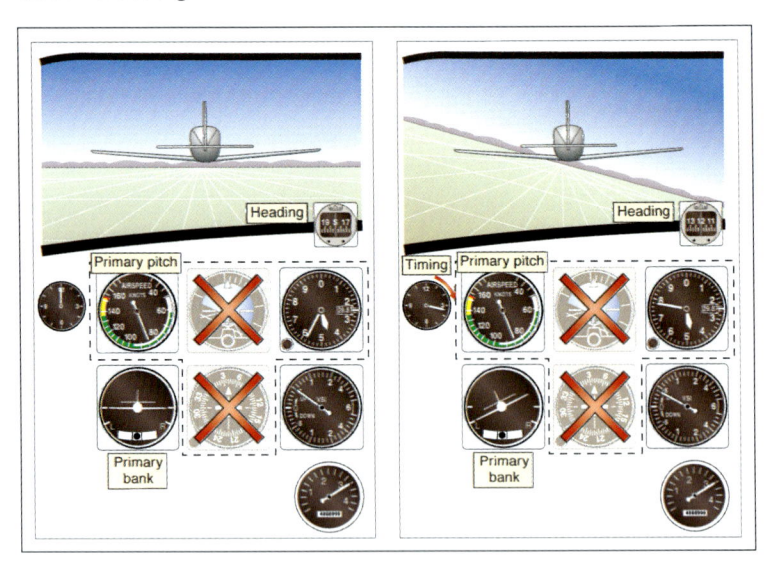

Maintain the climbing turn with reference to the turn coordinator and the ASI, and bring the direction indicator (DI, clock or magnetic compass) into the scan as the desired heading is approached.

Roll out of the climbing turn into a straight climb with coordinated aileron and rudder, achieving wings level with the turn coordinator, balance ball centred, and maintaining climb airspeed with reference to the ASI.

Descending Turn on a Limited Panel

The descending turn is normally entered from a straight descent, and is more easily achieved if the aeroplane is well established and trimmed in the straight descent. Descent airspeed should be maintained in the descending turn, therefore the primary performance guide to pitch attitude is the ASI.

To enter a descending turn, roll on bank with coordinated aileron and rudder until the desired rate of turn is indicated on the turn coordinator. Adjust the pitch attitude with reference to the ASI. Pitch attitude in a descending turn will be slightly lower than in the straight descent.

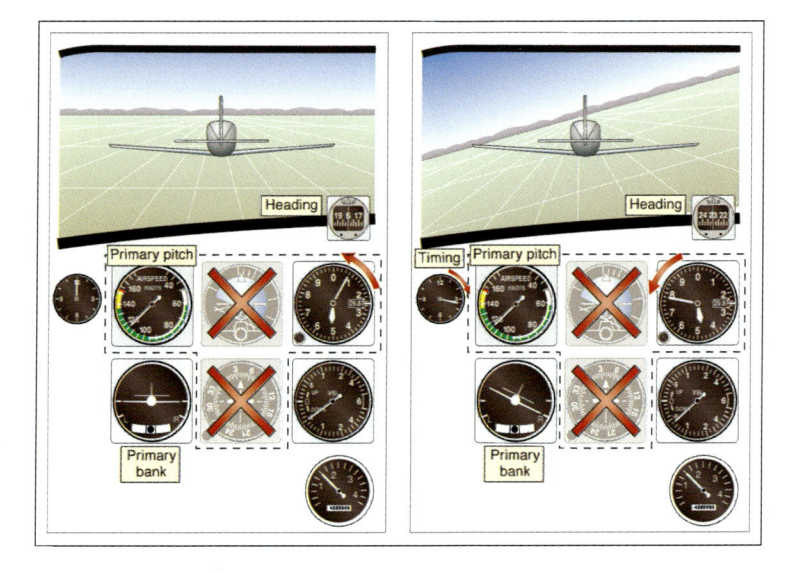

Entering and maintaining a descending turn using a limited panel

To maintain the descending turn, hold bank angle with reference to the **turn coordinator**, and hold pitch attitude with reference to the **ASI**. Bring the direction indicator (DI, clock or magnetic compass) into the scan as the desired heading is approached.

Roll out of the descending turn into a straight descent with coordinated aileron and rudder, achieving wings level with the turn coordinator, balance ball centred, and maintaining descent airspeed with reference to the ASI.

(e) LIMITED PANEL

Calculating timed turns:-

In normal operations the DI is aligned to the compass, either manually or automatically. Thanks to the stability of the gyro, it makes turning onto headings very easy. Unfortunately, you have to demonstrate the ability to turn onto set headings using the compass, simulating radar vectors to better weather for example. The standby compass is only useable in straight and level flight as it is affected by acceleration and turning errors. You will have seen these errors in your PPL or basic training.

When turning at rate 1 the aircraft turns at a rate of 3° per second. Therefore, you can calculate the time needed to turn. Begin the stopwatch as you roll in and then roll out at the elapsed time. The only other problem is deciding in which direction to turn. This can be solved by using a VOR/ADF rose.

When in straight and level flight glance quickly at the standby compass and rotate the OBS so that it reads the same as the heading. Do this in stages so that the primary scan is maintained. Aligning the OBS to the compass helps you to work out which is the quickest direction to turn. A rule of thumb for calculating the timing is to allow 10 seconds per 30° segment. Remember that the OBS will not change heading when you turn. You have to keep adjusting the indication every time a change of heading occurs! Enter a level coordinated rate 1 turn and begin the stopwatch. Once established in the turn, maintain the level turning scan and glance at the stopwatch. At the elapsed time roll wings level, coordinated with rudder and regain the straight and level scan. You will find that the standby compass takes a few seconds to stabilize, then check you're on the selected heading, correct using the same method if required.

Compass & OBS/ADF
Align the compass and the OBS or ADF rose to help calculate timed turns

$$\text{Time to turn at rate 1} = \frac{\text{Number of degrees to change}}{3}$$

ie. 30 degrees = 10 seconds

(e) LIMITED PANEL

5 - GENERAL HANDLING

Execute recovery on limited panel instruments from unusual attitudes with minimum height loss, applying the correct recovery techniques within aeroplane limitations, to return the aeroplane to stabilised level flight

The hardest recovery actions are performed on limited panel, hence the reason why they are assessed on the test.

You are taught to trust the instruments at all times, specifically the attitude indicator. Consider what happens, if the AI fails but no warning flag is shown, or you become distracted when all instruments are fully serviceable, or you simply don't trust the instruments. The aircraft will eventually enter an unusual attitude, characterised by an extreme in pitch and/or roll. A sad statistic is the number of fatalities through pilots flying in IMC when not qualified or current, consequently entering a stall or spiral dive or simply flying into terrain. Currency, practice and training are all key elements to a safe instrument flight. You must demonstrate that you can recognise and recover to straight and level flight from unusual attitudes. The examiner will brief you and then enter the unusual attitude. It will be no different from those experienced during visual flight; however, it may feel a little strange due to the lack of visual references. The examiner will hand over control and expect you to recover. Remember the correct response and actions when handing over controls:-

EXAMINER: **YOU HAVE CONTROL**.
CANDIDATE: **I HAVE CONTROL**.

All recoveries follow the same method of recognition, all you need to do is remember A, B, C, D:-

Airspeed - check, adjust power as required;
Bank – check, roll wings level maintaining balance;
Climb/Descent – check the altimeter, and adjust the pitch accordingly.

NOTE *that the VSI is not used as a primary flight instrument during the recovery, as it can give reverse indications and can lag as your instructor will demonstrate. Always recover back to trimmed straight and level flight.*

(e) LIMITED PANEL

Regaining normal flight from a spiral dive – full panel

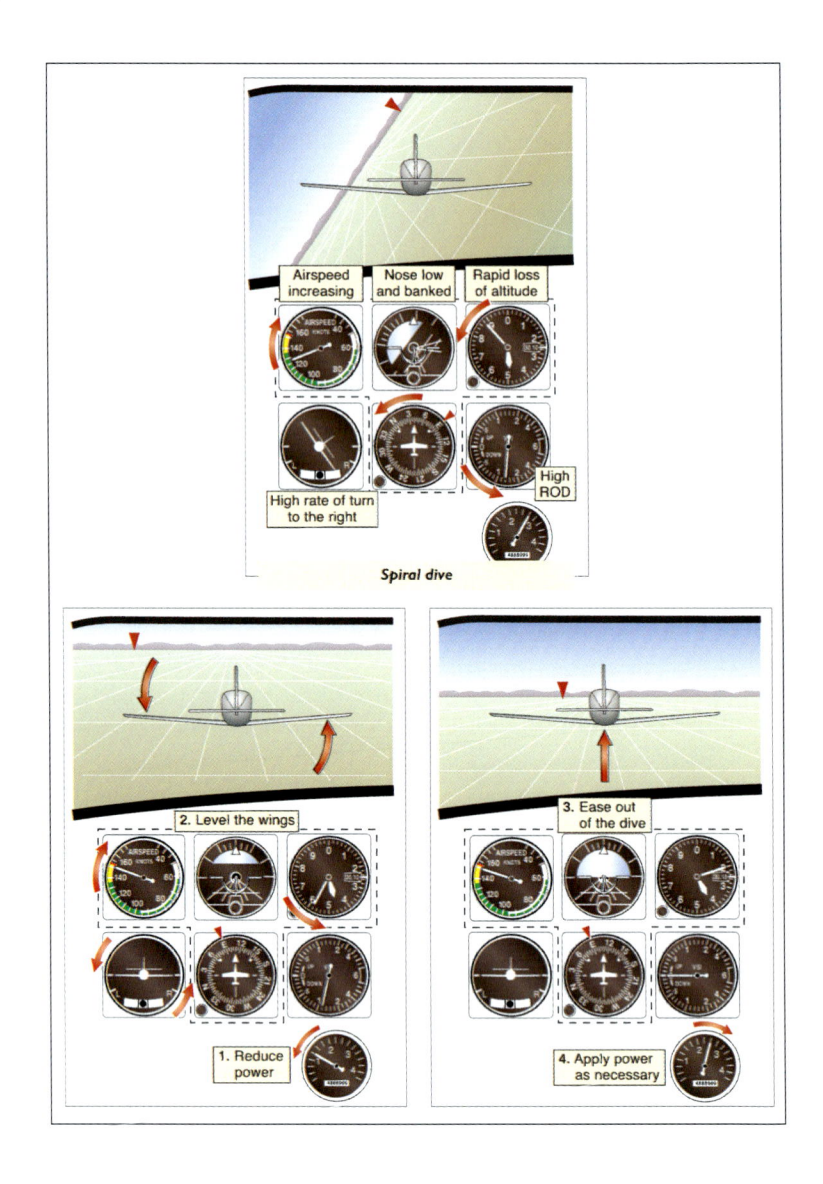

CHAPTER FIVE   (e) LIMITED PANEL

5 - GENERAL HANDLING

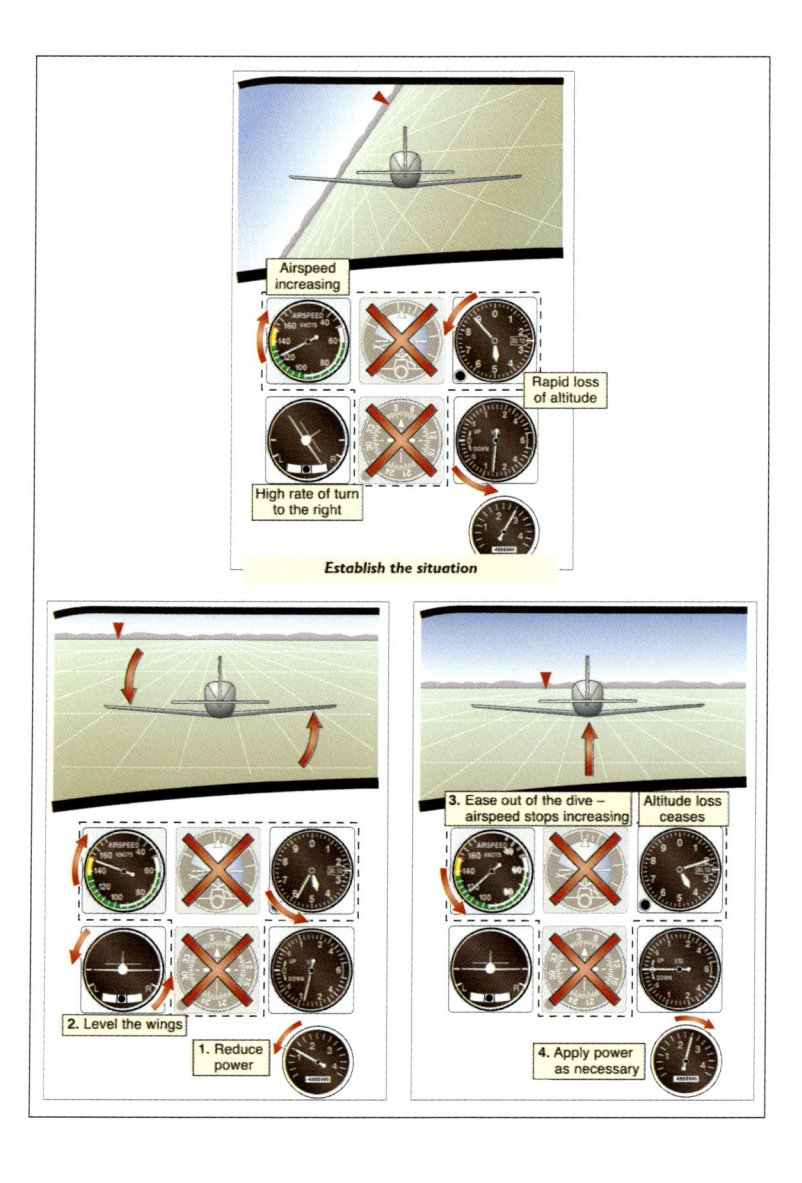

Recovery from nose-low and high airspeed – limited panel

Establish the situation
- Airspeed increasing
- Rapid loss of altitude
- High rate of turn to the right

1. Reduce power
2. Level the wings
3. Ease out of the dive – airspeed stops increasing
4. Apply power as necessary

Altitude loss ceases

(e) LIMITED PANEL

5 - GENERAL HANDLING

Regaining normal flight using the full panel

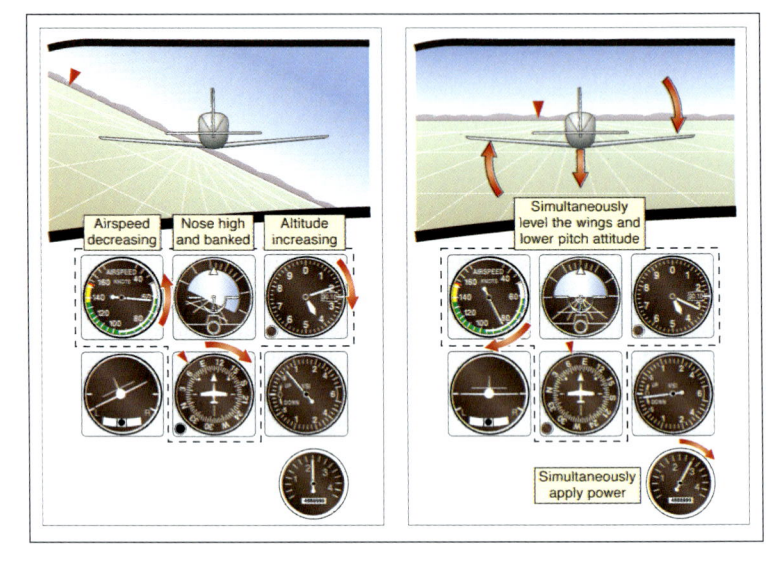

Recovering from nose-high and decreasing airspeed on the limited panel

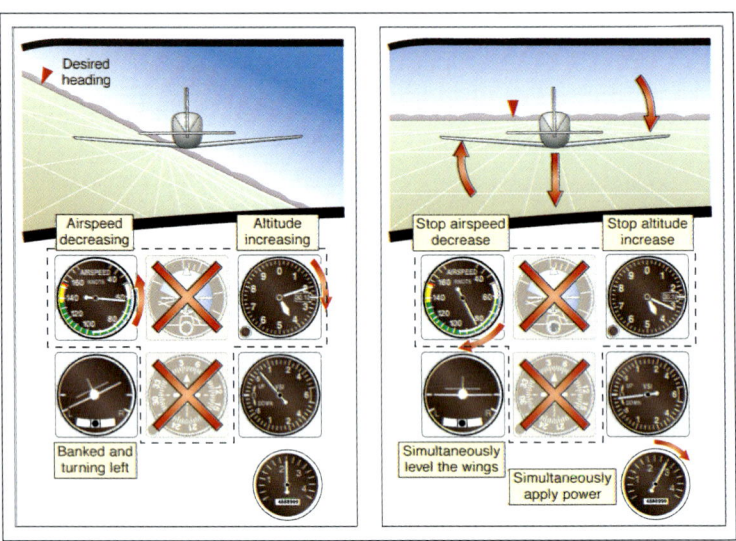

CHAPTER FIVE — (e) LIMITED PANEL

Recovery from Unusual Attitudes on electronic flight instruments

EFIS aircraft are not equipped with a turn coordinator that the pilot can use; although some are fitted behind the instrumentation for the autopilot to detect roll. If the AHRS unit fails, the pilot has no reference to the roll axis, only the vertical via the remaining pressure instruments. Consequently, traditional methods using the turn co-ordinator to interpret roll on limited panel are not possible.

To overcome this problem and allow the pilot to recover from unusual attitudes, analogue standby flight instrumentation is fitted to allow the pilot to remain in control of the aircraft following an AHRS failure. These comprise AI, ASI, ALT and magnetic compass.

Standby instruments on EFIS aircraft

On more advanced aircraft the traditional analogue instruments are combined into an Electronic Horizontal Situation Indicator (EHSI). This also has an input from one of the VOR/ILS receivers which can then display ILS indicators and speed bugs. Protracted flight on the standby flight instruments is not easy; it requires a high level of discipline and accuracy as the size and information available is limited.

(e) LIMITED PANEL (ELECTRONIC FLIGHT INSTRUMENTS)

Recoveries on the standby flight instruments are the same as on full panel analogue instruments. The AI may topple in extreme attitudes. If the AHRS unit has failed then the ADC will still provide valid information and the remaining performance instruments are available to aid recovery. The AI becomes the master instrument; avoid the temptation to fixate on the PFD. Another benefit of electronic flight instrumentation is that when the AHRS unit fails, a red cross appears on the PFD together with '**ATTITUDE FAIL**' or a similar message depending on the manufacturer. This makes it quite clear that the unit is no longer serviceable. Once the aircraft is stable, consult the checklist to see if it is possible to recover the situation. Some AHRS units can be realigned in flight. It should be noted that when the AHRS unit fails all unusual attitude protection is lost as well as all autopilot functions except roll and altitude hold mode.

AHRS failure

Note the red cross through the AI

If both the AHRS and ADC computers fail then the PFD gives no useful attitude or performance information, so you must focus fully on the standby flight instruments. The PFD soft keys and audio features are still available.

5 - GENERAL HANDLING

AHRS and ADC failure
Note red crosses through the attitude indicator and pressure instruments

If the individual display unit fails rather than the AHRS, a reversionary mode will enable the PFD to be seen on the MFD in a compressed mode and vice versa. You must read and understand the user manual thoroughly regarding failures and redundancy applicable to your aircraft type.

Some essential tips when using EFIS:-

- Correctly interpret flight and navigation instrument information displayed on the PFD.
- Determine what redundancy modes are installed and available. Recognise and compensate appropriately for failures of the PFD and supporting instrument systems.
- Accurately determine system options installed and actions necessary for functions, data entry and retrieval.
- Know how to select essential presentation modes, flight modes, communication and navigation modes, as well as cancellation.
- Be able to determine extent of failures and reliable information remaining available, to include procedures for restoring function(s) or moving displays to the MFD or other display.

Autopilot use

Depending on the EFIS fitted, some have a turn coordinator fitted behind the display unit so that the autopilot can detect roll when engaged. This can be used as a wing leveller. This protection will always be available, barring a failure of the turn coordinator (to aid the pilot if the aircraft attains an unusual attitude).

(e) LIMITED PANEL (ELECTRONIC FLIGHT INSTRUMENTS)

Always recover from an unusual attitude in manual flight and use the roll function of the autopilot once the aircraft is stable. This will protect you from entering any further unusual attitudes.

A turn coordinator is fitted behind the display unit so that the autopilot can detect roll when engaged

Training

EFIS equipped aircraft have changed the way in which a pilot is trained to operate in IFR conditions. Because of the very different way in which digital instrumentation works and displays data, the instructor can no longer simulate limited panel by the traditional method; which is to place a shield over the AI and DI. This is not suitable in glass cockpit aircraft as you would cover all of the instruments. Manufacturers give guidance to instructors and examiners on how to simulate failures in flight. The ideal platform on which to practise failures is an approved simulator, with the same instrumentation as the aircraft you are training. You will be able to stop the simulator and analyse the effect and then look at ways to regain the system. You will also be able to see the exercise through to its natural conclusion. Flying an instrument approach on limited panel is extremely challenging and it is difficult to achieve in live flight. If completing training in the aircraft, be very careful before pulling circuit breakers or turning equipment off in flight, as the systems may not be recoverable until safely on the ground. Always follow your instructor's guidance and information in the systems manual.

CHAPTER SIX

2D Approach

'Two-dimensional (2D) instrument approach operation' means an instrument approach operation using lateral navigation guidance only.

A)   NAVIGATION AIDS

Confirms the serviceability of selected navigation equipment

Select the appropriate radio aid for the procedure and identify it. Usually the aid will be based at the airfield, which should allow you to identify it early on. The examiner will expect you to demonstrate **single needle tracking** whilst returning to the airfield. The examiner will ask you to nominate the track and assess whether you can track accurately and within test tolerances. Be aware that an NDB has limited range. You may have to use either **GPS** or use dead reckoning technique until you are within the promulgated range.

Whichever type of beacon used, identify it before use and make sure that there are no failure flags. If you have been using the **RNAV** function of the GPS unit make sure that you know how to revert back to raw data tracking.

MAKE SURE THAT YOU KNOW HOW TO REVERT BACK TO RAW DATA INFORMATION

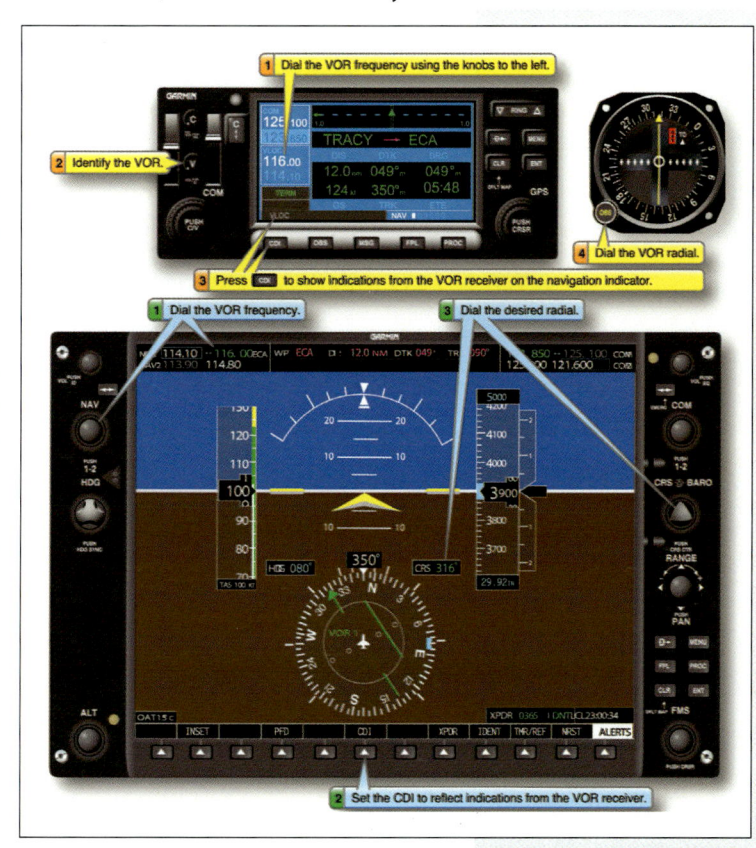

(a) NAVIGATION AIDS

6 - 2D APPROACH

CAP 773

Gives guidance on flying RNAV (GNSS) approaches

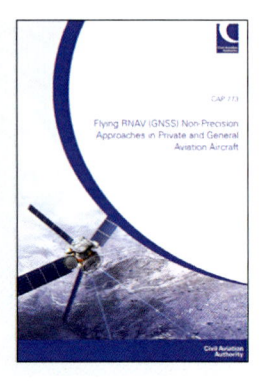

A typical GNSS approach plate

It is now acceptable to conduct a **RNAV (GNSS) approach;** however, it means that the precision approach will normally be completed procedurally including a hold. This may cause inconvenience to other traffic at a busy airfield, consequently you may be offered an alternative.

In the UK, **GNSS approaches** are relatively new, however, in other parts of the world have successfully been in use for many years. Before attempting a GNSS approach it is important that you study the user manual to understand the various functions and how to insert the correct approach procedure. The UK CAA publishes a safety sense guide on GNSS receivers and **CAP 773** has information for private and general aviation aircraft conducting GNSS approaches. Air Pilot's Manual volume 5 also has detailed information on flying them. Your ATO will also have information in the Training Manual on GNSS and RNAV approach procedures.

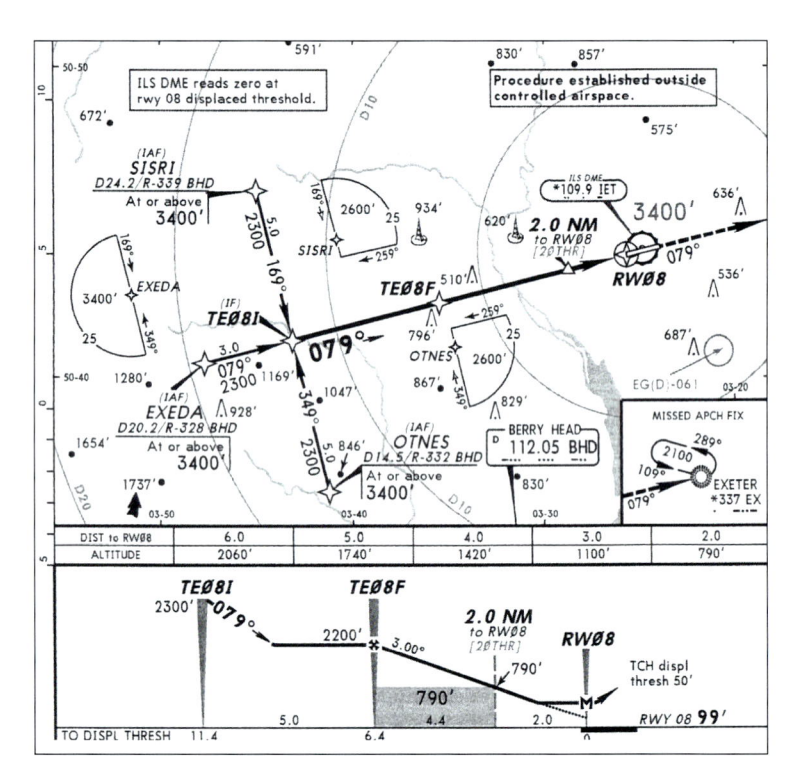

CHAPTER SIX (a) NAVIGATION AIDS

6 - 2D APPROACH

The RTF is slightly different when conducting a GPS approach, here is a typical example:

(PILOT) Exam 01, request RNAV approach via BEMBO, Runway 27

(ATC) Exam 01, cleared RNAV approach Runway 27, report at BEMBO

ATC may require a report at a certain point on the procedure:

(ATC) Exam 01, report 2 miles from final approach fix

(PILOT) Exam 01, wilco

If there is a failure of a satellite or system malfunction a **RAIM message** will appear. You have no alternative but to request an alternative approach:

(PILOT) Exam 01, Unable RNAV, Loss of RAIM, Request Beacon Approach

(ATC) Exam 01, Roger, cleared beacon approach, report beacon outbound

If you need to go-around during a GPS approach:

(PILOT) Exam 01, RAIM alert, going around

(ATC) Exam 01, Roger, standard missed approach

(PILOT) Exam 01, standard missed approach

(a) NAVIGATION AIDS

B) ARRIVAL PROCEDURES, DESCENT PLANNING AND CONSIDERATION OF MSA

Following the General Handling section of the test you will probably be in uncontrolled airspace and not operating within the ATS airway system. Consequently, the examiner will want to see you demonstrate excellent **situational awareness** with respect to the **MSA** as you won't have a **MORA** or MSA depicted on any chart. This is why you must carry a VFR 1:500,000 chart with you onboard. To calculate the MSA follow these steps:-

- Complete a radio navigation position fix;
- Plot the track to the destination IAF;
- Find the highest MEF along track and add 1000 ft to it-you could also add 1000 ft to the highest fixed obstacle within 5 nm of track, however, this is quite time consuming

Radio Position Fix

Complete a radio position fix, plot the track to the IAF, add 1000 ft to the highest MEF along the track to calculate a safety altitude

The examiner may liaise with ATC and arrange clearance to enter controlled airspace. However, it is your responsibility to make sure you have positive clearance to enter controlled airspace. Contact ATC at least 10 minutes before the airspace boundary.

ATC will require an estimate for the beacon and expect you to be at that level 5 minutes before the beacon if operating under a procedural service. The examiner will take this opportunity to take control and reconfigure the aircraft to trimmed asymmetric flight.

Once the examiner has handed control back to you, check that you are happy with the aircraft's position in relation to the beacon. ATC will give you a level or altitude to enter the hold, adjust accordingly. You may have to climb if you are not first for the approach.

C) **APPROACH AND** LANDING BRIEFING

Selects and complies with the appropriate VOR/NDB/GNSS instrument approach procedure

Select and review the correct approach plate for the procedure. Consider how you will fly it. If you are going to fly a GNSS approach, or back up a conventional approach with procedure stored in the GPS/FMS database, then make sure that you know how to load and activate it correctly. As each unit varies, you must consult the user manual before trying to do this. Avoid the temptation of getting too 'heads down' whilst programming the equipment-fly the aircraft first!

6 - 2D APPROACH

> **MAKE SURE YOU LOAD THE INSTRUMENT PROCEDURE FROM THE DATABASE CORRECTLY**

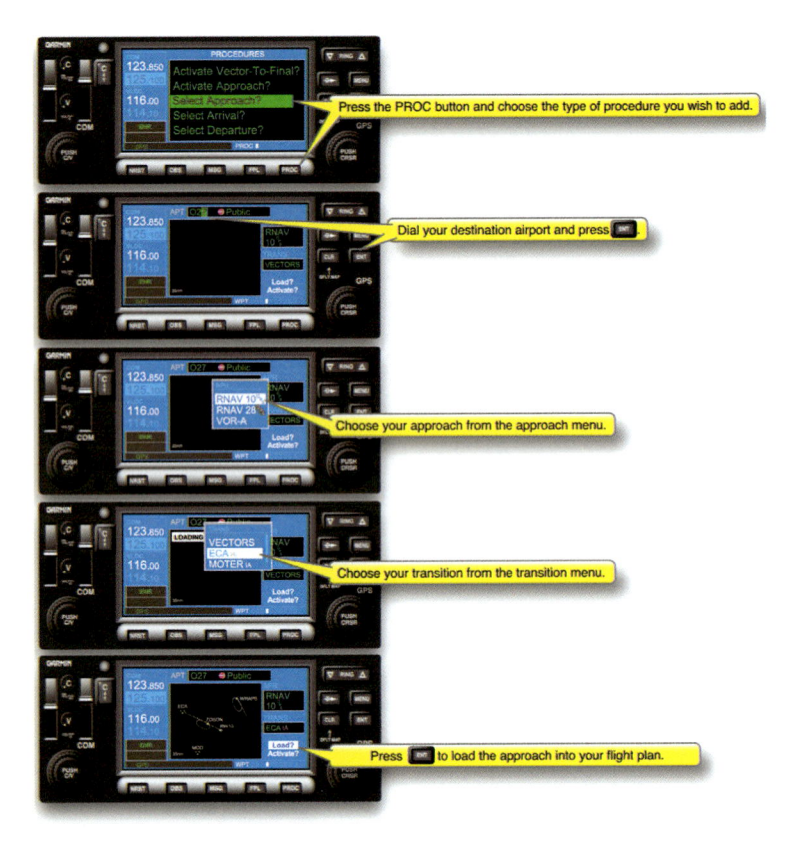

Press the PROC button and choose the type of procedure you wish to add.

Dial your destination airport and press ENT

Choose your approach from the approach menu.

Choose your transition from the transition menu.

Press ENT to load the approach into your flight plan.

Traditionally ATOs have taught students during a **2D** to descend to the MDA/MDH immediately after passing the FAF; the MDA/MDH is then maintained until reaching the missed approach point where either; a landing is made or a missed approach is flown. This is often referred to as the 'Dive and Drive' technique.

Typical 2D approach Procedure

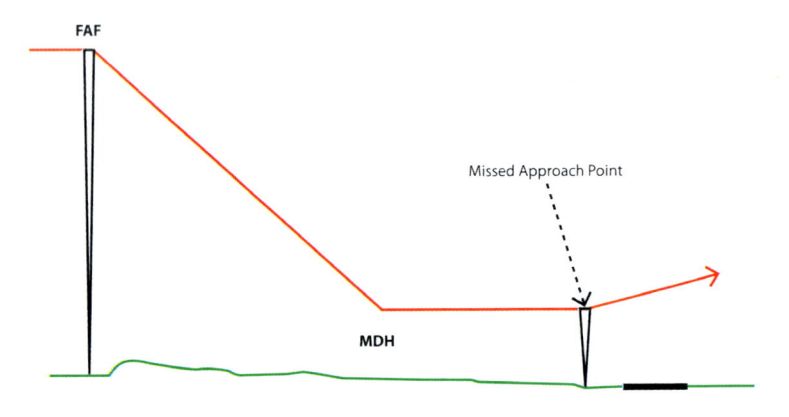

CHAPTER SIX   (c) APPROACH & LANDING BRIEFING

The **'Dive and Drive'** technique makes it difficult to achieve a stabilised approach and smooth transition to a visual approach. Many accidents have occurred using this technique. Consequently, it is not a suitable method for a large transport aeroplane to use when attempting to fly a NPA.

The UK CAA recommend ATOs to adopt the **CDFA** technique for NPAs as most IR candidates are aiming for commercial careers, however, they are not legally obliged to do so. If the CDFA technique is not adopted an increase to the approach minima is required. Consult the ATO Operations Manual for additions to minima.

A CDFA is a technique used for flying the final approach segment of a 2D instrument approach procedure as a continuous descent, without level-off, from an altitude/height at or above the FAF altitude/height to a point approximately 15 m (50ft) above the landing runway threshold, or the point where the flare manoeuvre should be started for the type of aeroplane flown. The only exception is a circling approach where a level flight segment is necessary to position the aircraft for safely landing.

(c) APPROACH & LANDING BRIEFING

Continuous Descent Final Approach (CDFA) Technique

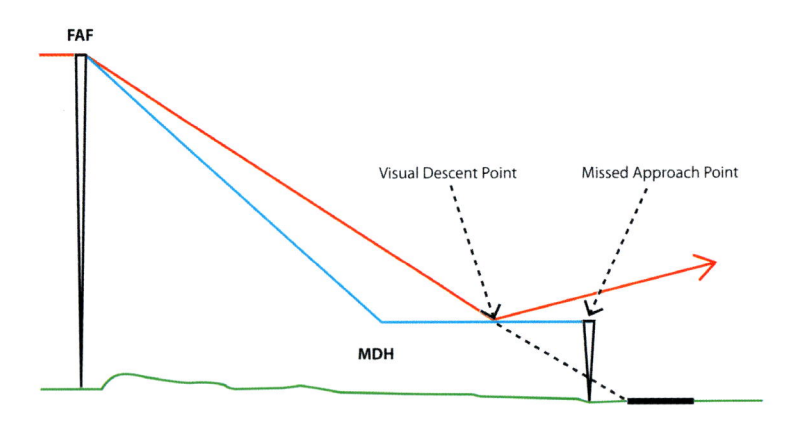

Most operators will use the following criteria when flying a 2D using the CDFA technique:-

1. If the required visual reference is not achieved, a prompt initiation of the missed approach procedure is required on reaching published DA, or Missed Approach Point (MAPt), whichever occurs first
2. The missed approach procedure must be flown (laterally) via the published MAPt, unless stated otherwise on the chart
3. In IMC, the aircraft must satisfy company 'Stable Approach Criteria' by 1000 ft ARTE, or DA, whichever is higher
4. If an approach requires a rate of descent greater than 1200 fpm it must be briefed

NOTE: *A CDFA 2D approach should normally be flown in the final landing configuration from the Final Approach Fix (FAF)*

Make sure that you read both your ATO's Operations and Training Manuals regarding 2D approaches. Pay specific attention to how the approach is to be flown and if any additions are required to the approach minima.

When you are calculating the approach minima consider the following:-

- There is no PEC correction required to the minima for a 2D approach
- Check in the Operations Manual for any additions to the MDA. 50 ft is usually added to the minima when using the CDFA technique to allow for altitude lost in the go-around
- The absolute minimum RVR required for single pilot operations is 800 m unless an autopilot is fitted

6 - 2D APPROACH

- If your ATO does not use the CDFA technique then you must add the RVR increment for a Category A aeroplane of 200 m to the published minima

The **CDFA technique** allows operators to use lower minima and is annotated as such on certain approach plates. ATOs will state if any additions are required to be added to CDFA minima. Commercial operators have to submit a comprehensive safety case to the CAA before they are exempt from adding an increment to the published MDA.

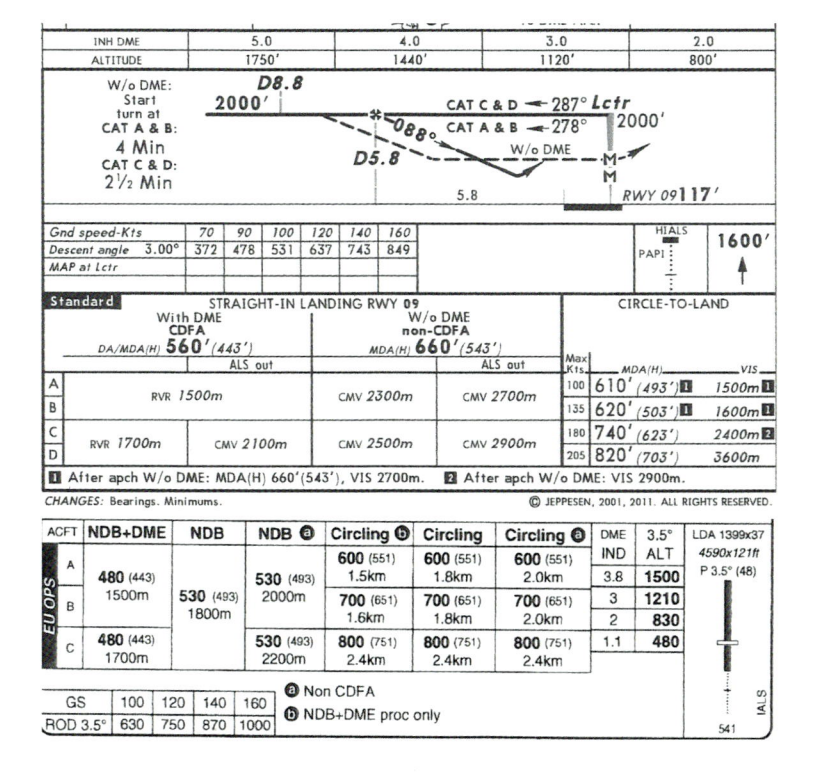

VARIOUS CDFA APPROACH MINIMA AS DEPICTED BY JEPPESEN & THALES APPROACH PLATES

The examiner will explain how he expects you to demonstrate the visual circle to land procedure. He will brief you on this. Make sure you note the appropriate minima in the brief.

(c) APPROACH & LANDING BRIEFING

Completes the necessary aeroplane checks and drills

Complete the approach checks once cleared to descend to an altitude. Complete the pre-landing checks once beacon outbound, with the exception of the landing gear and final flap. Re-identify the beacon. The examiner may de-tune the ILS if the airfield has one at this point. At approximately 4 nm from the runway confirm that you are configured for landing.

D)	HOLDING PROCEDURE

Completes any holding procedure with appropriate corrections for tracking and timing to achieve a standard hold

Before completing the final instrument approach the examiner needs to see you join and complete a holding pattern. This will then lead into a procedural approach.

Entering a holding pattern has no commercial benefit. There are certain conditions, however, where holding may be necessary. These are as follows:-

- ATC may instruct you to hold if the airspace is congested
- You may wish to hold to allow the weather to improve
- In an emergency you want to enter a hold to complete a checklist or to burn off fuel to reduce the landing mass
- If the runway becomes blocked or the airport closes

If directed to enter the hold by ATC, they should issue an **Expected Approach Time (EAT)** if the delay is expected to be more than 20 minutes.

6 - 2D APPROACH

An EAT is issued so you know when to expect commencement of the approach and in the event of radio failure. When you enter a holding pattern you should reduce to holding speed and calculate how much time you can spend there before you need to make an approach or divert. Take a note of the time you enter and always check that you are above the minimum holding altitude.

A standard ICAO hold is a right handed oval pattern and has a maximum IAS for category A and B aircraft of 170 kts. Turns are expected to be flown at rate 1 and use a maximum bank angle of 25°. The hold is designed in accordance with special criteria laid down by ICAO and has a buffer area surrounding it to ensure terrain separation, typically 1000 ft. This is usually increased to 2000 ft separation in mountainous areas.

Joining a Holding Pattern

There will usually be some manoeuvring required to join a holding pattern, since an aeroplane may approach the holding fix from any direction and, surprisingly, this is often the most difficult manoeuvre to perform. Three types of sector entry have been devised, based on the direction of the inbound holding track and an imaginary line angled at 70° to the inbound holding track. How the aeroplane joins the pattern depends on the aircraft's heading, since this determines the sector from which it is approaching.

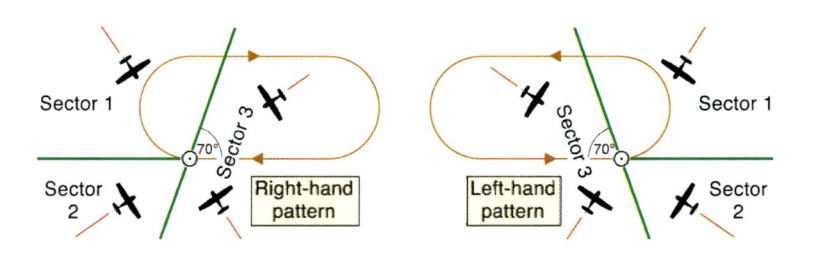

The Three Sectors

A Sector 1 Entry is a parallel entry

- Fly to the fix and turn onto an outbound heading to fly parallel to the inbound track. Do not backtrack on it – just fly parallel to it on the non-holding side for a period of 1 minute (plus or minus 1 sec/kt wind correction).

(d) HOLDING PROCEDURE

- Turn in the direction of the holding side through more than 180° either to intercept the inbound track or to return to the fix.
- On reaching the fix, turn to follow the holding pattern.

The Sector 1 Parallel Entry

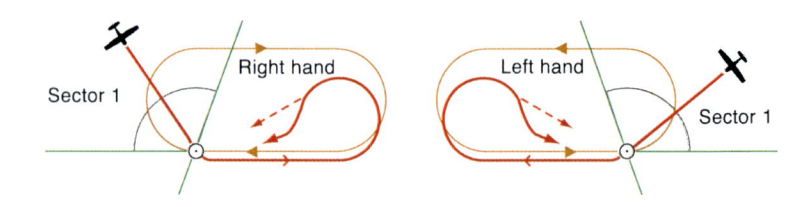

A Sector 2 Entry is an Offset entry

- Fly to the fix and turn onto a heading to fly a 30° teardrop, i.e. to make good a track within the pattern (on the holding side) at 30° to the reciprocal of the inbound leg for a period of 1 minute (plus or minus wind correction).
- Turn in the direction of the holding pattern to intercept the inbound track.
- Track to the fix, and proceed with normal holding patterns.

The Sector 2 Offset Entry

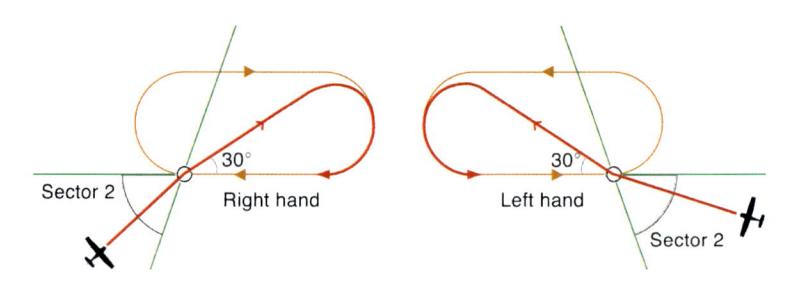

A Sector 3 Entry is a Direct Entry

- Fly to the fix and turn to follow the holding pattern.
- If a full 180° turn (or greater) is required to take up the outbound heading, then commence turning immediately when you reach overhead the fix. If, however, the turn onto the outbound leg is less than 180°, then hold heading for an appropriate time past the fix before commencing the rate-1 turn. For instance, if the turn is less than 180° by 45° (which at rate 1 of 3°/sec would take 15 sec), maintain the original heading for 15 seconds before turning.

6 - 2D APPROACH

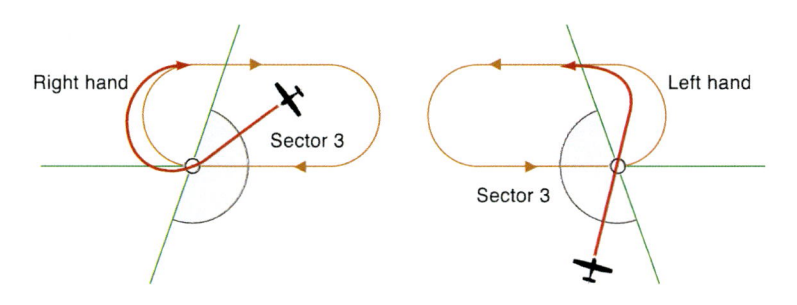

The Sector 3 Direct Entry

Entering a holding pattern correctly and efficiently (if one has to be entered) is a sign of a good instrument pilot. Holding patterns often precede an instrument approach, so a good holding pattern is a good start to the let-down.

USING THE ADF TO ENTER AND MAINTAIN A HOLDING PATTERN

Many holding patterns use an NDB or locator as the fix. In the figure opposite typical ADF indications are shown as the pilot initially tracks to the NDB, and then joins the holding pattern.

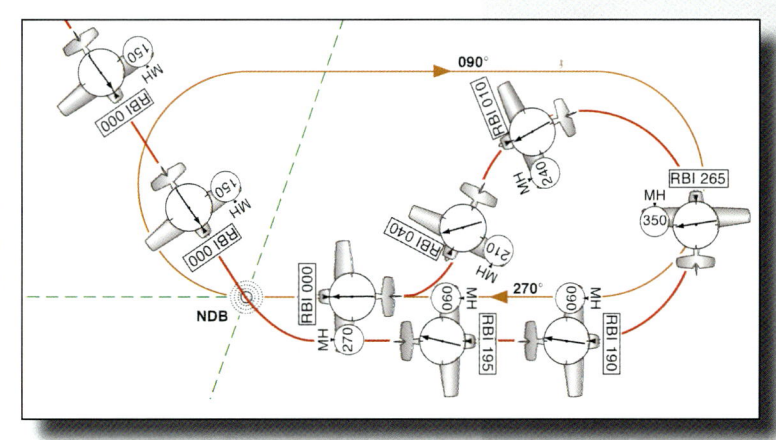

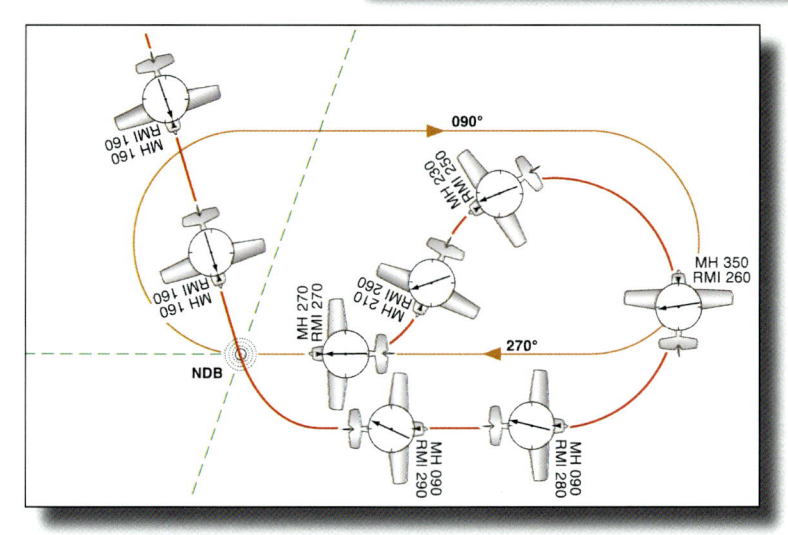

Making a similar sector 1 entry using an RMI

(d) HOLDING PROCEDURE

Making a Sector 2 Entry using the VOR

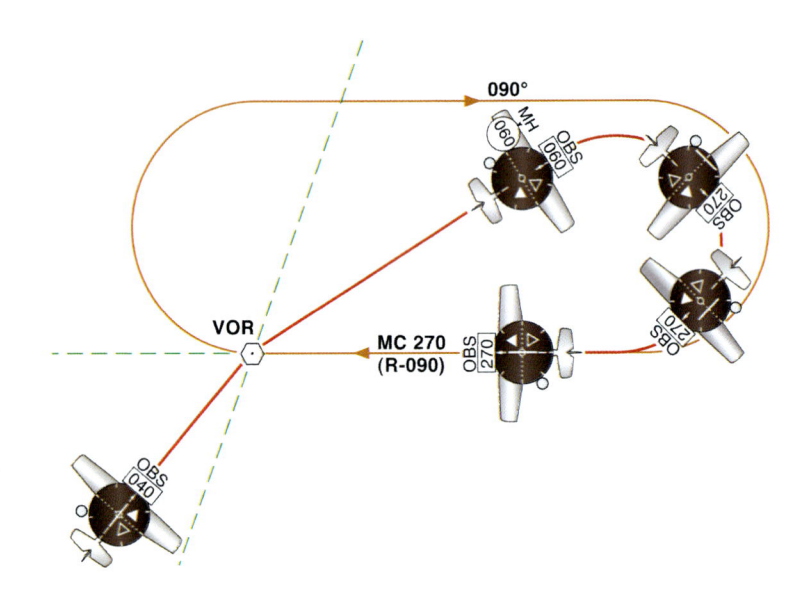

USING THE VOR TO ENTER AND MAINTAIN A HOLDING PATTERN

Some holding patterns use a VOR ground station as the fix. In the figure below typical VOR cockpit indications are shown as the pilot initially tracks to the VOR, and then joins the racetrack pattern.

Wind correction is vital to ensure that you stay within the protected area, although a buffer is built in when designing the holding pattern. It is your responsibility to compensate for any wind to ensure that you stay within the protected area. At the planning stage calculate single drift from the forecast wind. Remember to add magnetic variation to the forecast wind, as the published hold track is in degrees magnetic. As the forecast is just an estimate, adjustments in-flight are usually required. The examiner will expect you to do this on all subsequent holds.

Luckily, on aircraft fitted with an FMS this is all done for you. Unfortunately, for the IRT you are not allowed to use this function!

(d) HOLDING PROCEDURE

6 - 2D APPROACH

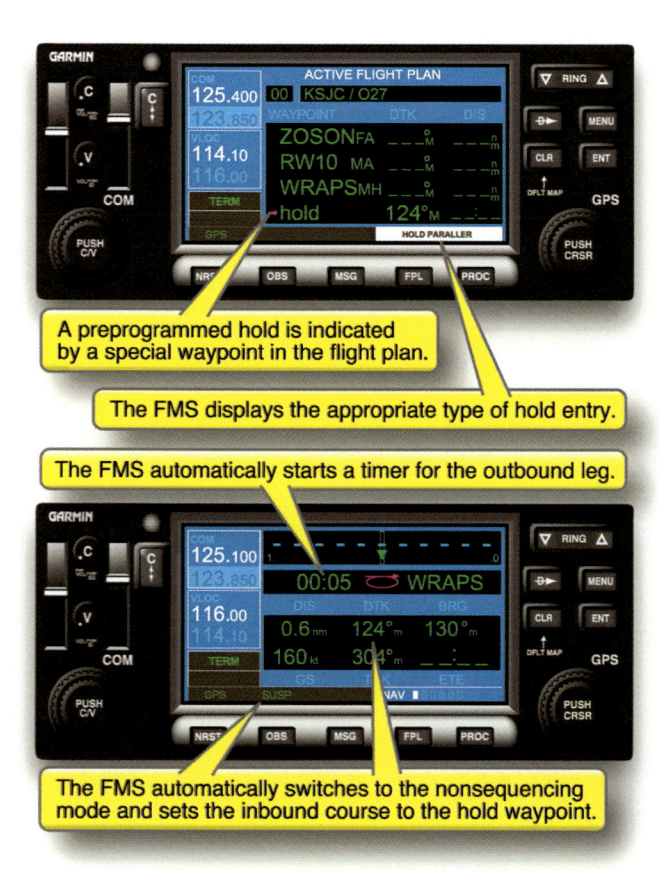

[Garmin GPS unit showing ACTIVE FLIGHT PLAN with COM 125.400, waypoints ZOSON FA, RW10 MA, WRAPS MH, hold 124°M, HOLD PARALLEL]

A preprogrammed hold is indicated by a special waypoint in the flight plan.

The FMS displays the appropriate type of hold entry.

The FMS automatically starts a timer for the outbound leg.

[Garmin GPS unit showing 00:05 WRAPS, DIS 0.6nm, DTK 124°m, BRG 130°m, GS 160kt, TK 304°m]

The FMS automatically switches to the nonsequencing mode and sets the inbound course to the hold waypoint.

> UNFORTUNATELY YOU ARE NOT ALLOWED TO USE THE GPS OR FMS TO DEMONSTRATE HOLDING!

There are many methods taught on how to compensate for the wind in the hold, these vary from the very minimal to some calculations which require a sound understanding of mathematics! Use a method which is simple and one that you understand. The whole point of a hold is to delay making the approach. If you ever need to enter the hold it is usually because you have to sort out a problem, so you don't want to be distracted with complex calculations. It is generally accepted to compensate for the wind as follows:-

- Adjust the time spent on the outbound leg by 1 sec per kt of head or tailwind component
- Adjust the outbound heading by 3 x single drift, unless this is greater than 30° or the resulting heading brings you within 30° of the wind direction, in which case apply 2 x single drift

(d) HOLDING PROCEDURE

If you are suddenly instructed to enter a hold which you did not plan and do not know the upper wind velocity; then as a very rough estimate this can be gained by adding 30° to the direction and doubling the strength of the surface wind velocity.

Below is an example using the clock code to determine the corrections in the hold. This is useful if you are instructed to take up the hold and you haven't prepared any heading or timings.

Using the Clockcode

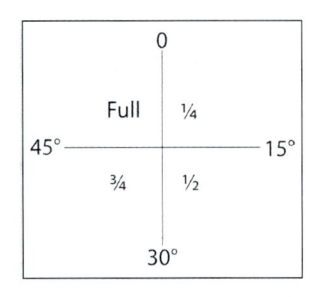

Hold corrections using the clock code method:

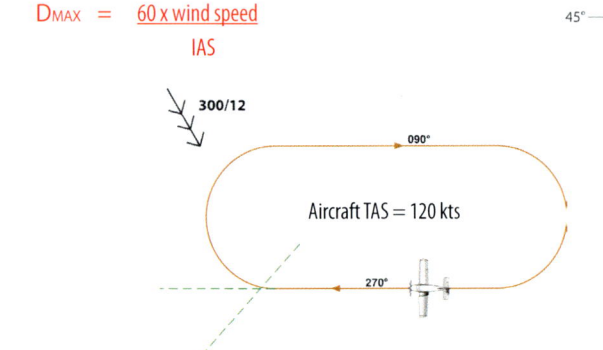

$$D_{MAX} = \frac{60 \times \text{wind speed}}{\text{IAS}}$$

300/12
090°
Aircraft TAS = 120 kts
270°

OUTBOUND HEADING:
1. Calculate D_{MAX}:
   $D_{MAX} = \frac{60 \times 12}{120}$
   $D_{MAX} = 6°$
2. Calculate actual drift:
   Difference between wind angle and hold axis = 30°
   Use clock code, 30° = ½
   ½ of D_{MAX} is = 3°
3. Apply drift to outbound heading:
   3 x Drift = 9° 090° - 9 = 081°
   Outbound heading = 081°

OUTBOUND TIMING:
1. Subtract wind angle from 90°
   90 – 30° = 60°
2. Use clock code to calculate proportion of ground speed
   60° = FULL
3. Apply timing correction
   (subtract if TWC)
   (add if TWC)
   12 kts is a tailwind
   Hold timing is 60 see - ½
   = 48 seconds outbound

OUTBOUND HEADING + TIME 081°/00:48

6 - 2D APPROACH

As the outbound leg of the hold is unlikely to have tracking guidance it is useful to have a marker to confirm that your corrections are accurate. This marker is often referred to as '**The Gate**'.

The **gate position** is the ideal bearing/radial achieved at the end of the outbound leg of the hold. This is typically 30° from the inbound track in still air. If this position is reached early, you have been blown inside the holding pattern due to the wind being stronger than expected. In this case, you must fly up the gate for the remaining time, before turning to intercept the inbound track. If the gate position is never reached at the end of the outbound leg, the wind has blown you out of the holding pattern and you must turn and roll out early to intercept the inbound track.

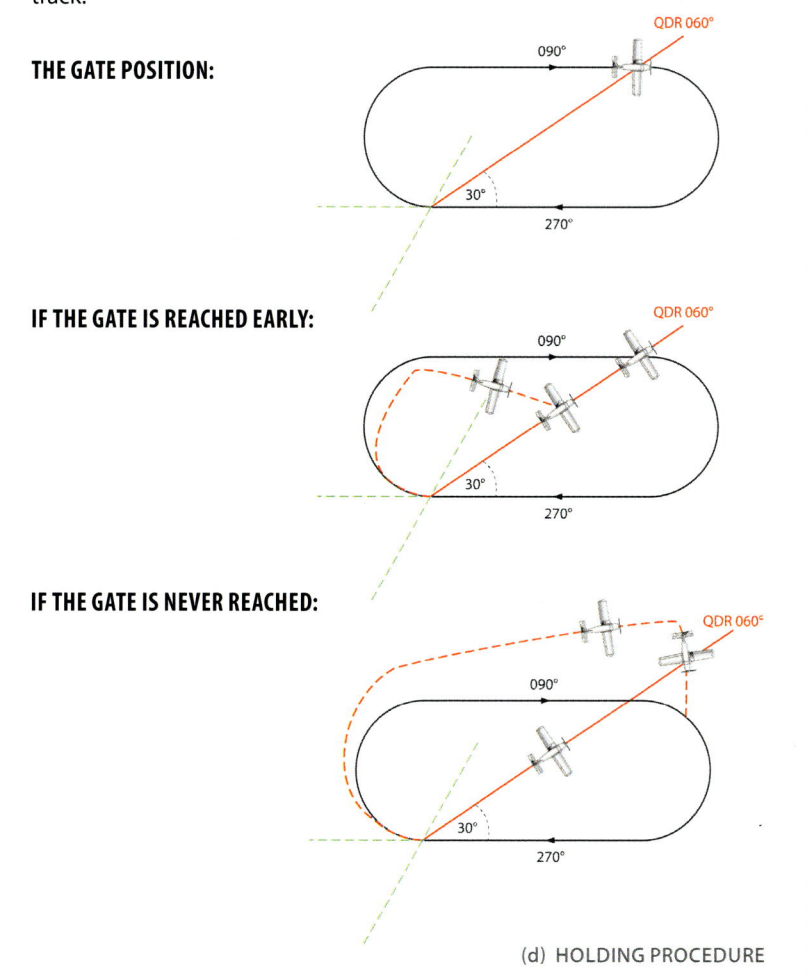

THE GATE POSITION:

IF THE GATE IS REACHED EARLY:

FLY UP THE GATE FOR THE REMAINING TIME AND THEN TURN TO INTERCEPT THE INBOUND TRACK

IF THE GATE IS NEVER REACHED:

TURN AT THE ELAPSED TIME BUT ROLL OUT EARLY TO INTERCEPT THE INBOUND TRACK

(d) HOLDING PROCEDURE

Some ATOs correct the gate for wind. Always follow your instructor's guidance on this.

In a hold based using an NDB, there are other markers during the turn inbound to help you roll out on the inbound track. They rely on having an RMI and you need to take into account dip error. Using too many markers can get complicated. Half way round the turn onto the inbound track you should be approximately 15° from the required inbound track and with about 60° to go you should be approximately 10° off. Make sure you account for ADF dip error when you monitor the progress in the turn; most light aircraft have a typical error of about 10°.

Most published holds are now based on a VOR radial and DME distance, or an RNAV/ GPS defined waypoint which makes the process easier and more accurate. RNAV/GPS waypoints do not require ground based aids and thus the holding pattern can be situated in the most convenient position. NDBs tend to be located at small or isolated airfields, as they are cheaper to install and maintain.

Procedure Turns

Unless suitable fixes, or radar vectoring by ATC, permits a direct entry into an instrument approach procedure, a positioning turn of some kind may be necessary. Course reversals can be made using procedure turns or teardrop turns. Positioning turns can also be made by following the appropriate sector entry into the racetrack pattern.

The 45°/180° Procedure Turn

The 45° procedure turn consists of:
- an outbound track from the fix;
- a turn of 45° away from the outbound track for 1 minute from
- the start of the turn (plus or minus wind correction in terms of both drift and time); and then
- a 180° turn in the opposite direction to intercept the inbound track.

6 - 2D APPROACH

Base Turn

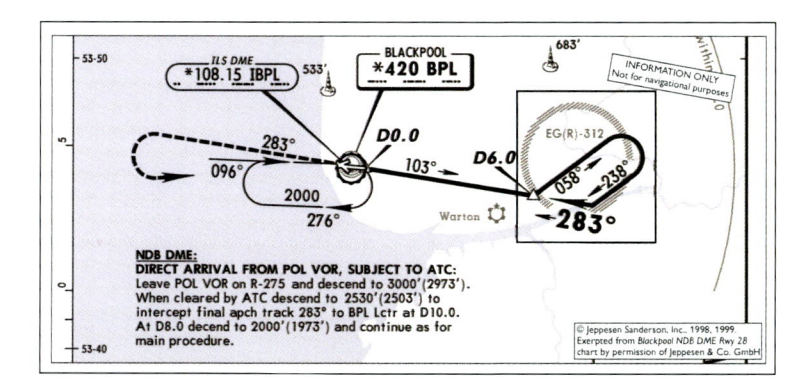

Left or right in a description of the procedure turn refers to the direction of the initial turn.

The 80°/260° Procedure Turn

The 80° procedure turn is less common in the UK. It consists of:
- an outbound track away from the fix;
- a turn of 80° away from the outbound track
- followed almost immediately by a 260° turn in the opposite direction to intercept the inbound track.

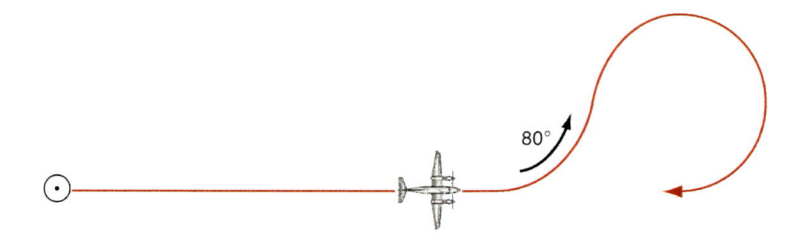

The 80°/260° Procedure Turn

If the initial turn is into a strong headwind, then the 80° heading can be held for a brief time (e.g. an extra one second per knot of headwind), before the 260° turn is commenced.

If the initial turn puts a strong tailwind behind the aeroplane, then stop turning before 80° is reached, and gently roll immediately into the reversal turn.

(d) HOLDING PROCEDURE

The Base Turn

The base turn, used to reverse direction by more than 180°, is a teardrop pattern which consists of:
- a specified outbound track and timing or distance limit;
- followed by a turn to intercept the inbound track.

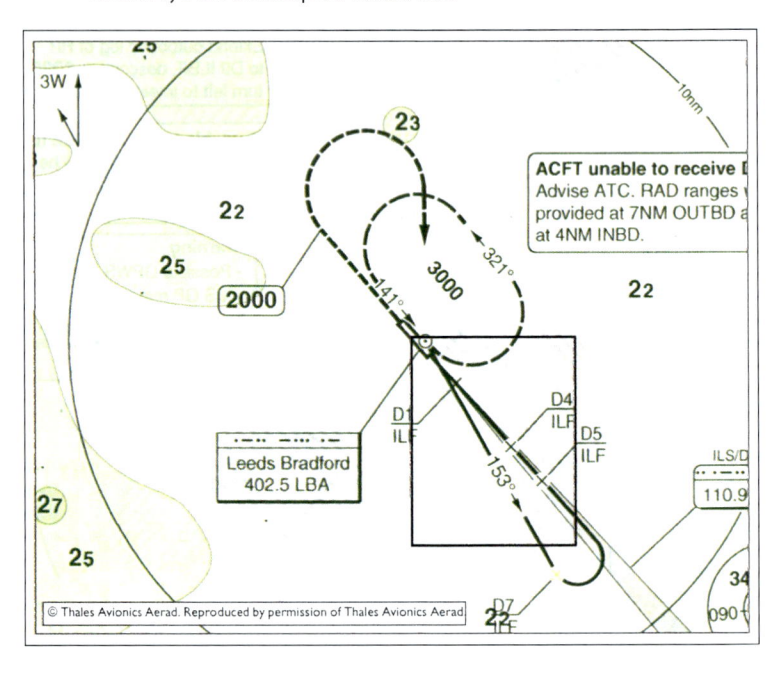

A Base Turn

Positioning in a Racetrack Pattern for an Approach

Many instrument approaches commence at the holding fix, and simply by carrying out a sector entry to the holding pattern (even if a full pattern is not required) the aeroplane is in position to commence the approach. For example, an aeroplane approaching the LBA NDB at Leeds Bradford from the east, could enter the holding pattern with a sector 1 parallel entry, and be ready immediately on reaching the fix on the inbound leg of the pattern to begin the approach. If there is any delay in approval to begin the approach, the aeroplane can simply remain in the holding pattern.

(d) HOLDING PROCEDURE

6 - 2D APPROACH

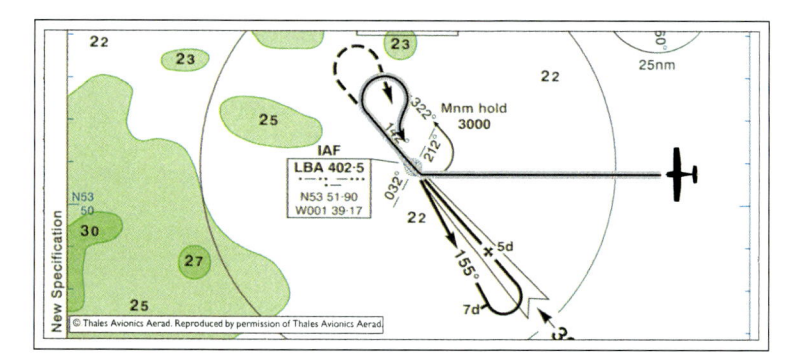

Positioning in a holding pattern

Sometimes alternative procedures are marked on the instrument approach chart. On the East Midlands chart, for instance, there is a 45° procedure turn specified, but there is also an alternative, and simpler, procedure: "Extend the outbound leg of the holding pattern to 8 DME (Cat A, B; 2 min if no DME), and then turn left to intercept the localiser." Only one turn will be required, instead of three.

Manoeuvring at East Midlands

(d) HOLDING PROCEDURE

The RTF associated with the holding is described later as it would be used during the test. As ATC usually instruct you to take up the hold the standard phraseology used is as follows:-

(ATC) Exam 01 hold at DAYNE, FL 70, expected approach time at 10, landing delays at Manchester 20 minutes

(PILOT) Hold at DAYNE, FL70 expected approach time at time 10, Exam 01

E) PUBLISHED APPROACH PROCEDURE

Completes the manoeuvring pattern as required to establish the final approach segment within the specified limits

The tolerances for the NPA are as follows:-

- Starting go-around from MDA +50 ft/-0 ft (single engine +100 ft/-0 ft)
- 'Not below' minima (from FAF altitude down to MDA) – 0ft
- Circling minima + 100 ft/-0 ft
- Heading +/- 5 kts (single engine +/- 10°)
- Tracking on radio aids +/-5°
- Approach +/-5 kts
- Vat or VREF +5/-0 kts
- Vyse +/-5 kts
- 2D (LNAV) and 3D (LNAV/VNAV) "linear" lateral deviations cross-track error/deviation shall normally be limited to ± ½ the RNP value associated with the procedure. Brief deviations from this standard up to a maximum of 1 time the RNP value are allowable.
- 3D linear vertical deviations (e.g. RNP APCH (LNAV/VNAV) using BaroVNAV) not more than – 75 feet below the vertical profile at any time, and not more than + 75 feet above the vertical profile at or below 1 000 feet above aerodrome level.

Establishes the final approach segment and maintains the approach track and vertical profile to MDA or circling minima and continues until visual flight conditions are established so as to complete transition to a visual approach or manoeuvre for landing

Complies with all ATC instructions and clearances

On the final outbound leg of the hold inform ATC that you are ready to commence the approach. As long as clearance is given, you can commence the approach when you pass the beacon. ATC may give you an altitude restriction during the outbound leg until traffic has passed beneath you. You must not descend until further clearance has been given by ATC.

When passing the fix use the following as an aid to the order of events:-

Twist-Time-Turn-Talk

Pay particular attention to maintaining the correct track during the approach. If you are flying the approach with a simulated failed engine, any change in power will need a rudder and trim input. Keeping the aircraft in balance and in trim is critical.

Once the outbound leg has been completed, twist the heading bug to an appropriate intercept heading and turn onto it. Establish on the inbound track early, confirm that you are at the correct platform altitude.

During the final instrument approach, you will be expected to demonstrate a circling approach and landing. Circling is the term used to describe the visual phase of an instrument approach to bring an aircraft into position for landing on a runway which is not suitably located for a straight in approach. It is a visual manoeuvre conducted under IFR.

Circling approaches are needed where:-

- The wind favours a runway which has no instrument approach
- The final approach track is offset by more than 30°, precluding straight in approach minima
- The final approach gradient is too steep to allow a straight in approach and landing

At aerodromes, where circling is permitted, a circling (visual manoeuvring) area is established. Its dimensions depend on the aircraft category.

Radius of the arcs

(R) varies with the aircraft category

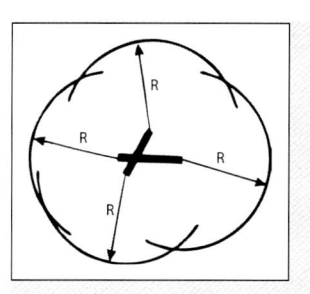

(E) PUBLISHED APPROACH PROCEDURES

The radii (R) from the threshold and minimum OCH is defined as:-

Aircraft category	Maximum speeds for circling	Circling area maximum radii from RWY THR (nm)	Minimum obstacle clearance (ft)	Lowest permissible OCH aal (ft)
A	100kt	1.68	300	400
B	135kt	2.66	300	500
C	180kt	4.20	400	600
D	205kt	5.28	400	700
E	240kt	6.94	500	800

The **aircraft category** is based on the airspeed at the threshold (vat), which is 1.3 x the stalling speed in the landing configuration at maximum certified landing mass, e.g.

Aircraft Category A - nominal Vat less than 91 kts IAS
Aircraft Category B - nominal Vat 91 kts to 120 kts IAS
Aircraft Category C - nominal Vat 121 kts to 140 kts IAS
Aircraft Category D - nominal Vat 141 kts to 165 kts IAS
Aircraft Category E - nominal Vat 166 kts to 210 kts IAS

The important point to note is that there is only a small margin above obstacles whilst circling. It is a difficult manoeuvre to fly in any aircraft especially in poor weather. Operationally, it is often safer to fly a straight in approach and landing if the tailwind and performance allows.

There may be parts of the aerodrome which are unsuitable for circling which will be shown on the approach plate. Prescribed tracks may be given, however navigation is done by visual reference.

6 - 2D APPROACH

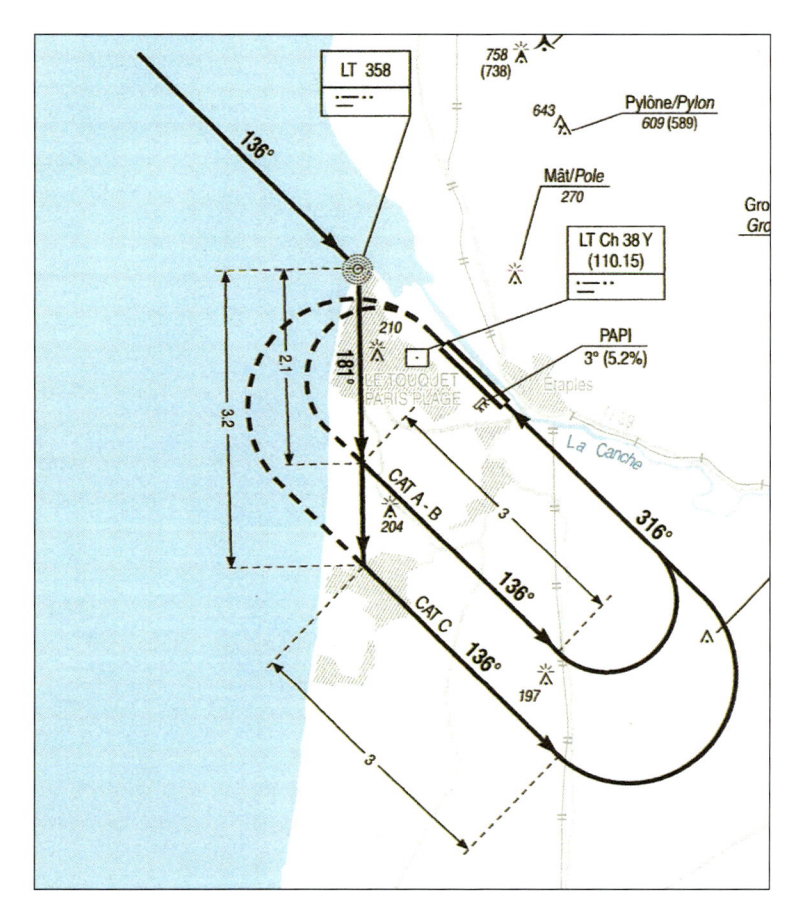

Circling Procedure

With prescribed tracks and distances

If no prescribed tracks are shown, it is up to the pilot to decide on a suitable circuit to the landing runway. Typical examples are as follows:-

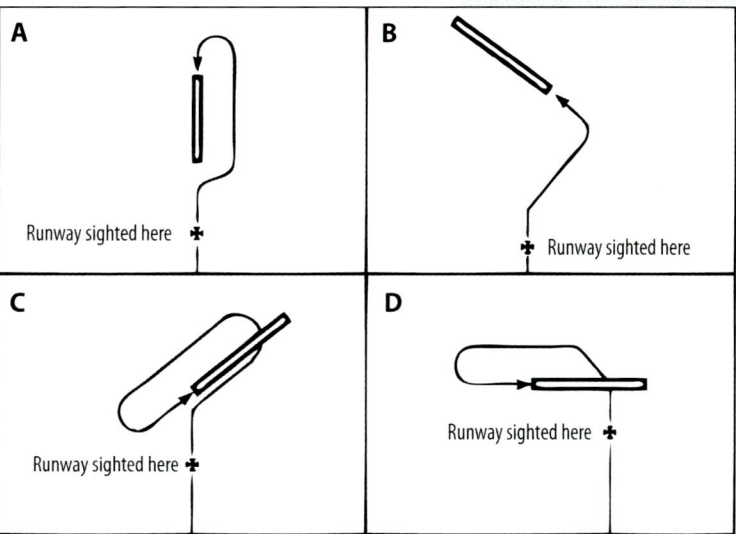

(E) PUBLISHED APPROACH PROCEDURES

Pattern A is the most common type to be flown. At MDA with the runway in sight you should level off and turn approximately 45° from the runway track. Start timing as you turn and fly for approximately 30 sec corrected for wind. Turn downwind, do not descend below MDA and remain within the defined circling area. Complete the pre-landing checks abeam the runway, inform ATC that you are downwind. Once abeam the threshold reset the stopwatch. Timing to fly further downwind is calculated as follows:-

Timing (seconds) = 3 x Height aal (+/- wind component)

Turn onto base and do not descend below MDA until intercepting the final approach path for landing. Configure as appropriate and complete the landing checklist. Fly a normal approach and landing.

6 - 2D APPROACH

Circling Approach Profile

AIRMANSHIP: Approach Ban, AOM, Wind Limitations, Appropriate Missed Approach Procedure, Aircraft Limitations

NOTES: If a missed approach is needed at anytime while circling make an initial climbing turn towards the landing runway, and intercept the missed approach of the instrument approach flown.

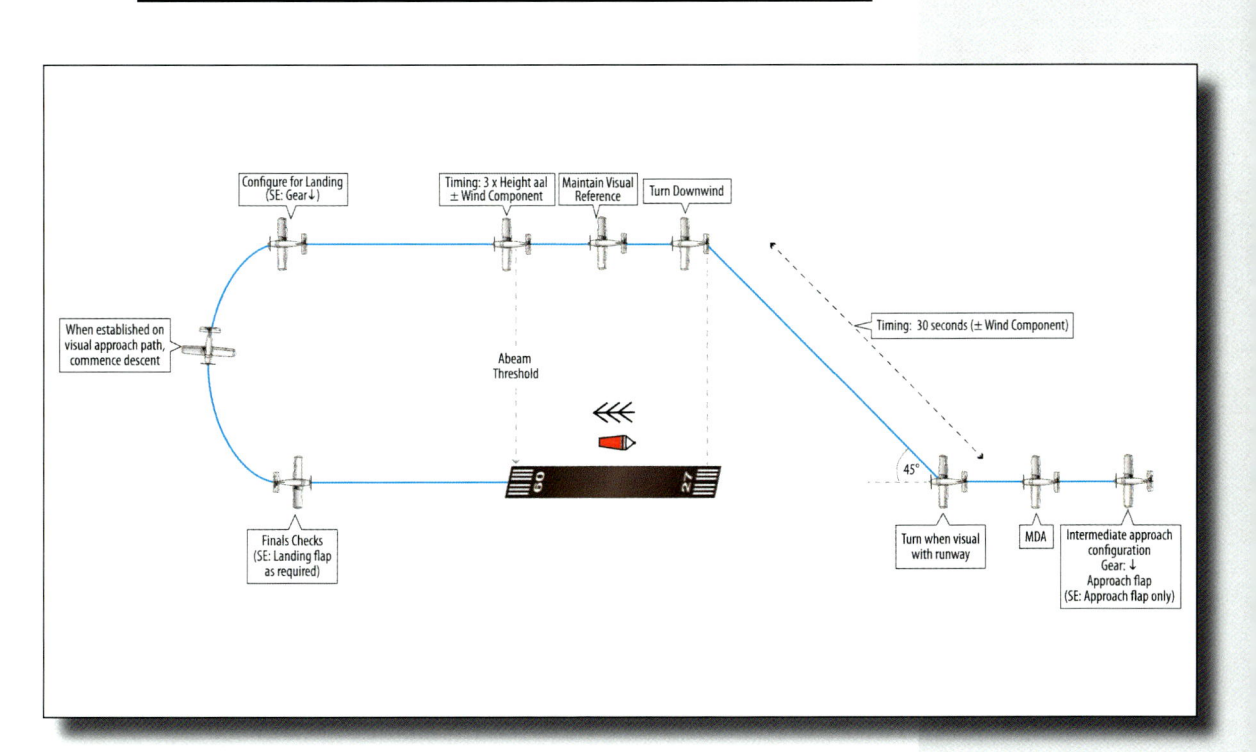

Configure for Landing (SE: Gear↓)

Timing: 3 x Height aal ± Wind Component

Maintain Visual Reference

Turn Downwind

When established on visual approach path, commence descent

Abeam Threshold

Timing: 30 seconds (± Wind Component)

45°

Finals Checks (SE: Landing flap as required)

Turn when visual with runway

MDA

Intermediate approach configuration
Gear: ↓
Approach flap
(SE: Approach flap only)

(E) PUBLISHED APPROACH PROCEDURES

The examiner may ask in the briefing:-

'What should you do if visual references are lost during the circle to land manoeuvre?'

ANSWER:- *If visual reference is lost when circling from an instrument approach, the missed approach specified for that particular procedure will be followed. An initial climbing turn will be made towards the runway and, when overhead the airfield, the aircraft will be established in a climb on the missed approach track. Where there is a choice of direction in which the circling manoeuvre may be flown, and depending when visual reference is lost, different patterns will be required to establish the aircraft on the appropriate missed approach track.*

F) APPROACH TIMING

If there is no DME associated with the procedure, the point at which you turn inbound will be defined by timing. During the planning stages you must adjust this timing by:

1 sec per 1kt of HWC or TWC for every minute flown

It is good airmanship to cross check the groundspeed given by the DME or GPS and adjust the timing accordingly. This will be more accurate.

A good habit to develop is always to reset the stopwatch every time you pass a fix. If the DME fails you may be able to continue the approach based on timing.

A common mistake is forgetting to reset the stopwatch as you pass over the beacon/fix. ATC may give range checks if radar is available, failing that you could estimate how long you have been outbound for and adjust accordingly.

G) **CONTROL OF** THE AEROPLANE

Establishes the appropriate aeroplane configuration and airspeed for all phases of the approach

Approximately 0.5 nm before the FAF, configure the aircraft for the final approach. Aim to fly a stabilised approach; when changing configuration use:-

LIMITATION – OPERATION – INDICATION

Ideally, once the aircraft is configured, it should be time to reduce the power and descend. If you configure too early a large power input is required to counteract the increase in drag. This increase in power causes yaw which requires a rudder input. If left uncorrected the aircraft will alter heading. The inbound tracking may then exceed tolerances. It is acceptable to begin the descent up to 0.3 nm before the FAF to allow for aircraft inertia.

As you descend, you must adjust the rate of descent to follow the vertical profile of the procedure, typically 300 ft/nm. Monitor the altitude against the range checks published on the approach plate. The key is to establish the aircraft early on at the correct rate of descent, in trim. You can then concentrate on tracking the inbound course.

To enable you to utilise the CDFA technique, approach plates will have a range/altitude table along with an advisory ROD to allow you to maintain the correct descent angle.

IXR DME	2.0	3.0	4.0	5.0
ALTITUDE	900'	1270'	1640'	2010'

TO ACHIEVE THE CORRECT VERTICAL PROFILE CROSS CHECK WITH THE RANGE/ ALTITUDE TABLE

(g) CONTROL OF THE AEROPLANE

During the approach scan to check that you are achieving these check altitudes, if not on the vertical profile, adjust as follows:-

High - Reduce power, lower the pitch attitude, configure fully *(if not already done so)*;
Low - Increase power, raise the pitch attitude.

When making corrections only small changes in pitch and/or power should be required, do not over control. It is often easier to regain the approach path from below than above, as only a small reduction in the rate of descent should allow the aircraft to intercept the approach path. Once you have regained the ideal approach angle, adjust the pitch and power to maintain it. Consider if a change from the original setting is required.

2D Approach

AIRMANSHIP:	Approach Plate, CDFA Technique, AOM, Approach Ban, Aircraft Limitations

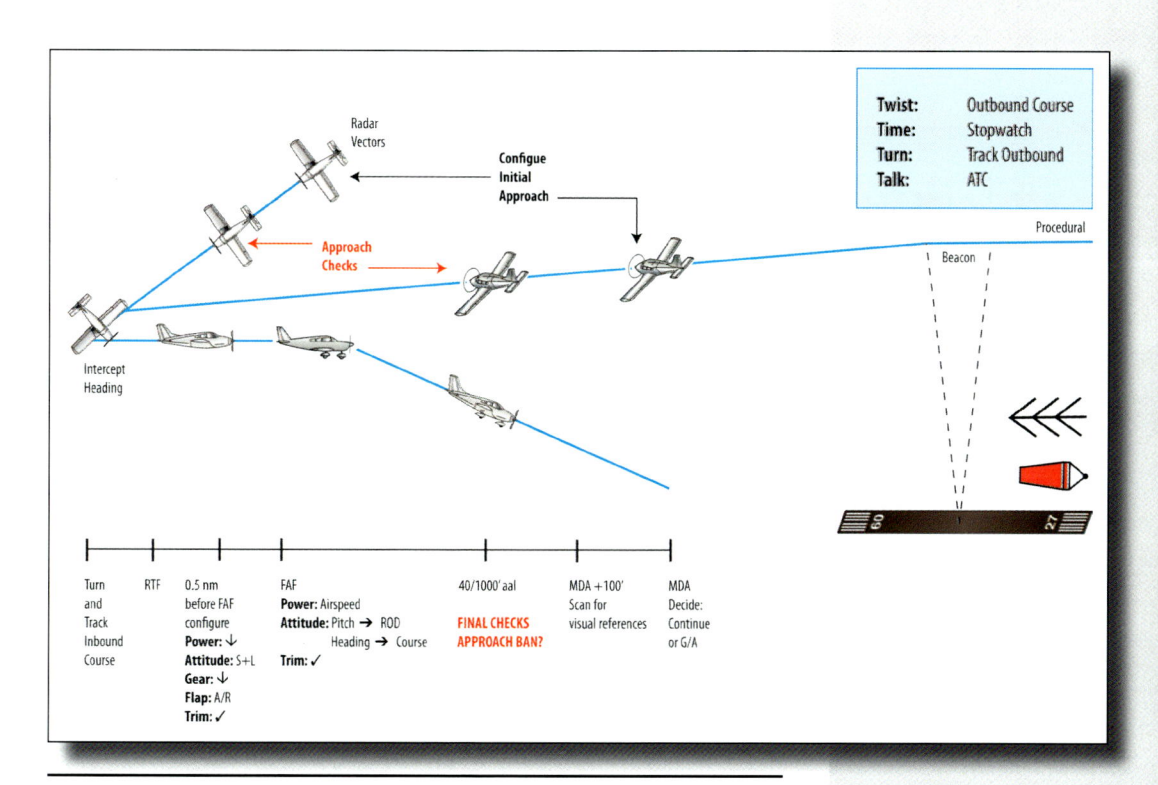

Twist: Outbound Course
Time: Stopwatch
Turn: Track Outbound
Talk: ATC

Radar Vectors
Configure Initial Approach
Approach Checks
Procedural
Beacon
Intercept Heading

| Turn and Track Inbound Course | RTF | 0.5 nm before FAF configure
Power: ↓
Attitude: S+L
Gear: ↓
Flap: A/R
Trim: ✓ | FAF
Power: Airspeed
Attitude: Pitch → ROD
Heading → Course
Trim: ✓ | 40/1000' aal
FINAL CHECKS
APPROACH BAN? | MDA +100'
Scan for visual references | MDA
Decide: Continue or G/A |

NOTES:
- Adjust the ROD to achieve a constant angle of descent, cross check altitude against the range/altitude table on the approach plate.
- SE = Delay landing configuration until just before beginning the descent.
- When using landing gear or flap remember:
  LIMITATION **OPERATION** **INDICATION**

(g) CONTROL OF THE AEROPLANE

H) & I) GO-AROUND/LANDING

If this is the final instrument approach, the examiner will take the instrument shields down during the missed approach. When visual, the examiner will expect you to level off at circling minima and demonstrate a visual circuit.

You must not go below the circling minima, so it is wise to add a small buffer but no more than about 50 ft as the test tolerance is circling minima + 100 ft. Do not relax. Many candidates fail this section of the test because they think the hard work is over. You have not seen outside the aircraft for a while, consequently you will take time to adjust to flying visually. Fly a visual circuit, approach and landing and correct for wind. Do not descend below the circling minima until turning to intercept the final approach path.

J) ATC LIAISON

Uses correct RTF for VOR/NDB procedures

Rather than just include the correct RTF for non precision approaches, here are examples of typical IRT profiles from various regional airports which are popular test routes.

6 - 2D APPROACH

Flight 6 Bournemouth to Alderney via Airway

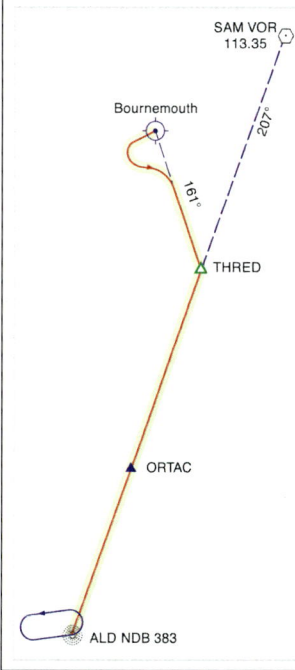

SAM VOR 113.35
Bournemouth
207°
161°
THRED
ORTAC
ALD NDB 383

Bournemouth Ground

🛬 Bournemouth Ground
Exam 40

🎙 Exam 40
Bournemouth Ground
Pass your message

🛬 West Apron
Information Foxtrot
Request taxi
Exam 40

🎙 Exam 40
Taxi holding point Golf One
Runway 26
QNH 1004

🛬 Taxi holding point Golf One
Runway 26
QNH 1004
Exam 40

🎙 Exam 40
Airways clearance when ready

🛬 Pass your message
Exam 40

🎙 London Control clears
Exam 40 on track THRED
climbing flight level 60
Squawk 6621 frequency 135.050
when instructed

🛬 Cleared on track THRED climbing
flight level 60
Squawk 6621 frequency 135.050
when instructed
Exam 40

🎙 Exam 40
Readback correct
Report ready for departure

🛬 Wilco Exam 40

🛬 Exam 40
Ready for departure

🎙 Exam 40
Hold position
Contact Bournemouth Tower 125.6

🛬 Hold position
Contact Bournemouth Tower 125.6
Exam 40

Bournemouth Tower

🛬 Bournemouth Tower
Exam 40

🎙 Exam 40
Bournemouth Tower hold position
After the landing Boeing 737
4-mile final, line up Runway 26

🛬 Hold position. After the landing
Boeing 737 4-mile final, line up Runway 26
Exam 40

🎙 Exam 40
After departure climb on track to altitude
three thousand feet
When instructed contact Bournemouth
Radar 119.475

🛬 After departure climb on track to
altitude three thousand feet
When instructed contact Bournemouth
Radar 119.475
Exam 40

🎙 Exam 40 correct
Runway 26 cleared for take-off
Surface wind 220 11 knots

🛬 Runway 26 cleared for take-off
Exam 40

🎙 Exam 40
Contact Bournemouth Radar 119.475

🛬 Contact Bournemouth Radar 119.475
Exam 40

Bournemouth Radar

🛬 Bournemouth Radar
Exam 40

🎙 Exam 40
Passing altitude two thousand feet, climbing
to altitude three thousand feet

🛬 Exam 40
Bournemouth Radar squawk ident

🛬 Squawk ident
Exam 40

🎙 Exam 40
Maintain altitude three thousand feet
Bournemouth QNH 1004

🛬 Maintain altitude three thousand feet
Bournemouth QNH 1004
Exam 40

🎙 Exam 40
Climb flight level 60

🛬 Climb flight level 60
Exam 40

🎙 Exam 40
Contact London Control 135.050

🛬 Contact London Control 135.050
Exam 40

London Control

🛬 London Control
Exam 40 passing flight level 50 for
flight level 60

🎙 Exam 40
London Control
Report reaching flight level 60
Route direct ORTAC

🛬 Wilco, direct ORTAC
Flight level 60
Exam 40

🎙 Exam 40
Flight level 60

🎙 Exam 40 Roger

🎙 Exam 40
Contact Jersey Zone 125.2

🛬 Jersey Zone 125.2
Exam 40

Jersey Zone

🛬 Jersey Zone
Exam 40

🎙 Exam 40
Jersey Zone
Report ORTAC

🛬 Wilco Exam 40

🛬 Exam 40
ORTAC

🎙 Exam 40
Descend to altitude three thousand feet
Jersey QNH 1003
Route direct ALD

🛬 Descend to altitude three thousand
feet
Jersey QNH 1003
Route direct ALD
Exam 40

🎙 Exam 40
Contact Guernsey Approach 128.650

🛬 Guernsey Approach 128.650
Exam 40

Guernsey Approach

🛬 Guernsey Approach
Exam 40

🎙 Exam 40
Guernsey Approach
Descend to altitude two thousand feet
QNH 1003

🛬 Descend to altitude two thousand
feet QNH 1003
Exam 40

🎙 Exam 40
Cleared to enter the hold at the ALD,
altitude two thousand feet, report entering
the hold

🛬 Cleared to enter the hold at the
ALD, altitude two thousand feet, report
entering the hold
Exam 40

🛬 Exam 40
Entering the hold ALD

🎙 Exam 40 roger
Report ready for the procedure

🛬 Wilco Exam 40

🎙 Exam 40
Request procedural NDB approach

🎙 Exam 40
Cleared Beacon approach runway 26
Report beacon outbound

🛬 Cleared Beacon approach Runway 26
Wilco
Exam 40

🛬 Exam 40
Beacon outbound

🎙 Exam 40
Descend with the procedure, report
established on the final approach track

🛬 Descend with the procedure, report
established on the final approach track
Exam 40

🛬 Exam 40
Established final approach 26

🎙 Exam 40 cleared low approach and
go-around Runway 26
Standard missed approach
Report going around
Wind 200 09 knots
Threshold elevation 290 feet

🛬 Cleared low approach and go-around
Runway 26
Standard missed approach
Threshold elevation 290 feet
Wilco Exam 40

🛬 Exam 40
Going around

🎙 Exam 40 roger
Route direct ORTAC
Climb to altitude three thousand feet
QNH 1003

🛬 Route direct ORTAC
Climb to altitude three thousand feet
QNH 1003
Exam 40

🎙 Exam 40
Squawk 3706
Report ORTAC

🛬 Squawk 3706
Wilco Exam 40

🛬 Exam 40
ORTAC

🎙 Exam 40
Radar Service terminated
Squawk 7000
Freecall Bournemouth Approach 119.475

(j) ATC LIAISON

6 - 2D APPROACH

✈ Squawk 7000
Radar Service terminated
Freecall Bournemouth Approach 119.475
Exam 40

General handling

✈ Bournemouth Approach
Exam 40

✈ Exam 40
Bournemouth Approach
Pass your message

✈ Exam 40
Seneca
ORTAC
Altitude three thousand feet
Request Basic Service

✈ Exam 40
Basic Service
QNH 1004

✈ QNH 1004
Exam 40

General handling complete, listen to Bournemouth ATIS

✈ Bournemouth Approach
Exam 40

✈ Exam 40
Bournemouth Approach
Pass your message

✈ Exam 40
Inbound, information India
Altitude three thousand feet
Estimating BIA at 56 IFR
Request Traffic Service and radar vectored ILS.

✈ Exam 40
Squawk 1737
QNH 1004

✈ Squawk 1737
QNH 1004
Exam 40

✈ Exam 40
Identified 18 miles south of Bournemouth
Traffic Service

✈ Traffic Service
Exam 40

✈ Exam 40
Vectoring for the ILS Runway 26
Bournemouth
QNH 1004

✈ Vectoring for the ILS Runway 26
Bournemouth
QNH 1004
Exam 40

✈ Exam 40
Turn left heading 040

✈ Left heading 040
Exam 40

✈ Exam 40
Descend to altitude two thousand feet
Bournemouth QNH 1004

✈ Descend to altitude two thousand feet
Bournemouth QNH 1004
Exam 40

✈ Exam 40
Turn left heading 010
Left base Runway 26
15 miles from touchdown

✈ Left heading 010
Exam 40

✈ Exam 40
Radar Control Service within the Bournemouth zone

✈ Radar Control Service
Exam 40

✈ Exam 40
Turn left heading 300 degrees when established on localizer descend with glidepath

✈ Left heading 300 degrees when established on localizer descend with the glidepath
Exam 40

✈ Exam 40
Threshold elevation 36 feet
Contact Bournemouth Tower 125.6

✈ Contact Bournemouth Tower 125.6
Exam 40

Bournemouth Tower

✈ Bournemouth Tower
Exam 40
Fully established Runway 26

☎ Exam 40
Runway 26 cleared to land
Surface wind 200 12 knots

✈ Runway 26 cleared to land
Exam 40

Flight 7 Cranfield to East Midlands

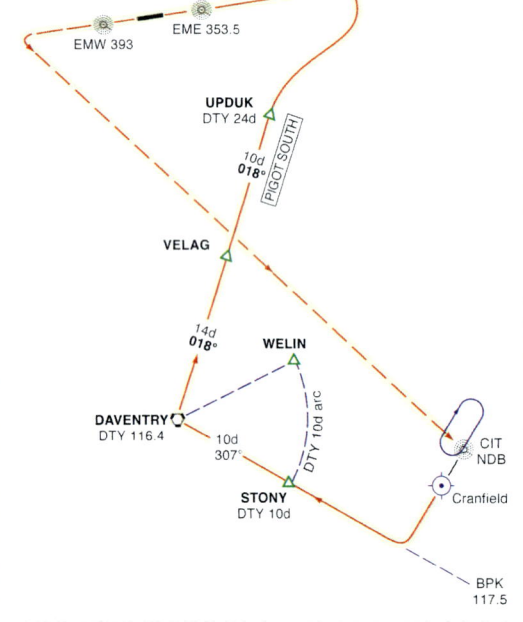

Cranfield Tower

✈ Cranfield Tower
Exam 40

☎ Exam 40
Cranfield Tower
Pass your message

✈ Exam 40
Seminole GTWIN
Information Zulu
QNH 998 millibars
Two on board
Request taxi IFR to East Midlands

✈ Exam 40
Cross Runway 18 holding point Alpha 1
Departure Runway 21

✈ Cross Runway 18 holding point Alpha 1
Departure Runway 21
Exam 40

☎ Exam 40
Your clearance

✈ Pass your message
Exam 40

✈ London Control clears Exam 40 to join controlled airspace on track Daventry climb flight level 70, squawk 6621, frequency for London Control 130.925 when instructed

✈ Cleared to join controlled airspace on track Daventry, after departure STONY-WELIN climb flight level 70, squawk 6621, frequency for London Control 130.925 when instructed
Exam 40

☎ Exam 40
Readback correct
Report ready for departure

✈ Wilco Exam 40

✈ Exam 40
Ready for departure

☎ Exam 40 roger
Line up Runway 21
After departure Stony Daventry climb to altitude three thousand feet
Contact Cranfield Approach 122.850

✈ Line up Runway 21
After departure Stony Daventry climb to altitude three thousand feet
Contact Cranfield Approach 122.850

☎ Exam 40
Runway 21 cleared for take-off
Surface wind 280 15 knots

✈ Runway 21
Cleared for take-off
Exam 40

CHAPTER SIX   (j) ATC LIAISON

6 - 2D APPROACH

Exam 40
Contact Cranfield Approach 122.850

→ *Cranfield Approach 122.850 Exam 40*

Cranfield Approach

→ *Cranfield Approach Exam 40*
Passing altitude two thousand feet for altitude three thousand feet

Exam 40
Cranfield Approach
Climb to altitude four thousand feet
Report passing altitude three thousand feet

→ *Climb to altitude four thousand feet
Report passing altitude three thousand feet Exam 40*

Passing altitude three thousand feet Exam 40

→ *Exam 40 roger
Climb flight level 70*

Climb flight level 70 Exam 40

*Exam 40
Contact London Control 130.925*

→ *London Control 130.925 Exam 40*

London Control

→ *London Control Exam 40*

*Exam 40
London Control
Squawk ident*

→ *Squawk ident Exam 40*

*Exam 40
Identified 12 miles south-east of Daventry
Traffic Service
Cleared to enter controlled airspace route Daventry–UPDUK–EME
Climb flight level 70*

→ *Traffic Service
Cleared to enter controlled airspace route Daventry–UPDUK–EME
Climb flight level 70 Exam 40*

*Exam 40
Radar Control Service*

→ *Radar Control Service
Maintaining flight level 70 Exam 40*

→ *Exam 40 roger
Request descent*

*Exam 40
Descend flight level 60*

→ *Descend flight level 60 Exam 40*

*Exam 40
Descend to altitude four thousand feet
East Midlands QNH 999 millibars*

→ *Descend to altitude four thousand feet East Midlands QNH 999 millibars Exam 40*

*Exam 40
Contact East Midlands Approach 134.175*

→ *East Midlands Approach 134.175 Exam 40*

East Midlands Approach

→ *East Midlands Approach Exam 40
Descending to altitude four thousand feet*

*Exam 40
East Midlands Approach
Vectoring for an ILS approach Runway 27
Information Delta
QNH 999 millibars*

→ *Vectoring for an ILS approach Runway 27
Information Delta received
QNH 999 millibars
Exam 40*

*Exam 40
Turn right heading 030
Descend to altitude three thousand feet
QNH 999 millibars*

→ *Right heading 030
Descend to altitude three thousand feet
QNH 999 millibars
Exam 40*

*Exam 40
Descend to altitude two thousand feet
Turn right heading 080
Downwind left-hand
20 miles from touchdown*

→ *Descend to altitude two thousand feet
Turn right heading 080
Exam 40*

*Exam 40
After missed approach climb straight ahead to altitude two thousand feet
On reaching, turn left to leave the Control Zone on track IFR*

→ *After missed approach climb straight ahead to altitude two thousand feet
On reaching, turn left to leave the Control Zone on track IFR*

*Exam 40
Turn left heading 350, base leg*

→ *Left heading 350
Exam 40*

→ *Exam 40
Turn left heading 300, when established on localizer descend with glidepath
Report established*

→ *Left heading 300 when established on localizer descend with glidepath. Wilco Exam 40*

→ *Localizer established
Exam 40*

→ *Exam 40
Runway 27 cleared low approach and go-around not below height 400 ft above threshold elevation
Inspection vehicle on the runway
Report going around*

→ *Runway 27 cleared low approach and go-around not below height 400 ft above threshold elevation
Wilco Exam 40*

→ *Exam 40
Going around*

→ *Exam 40 roger*

→ *Exam 40
Squawk 4555*

→ *Squawk 4555
Exam 40*

→ *Exam 40
Traffic Service outside controlled airspace*

→ *Traffic Service
Exam 40*

→ *Exam 40
Unknown traffic left ten o'clock, range 3 miles, crossing left to right, no height information*

→ *Exam 40 roger*

→ *Exam 40 visual*

→ *Exam 40 roger*

→ *Exam 40
Leaving my radar cover
Basic Service
Report leaving the frequency*

→ *Exam 40
Basic Service
Changing to Cranfield Approach 122.850*

→ *Exam 40 roger
Squawk 7000*

→ *Squawk 7000
Exam 40*

General handling

→ *Cranfield Approach
Exam 40*

→ *Exam 40
Cranfield Approach
Pass your message*

→ *Exam 40
Seminole
20 miles east of Daventry
Altitude three thousand feet
Request Basic Service*

→ *Exam 40 roger
Basic Service
Cranfield QNH 1000*

→ *QNH 1000
Exam 40*

General handling complete – Listen to Cranfield

→ *Exam 40
Request rejoin
Estimating CIT at 48
Request your weather*

→ *Exam 40 Procedural Service
Cleared to the CIT at altitude four thousand five hundred feet for conspicuity squawk 0247
Runway 21
QNH 1001*

→ *Procedural Service. Cleared to the CIT at altitude four thousand five hundred feet. QNH 1001
Squawk 0247
Runway 21
Exam 40*

→ *Exam 40
Report reaching four thousand five hundred feet and entering the hold CIT*

→ *Wilco Exam 40*

→ *Exam 40
Four thousand five hundred feet*

→ *Exam 40 roger*

→ *Exam 40
CIT entering the hold*

→ *Exam 40
Report ready for the approach*

→ *Wilco Exam 40*

→ *Exam 40
Ready for approach*

→ *Exam 40
Descend to altitude three thousand five hundred feet
Report reaching*

→ *Descend to altitude three thousand five hundred feet
Wilco Exam 40*

→ *Exam 40
Three thousand five hundred feet*

→ *Exam 40
Cleared Beacon approach Runway 21
Report beacon outbound*

→ *Cleared Beacon approach Runway 21
Report beacon outbound
Exam 40*

→ *Exam 40
Beacon outbound*

→ *Exam 40
Report base turn complete*

→ *Report base turn complete
Exam 40*

→ *Exam 40
Base turn complete*

→ *Exam 40
Report beacon inbound*

→ *Wilco Exam 40*

→ *Exam 40
Beacon inbound*

(j) ATC LIAISON

6 - 2D APPROACH

Exam 40
Threshold elevation 358 feet
Contact Cranfield Tower 134.925

Contact Cranfield Tower 134.925
Exam 40

Cranfield Tower
Cranfield Tower
Exam 40
Final runway 21 for go-around into visual circuit

Exam 40
Cranfield Tower
Runway 21 cleared low approach and go-around
Surface wind 240 10 knots
Visual left-hand circuit
report going around

Cleared low approach and go-around
Visual left-hand circuit
Wilco Exam 40

Exam 40
Going around

Exam 40 roger

Exam 40
Downwind to land

Exam 40
Report final
Number two follow a Tomahawk
2-mile final

Report final, number two, visual
Exam 40

Exam 40 final

Exam 40
Cleared to land
Surface wind 250 9 knots

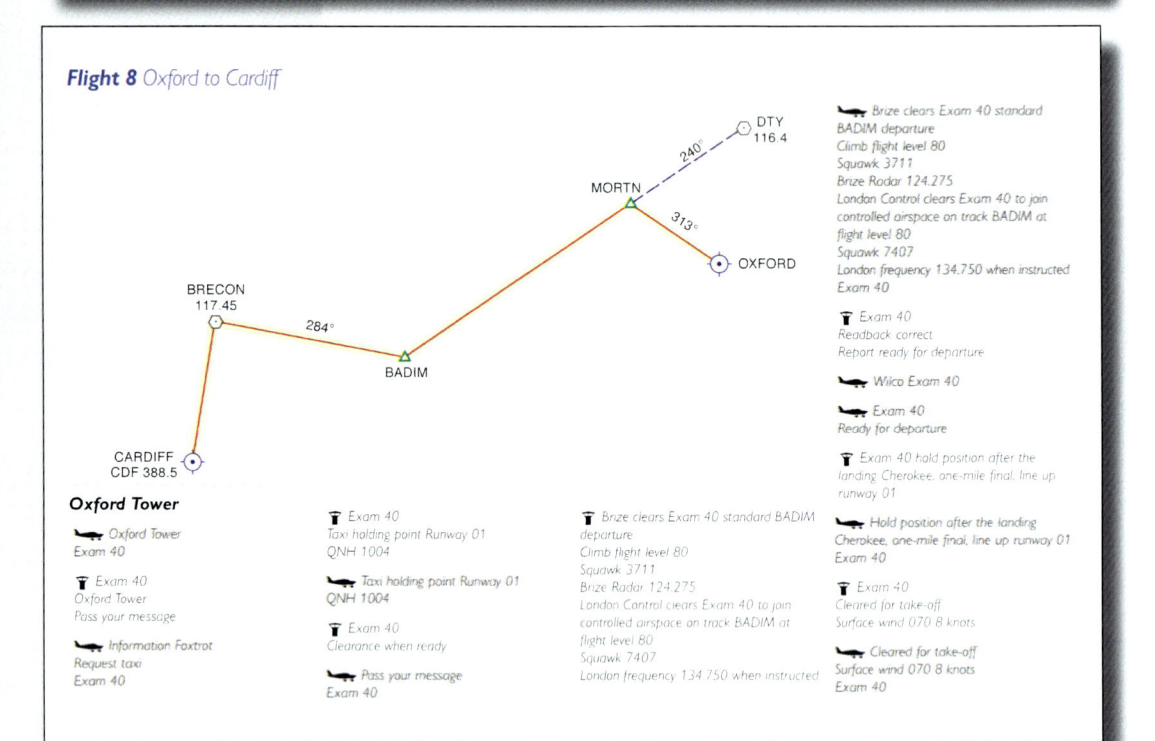

Cleared to land
Exam 40

Flight 8 *Oxford to Cardiff*

DTY 116.4
240°
MORTN
313°
OXFORD
BRECON 117.45
284°
BADIM
CARDIFF CDF 388.5

Oxford Tower

Oxford Tower
Exam 40

Exam 40
Oxford Tower
Pass your message

Information Foxtrot
Request taxi
Exam 40

Exam 40
Taxi holding point Runway 01
QNH 1004

Taxi holding point Runway 01
QNH 1004

Exam 40
Clearance when ready

Pass your message
Exam 40

Brize clears Exam 40 standard BADiM departure
Climb flight level 80
Squawk 3711
Brize Radar 124.275
London Control clears Exam 40 to join controlled airspace on track BADIM at flight level 80
Squawk 7407
London frequency 134.750 when instructed
Exam 40

Brize clears Exam 40 standard BADiM departure
Climb flight level 80
Squawk 3711
Brize Radar 124.275
London Control clears Exam 40 to join controlled airspace on track BADIM at flight level 80
Squawk 7407
London frequency 134.750 when instructed

Exam 40
Readback correct
Report ready for departure

Wilco Exam 40

Exam 40
Ready for departure

Exam 40 hold position after the landing Cherokee, one-mile final, line up runway 01

Hold position after the landing Cherokee, one-mile final, line up runway 01
Exam 40

Exam 40
Cleared for take-off
Surface wind 070 8 knots

Cleared for take-off
Surface wind 070 8 knots
Exam 40

CHAPTER SIX   (j) ATC LIAISON

6 - 2D APPROACH

🛩ℹ Exam 40
Contact Oxford Approach 125.325

📻 Contact Oxford Approach 125.325
Exam 40

Oxford Approach

📻 Oxford Approach
Exam 40
Standard BADIM departure
Passing altitude 1000 feet, climbing flight level 80

🛩ℹ Exam 40
Oxford Approach
Report passing altitude two thousand five hundred feet

📻 Wilco Exam 40

📻 Exam 40
Passing altitude two thousand five hundred feet

🛩ℹ Exam 40
Contact Brize Radar 124.275

📻 Contact Brize Radar 124.275
Exam 40

Brize Radar

📻 Brize Radar
Exam 40
Standard BADIM departure passing altitude two thousand eight hundred feet, climbing flight level 80
Request Traffic Service

🛩ℹ Exam 40
Brize Radar
squawk ident

🛩ℹ Exam 40
Turn right heading 090 when established on localizer descend with the glidepath

📻 Turn right heading 090 when established on localizer descend with the glidepath
Exam 40

🛩ℹ Exam 40
Runway 12 cleared low approach and go-around
Report going around
Surface wind 070 9 knots

📻 Runway 12 cleared low approach and go-around
Wilco Exam 40

📻 Exam 40
Going around

🛩ℹ Exam 40 roger

🛩ℹ Exam 40
Report taking up the hold CDF

📻 Wilco Exam 40

📻 Exam 40
Entering hold

🛩ℹ Exam 40
Report ready for approach

📻 Squawk ident
Exam 40

🛩ℹ Exam 40
Identified 3 miles north-west of Oxford
Traffic Service

📻 Traffic Service
Exam 40

🛩ℹ Exam 40
Change squawk 6112

📻 Squawk 6112
Exam 40

🛩ℹ Exam 40
Contact London Control 136.075

📻 Contact London Control 136.075
Exam 40

London Control

📻 London Control
Exam 40

🛩ℹ Exam 40
London Control
Entering controlled airspace
Radar Control Service
Maintain flight level 80

📻 Radar Control Service
Maintain flight level 80
Exam 40

📻 Exam 40
Report BCN

📻 Wilco Exam 40

📻 Exam 40
Ready for approach

🛩ℹ Exam 40
Cleared NDB approach Runway 12
Report beacon outbound

📻 Cleared NDB approach Runway 12
Report beacon outbound
Exam 40

📻 Exam 40
Beacon outbound

🛩ℹ Exam 40
Report base turn complete

📻 Wilco Exam 40

🛩ℹ Exam 40
After go-around climb straight ahead to altitude three thousand feet, leave the Control Zone IFR

📻 After go-around climb straight ahead to altitude three thousand feet, leave the Control Zone IFR
Exam 40

📻 Exam 40
Base turn complete

🛩ℹ Exam 40
Report established on final approach track

📻 Wilco Exam 40

📻 Exam 40
Final

📻 Exam 40
BCN time 24
Flight level 80
Estimating CDF 32
Request descent

🛩ℹ Exam 40
Descend flight level 60

📻 Descend flight level 60
Exam 40

🛩ℹ Exam 40
Descend to altitude four thousand feet
Cardiff QNH 1002

📻 Descend to altitude four thousand feet
Cardiff QNH 1002
Exam 40

🛩ℹ Exam 40
Contact Cardiff Approach 125.850

📻 Cardiff Approach 125.850
Exam 40

Cardiff Approach

📻 Cardiff Approach
Exam 40
Descending to altitude four thousand feet

🛩ℹ Exam 40
Cardiff Approach
Vectoring ILS approach Runway 12, Information Hotel

📻 Vectoring ILS Approach Runway 12
Information Hotel
Exam 40

🛩ℹ Exam 40
Runway 12 cleared low approach and go-around
Report going around
Surface wind 060 12 knots

📻 Runway 12 cleared low approach and go-around
Wilco Exam 40

📻 Exam 40
Going around

🛩ℹ Exam 40 roger

🛩ℹ Exam 40
Traffic Service outside controlled airspace

📻 Traffic Service
Exam 40

The approaches are followed by the general handling segment outside controlled airspace, and if both were completed at the out station, as in the example above, a visual join at Oxford.

🛩ℹ Exam 40
Descend to altitude three thousand feet
Cardiff QNH 1002
Squawk 3604

📻 Descend to altitude three thousand feet
Cardiff QNH 1002
Squawk 3604
Exam 40

🛩ℹ Exam 40
Turn right heading 210 positioning downwind right-hand, number three

📻 Right heading 210
Exam 40

🛩ℹ Exam 40
Turn right heading 310, downwind 25 miles from touchdown
Descend to altitude two thousand feet

📻 Right heading 310, downwind
Descend to altitude two thousand feet
Exam 40

🛩ℹ Exam 40
After the go-around standard missed approach climb to altitude two thousand five hundred feet

📻 After the go-around standard missed approach climb to altitude two thousand five hundred feet
Exam 40

🛩ℹ Exam 40
Turn right heading 035, right base

📻 Right heading 035
Exam 40

(j) ATC LIAISON

intentionally blank

CHAPTER SEVEN

Simulated Asymmetric Flight

The examiner will brief you on the ground where he will conduct the asymmetric parts of the test. The final instrument approach will be conducted under asymmetric power and will include an asymmetric go-around and landing.

A)   **ENGINE FAILURE** AFTER TAKE OFF

Maintains control following a simulated engine failure after take-off; completes the necessary checks and drills; maintains the correct speed and continues to follow ATC instructions

Once you have safely established the aircraft in the climb at a safe height and once the after take-off checks are complete, the examiner will shield the throttle quadrant and simulate an engine failure. He will do this by retarding one of the throttles. The examiner is looking to see the following:-

- Apply the correct rudder input to counteract the yaw, and trim the aircraft correctly. Maintain heading
- Level wings or apply approximately 5° angle of bank towards the live engine
- Adjust pitch and trim the aircraft to maintain **Vyse** +/- 5kts
- Confirm full power is applied to the 'live' engine, propeller levers and mixture controls are set accordingly and that the undercarriage and flap are retracted
- Cowl flaps set accordingly

The test tolerances are as follows:-

- Altitude with simulated engine failure +/- 100 ft
- Heading with simulated engine failure +/- 10°
- Speed with simulated engine failure +10/-5 kts
- **Vyse** +/-5kt

(a)   ENGINE FAILURE AFTER TAKE OFF

Identify the failed engine by confirming which of your legs is not applying force to the rudder pedals. It may help to confirm this by removing the pressure from the controls briefly i.e. dead leg = dead engine. Tell the examiner which engine has failed and be specific, e.g. 'the right engine has failed'. Don't fall into the classic trap and say 'right, the left engine has failed'! He will then remove the shield from the quadrant.

For the purposes of the test, use touch drills to confirm which engine controls you would move. However, if you have a real engine failure, you MUST confirm the failure by slowly retarding the throttle on the failed engine; if there is any change in yaw or significant noise, then immediately apply full throttle.

Once you have feathered the failed engine, the examiner will set zero thrust. At this point check that you are following the missed approach procedure correctly and adjust accordingly. You need to make sure you can achieve any altitude restrictions contained within the missed approach procedure; if you cannot inform ATC.

Any emergency radio calls associated with the **EFATO** should be made aloud but not transmitted. However, it is good airmanship to inform ATC that you are practising asymmetric conditions.

Complete any securing checks once above the MSA or established in the hold. Back these up with reference to the **EAFTO** checklist. Don't assume that the engine failure exercise is over until informed by the examiner.

B) **ASYMMETRIC APPROACH** AND PROCEDURAL GO AROUND

Completes an asymmetric go-around into a circling approach or other appropriate manoeuvre maintaining control at safe speeds

On the final approach, the examiner needs to see an asymmetric go-around from DA/MDA. This will require a climb to circling MDA, level-off and visual circle to land. The examiner will remove the screens at a suitable point during the missed approach. At the planning stage always check the **Asymmetric Committal Altitude (ACA)** against the approach minima as the higher will apply.

The ATO will stipulate the ACA in the Training Manual to be used when simulating asymmetric flight, 200 ft is a typical value. However, some light aircraft have a much higher ACA.

As you approach DA/MDA apply full throttle on the live engine, simultaneously feed in full rudder to counteract the yaw. If it helps, imagine that both your leg and throttle are connected. When the aircraft is in a clean configuration, adjust the attitude to maintain **Vyse**. Do not go below MDA! The aircraft is unlikely to climb away until both the undercarriage and flaps are retracted and then follow the actions shown in the diagram. The examiner wants to see that you can control the aircraft and establish the aircraft in a climb, maintaining speed and directional limits whilst retracting the undercarriage and flap. To help you maintain heading, set the heading bug on the runway QDM or if a strong wind exists, the heading used on final approach to maintain the final approach track. While you are flying the go-around manoeuvre, check the airspeed and heading regularly and adjust the attitude accordingly. The go-around in any aircraft is a tricky manoeuvre. Time spent on the ground rehearsing the procedures pays dividends.

C) ASYMMETRIC APPROACH AND FULL STOP LANDING

Completes as asymmetric approach and landing; complies with ATC instructions and maintains satisfactory lookout to avoid other circuit traffic

Fly the circling manoeuvre as described earlier. Note, however, that when asymmetric performance is limited, it is wise to delay extension of flap and landing gear until starting the descent for landing.

ATC will inform you which direction to circle, make sure you follow this. ATC may, however, give you the option in which direction to fly. In an ideal scenario, break right and fly a left hand circuit, as this pattern will make it easier for you to see the runway.

The visual circuit will often be very busy, especially at an airfield with a lot of ATOs. You will be lower and closer to the runway, so you must maintain an excellent lookout, not only at the runway, but also for other traffic. Manoeuvre as instructed by ATC to maintain your position in the landing sequence.

Fly an asymmetric approach and landing as described in 'A Guide to the EASA CPL Flight Test'.

Once you have vacated the runway, complete the after landing checklist and taxi the aircraft back to the parking stand. Note the landing time and on blocks time on the navigation log. Once the engines have stopped and the aircraft is safely shutdown, the examiner will inform you that the test is complete. The examiner may give the result there or he may ask some questions back in the briefing room to check understanding. Make sure that the technical log and authorisation sheets have been filled in and signed with any defects correctly reported. It is, however, the examiner's responsibility to do this as he is the aircraft commander.

D)   ATC LIAISON

Compliance, RT Procedure, Airmanship

The examiner may ask some questions regarding ATC abnormal procedures when operating under IFR. Other than the standard RTF PAN and MAYDAY calls which are used to indicate an abnormal situation, the examiner may ask:-

'What are the actions in the event of radio failure when flying IFR?'

7 - SIMULATED ASYMMETRIC FLIGHT

ANSWER:- *Assuming that you cannot resolve the situation through checklist, or airmanship actions then you must follow the procedures found in the AIP ENR:-*

RADIO FAILURE PROCEDURES ARE FOUND IN THE UK AIP ENR SECTION

ENR 1-1-3-4 (30 Jul 09)   **UK AIP**

ENR 1.1 — GENERAL RULES
ENR 1.1.3 — GENERAL FLIGHT PROCEDURES

4.2.4   Instrument Meteorological Conditions (IMC)

4.2.4.1 A flight experiencing communication failure in IMC shall:

(a) Operate secondary radar transponder on Mode A, Code 7600 with Mode C.

(b) (i) Maintain, for a period of 7 minutes, the current speed and last assigned level or minimum safe altitude, if this higher. The period of seven minutes begins when the transponder is set to 7600 and this should be done as soon as the pilot has detected communications failure.

    (ii) If failure occurs when the aircraft is following a notified departure procedure such as a Standard Instrument Departure (SID) and clearance to climb, or re-routing instructions have not been given, the procedure should be flown in accordance with the published lateral track and vertical profile, including any stepped climbs, until the last position, fix, or waypoint, published for the procedure, has been reached. Then, for that part of the period of 7 minutes that may remain, maintain the current speed and last assigned level or minimum safe altitude, if this higher.

    (iii) Thereafter, adjust the speed and level in accordance with the current flight plan and continue the flight to the appropriate designated landing aid serving the destination aerodrome. Attempt to transmit position reports and altitude/flight level on the appropriate frequency when over routine reporting points.

(c) (i) If being radar vectored, or proceeding offset according to RNAV, without a specified limit, continue in accordance with ATC instructions last acknowledged for 3 minutes only and then proceed in the most direct manner possible to rejoin the current flight planned route. Pilots should ensure that they remain at, or above, the minimum safe altitude.

    (ii) If being radar vectored by an Approach Control Radar Unit (callsign DIRECTOR/RADAR/APPROACH), comply with the loss of communications procedures notified on the appropriate ATC Surveillance Minimum Altitude Chart (ATCSMAC) as detailed in the AD 2 section of the UK AIP.

(d) (i) Arrange the flight to arrive over the appropriate designated landing aid serving the destination aerodrome as closely as possible to the ETA last acknowledged by ATC. If no such ETA has been acknowledged, the pilot should use an ETA derived from the last acknowledged position report and the flight-planned times for the subsequent sections of the flight.

    (ii) Arrange the flight to arrive over the appropriate designated landing aid serving the destination aerodrome at the highest notified Minimum Sector Altitude taking account of en-route terrain clearance requirements.

    (iii) If following a notified Standard Arrival Route (STAR), after the seven minute period detailed in paragraph (b) (i) has been completed, pilots should arrange descent as close as possible to the published descent planning profile. If no descent profile is published, pilots should arrange descent to be at the minimum published level at the appropriate designated Initial Approach fix.

(e) On reaching the appropriate designated landing aid serving the destination aerodrome, begin further descent at the last acknowledged EAT. If no EAT has been acknowledged, the descent should be started at the ETA calculated in (d) (i), above, or as close as possible to this time. If necessary, remain within the holding pattern until the minimum holding level, published for the facility, has been reached. The rate of descent in holding patterns should not be less than 500 ft per minute. If 'Delay not determined' has been given, do not attempt to land at the destination aerodrome, divert to the alternate destination specified in the current flight plan or another suitable airfield.

(f) Carry out the notified instrument approach procedure as specified for the designated navigational aid and, if possible, land within 30 minutes of the EAT or the calculated ETA. When practical, pilots should take account of visual landing aids and keep watch for instructions that may be issued by visual signals from the ground.

(g) If communications failure occurs during an approach directed by radar, continue visually, or by using an alternative aid. If this is not practical, carry out the missed approach procedure and continue to a holding facility appropriate to the airfield of intended landing for which an instrument approach is notified and then carry out that procedure.

(d) ATC LIAISON

The examiner may also ask:-

'If you are intercepted by a military aircraft, where would you find the procedures to follow?'

ANSWER:- *This may seem a little farfetched but if you have a period of loss of communications you will be contacted on 121.500 Mhz and if you still do not respond a military aircraft will be sent to intercept you. ICAO procedures should be followed; these are described in the UK AIP ENR section. They should also be in the aircraft checklist. You are not expected to remember interception procedures, however, you do need to know where they are described.*

Signals Initiated by Intercepting Aircraft and Responses by Intercepted Aircraft

Series	INTERCEPTING Aircraft Signals	Meaning	INTERCEPTED Aircraft Signals	Meaning
1	DAY or NIGHT – Rocking aircraft and flashing navigational lights at irregular intervals *(and landing lights in the case of a helicopter)* from a position slightly above and ahead of, and normally to the left of, the intercepted aircraft and, after acknowledgement, a slow level turn, normally to the left onto the desired heading. **NOTE:** *1. Meteorological conditions or terrain may require the intercepting aircraft to reverse the positions and direction of turn given above in Series.* *2. If the intercepted aircraft is not able to keep pace with the intercepting aircraft, the latter is expected to fly a series of race-track patterns and to rock the aircraft each time it passes the intercepted aircraft.*	You have been intercepted. Follow me	DAY or NIGHT Rocking aircraft, flashing navigational lights at irregular intervals and following.	Understood, will comply
2	DAY or NIGHT – An abrupt breakaway manoeuvre from the intercepted aircraft.	You may proceed.	DAY or NIGHT Rocking the aircraft -	Understood, will comply
3	DAY or NIGHT – Lowering landing gear, showing steady landing lights and overflying runway in use.	Land at this aerodrome.	DAY or NIGHT – Lowering landing gear, showing steady landing lights and following the intercepting aircraft and, if, after overflying the runway in use, landing is considered safe, proceeding to land.	Understood, will comply

(d) ATC LIAISON

Signals Initiated by Intercepted Aircraft and Responses by Intercepting Aircraft continued..

Series	INTERCEPTING Aircraft Signals	Meaning	INTERCEPTED Aircraft Signals	Meaning
4	DAY or NIGHT – Raising landing gear and flashing landing lights while passing over runway in use at a height exceeding 300m *(1,000')* but not exceeding 600m *(2,000')* above the aerodrome level, and continuing to circle runway in use or helicopter landing area. If unable to flash landing lights, flash any other lights available.	Aerodrome you have designated is inadequate.	DAY or NIGHT – If it is desired that the intercepted aircraft follow the intercepting aircraft to an alternate aerodrome, the intercepting aircraft raises its landing gear *(if fitted)* and uses the Series 1 signals prescribed for intercepting aircraft.	Understood, follow me.
			If it is decided to release the intercepted aircraft, the intercepting aircraft uses the Series 2 signals prescribed for intercepting aircraft.	Understood, follow me
5	DAY or NIGHT – Regular switching on and off of all available lights but in such a manner as to be distinct from flashing lights.	Cannot comply.	DAY or NIGHT – Use Series 2 signals prescribed for intercepting aircraft.	Understood.
6	DAY or NIGHT – Irregular flashing of all available lights.	In distress.	DAY or NIGHT – Use Series 2 Signals prescribed for intercepting aircraft..	Understood.

(d) ATC LIAISON

7 - SIMULATED ASYMMETRIC FLIGHT

Abnormal operations during the test

With the advancement in technology fitted in light aircraft so too have the monitoring systems fitted in them to warn the pilot of failures. Electronic crew alerting systems are designed to monitor and if appropriate, warn the pilot of degradation in system capability. The pilot must then consult the appropriate abnormal checklist to resolve the situation. In recent years, as more technologically advanced aircraft are being used on initial IRTs, examiners are commenting that candidates often accept that the caution/warning is of a spurious nature and that there is no need to consult the appropriate checklist. Although it is not ideal to have a problem on the IRT, the checklist must be completed once the aircraft is in suitable position to do so. You must then decide whether to continue, return or divert.

Annunciation Window Text
L / R ENG TEMP
L / R OIL TEMP
L / R OIL PRES
L/R ENG FIRE
L / R GBOX TEMP
L / R ALTN AMPS
L / R STARTER
L / R FUEL TEMP
DOOR OPEN
AP TRIM FAIL

Annunciation Window Text
L / R ECU A FAIL
L / R ECU B FAIL
L / R FUEL LOW
L / R ALTN FAIL
L / R VOLTS LOW
L / R COOL LVL
PITOT FAIL
PITOT HT OFF
STAL HT FAIL
STAL HT OFF
L / R AUX FUEL E

Warning Alerts

You must consult the checklist if you receive any crew alert annunciations

(d) ATC LIAISON

intentionally blank

CHAPTER EIGHT

Oral Questioning

The examiner may ask practical questions relating to the flight on subjects such as altimetry, IFR procedures, performance, loading, icing procedures, emergency handling and the aircraft documents. It is usually used to clear up any misunderstandings, or to enable the examiner to check your knowledge.

Altimetry

1. Where will you find your ATO's rules regarding the setting of Altimeters?
2. Where is the designated location for pre-flight altimeter checks in the UK?
3. With QNH set on the apron what should the altimeter read?
4. What altimeter setting should you use when operating within the Bristol CTR?
5. How long is the Regional Pressure Setting valid for?
6. Where can you find information on altimetry within the AIP?
7. You are overhead MID VOR at 2400 ft, what altimeter setting would you use?
8. Which altimeter setting will give you the greatest separation above terrain?
9. Why are there two altimeters fitted in an IFR certified aircraft?
10. What is the usual civilian altimeter setting used in conducting instrument approaches?
11. Can you conduct an instrument approach using QFE?
12. If the QNH changes during the approach will ATC inform you and what are your actions?

13. In an airway flying above the transition altitude what is the primary altimeter setting and what is set usually on the secondary altimeter? Where would you find these procedures?
14. When ATC clear you to descend to an altitude when should you set the QNH?
15. If you think you have the incorrect QNH what should you do?

Flight Planning

1. Where would you find out your ATO's fuel planning policy?
2. A commercial flight in a MEP aircraft operating under an EU issued Air Operators Certificate must apply which fuel policy?
3. How much holding fuel is required for a MEP aircraft operating to EASA Commercial Air Transport regulations?
4. The weather is marginal at the destination aerodrome, can you as the pilot in command elect to take extra fuel when planning the fuel required?
5. Is outbound taxi time taken into account when planning the fuel required?
6. Where is the fuel uplift recorded?
7. Whose responsibility is it to ensure that the aircraft has sufficient fuel for the flight?
8. What is the basic EASA Part-CAT fuel planning policy for class B aeroplanes?
9. Does a flight operating IFR in controlled airspace require a flight plan?
10. How soon before a flight should an IFR flight plan be filed?
11. What time reference should be used on a flight plan?
12. How should a TAS of 160 kts be entered in the cruise speed box on the ATC flight plan?
13. If you want to go direct to a waypoint how is this entered on the flight plan?

14. Is the SID entered in the flight plan?
15. Where would you find standard routings between airports in the UK?
16. Why is it important to have a copy of the flight plan?
17. If you want to file the flight plan the night before for a early morning flight on the 17 September 2011, how would you indicate this on the flight plan?
18. What is the difference between an ATC flight plan and an Operational flight plan?

RTF

1. When is a full position report required?
2. What is the standard format for a position report?
3. What is the standard format on initial call to ATC when flying a SID?
4. Should you monitor 121.500 MHz during the flight?
5. What is the transponder code for radio failure?
6. In the UK where would you find the loss of communications procedure described?
7. Who are always available to help you if you need assistance?
8. If you want to check the weather at destination but are still out of range of the ATIS, how can you obtain the latest weather report without disturbing the airway controller?

Aerodrome Operating Minima

1. What are the single crew operating minima, without a serviceable autopilot fitted?
2. What are the lowest minima you can fly to with a serviceable autopilot on a precision approach?
3. When operating under single crew in a MEP aircraft can you fly a Category 3B approach?
4. Where would you find the minima for the approach?
5. How do you know whether to add a PEC error and where will the amount be stated?
6. Can you make an approach if the visibility is below limits?
7. What happens if the visibility drops below the operating minima when you are within 1000 ft aal?

Icing

1. How can you find out whether your aircraft is approved into known icing conditions?
2. Where are actions to be followed for flight in icing conditions described?
3. At the planning stage how can you check what the freezing level is?
4. If you encounter ice which you are unable to clear what should you do?
5. Do you need to check the anti/de-icing equipment before flight?
6. Whilst completing the pre-flight inspection of the aircraft, you discover that the de-icing boots are unserviceable, which document can you check to see whether you can legally depart with the defect?
7. When should the propeller de-ice system be operated?
8. When looking for ice, what should you check first?
9. Is it acceptable to depart with ice or frost on the wing?

Tolerances

1. What are the tolerances for an ETA?
2. What is the tolerance for tracking a VOR or NDB?
3. What are the tolerances during a 3D approach?
4. What allowance is there to achieve a CTOT?
5. During the cruise what is the tolerance on altitude?
6. Where are the tolerances found for the IRT?

intentionally blank

Answers for Oral Questions

Altimetry

1. ATO Operations Manual
2. The apron
3. The elevation of the airfield
4. Bristol QNH
5. 1 hr updated on the hour
6. ENR 1.7.
7. London QNH
8. Regional Pressure Setting
9. Firstly, in case one breaks, secondly so readings can be cross checked. It also allows you to monitor terrain separation.
10. Aerodrome QNH
11. Yes, the military use QFE based approaches
12. ATC will inform you of the new setting and expect you to read it back to them. You must then adjust to the new setting
13. SPS on the primary altimeter and RPS or aerodrome QNH on the secondary. Altimeter setting procedures are found in the Operations Manual
14. Immediately, unless they ask you to report passing a certain FL
15. Ask ATC to pass the appropriate QNH

Flight Planning

1. ATO Operations Manual
2. EASA Part CAT fuel policy fuel planning for Class B aeroplanes
3. 45 minutes
4. Yes
5. Yes
6. Technical log
7. Pilot-in-Command
8. Fuel Required = Taxi fuel + Trip + Contingency *(5% of trip)* + Diversion to alternate + Final Reserve Fuel *(45 minutes holding in a piston engine)* + Extra Fuel as required
9. Yes
10. At least 1 hr before the EOBT
11. GMT
12. N0160
13. DCT
14. No, just the first point on the airway. ATC will issue the appropriate instrument departure
15. UK AIP-SRD
16. In the event of a radio failure it is what ATC expect you to fly
17. DOF/110917 in the remarks section of the flight plan
18. The ATC flight plan is completed at the planning stage and is used to allow ATC to know where you are going and the route and level you would like to fly. It also has important safety information in the event that you are overdue and the emergency services need to find you. An operational flight plan is used in flight and has all the important information required to fly the route and monitor the progress of the fuel burn, MSA, frequencies, etc.

8 - ANSWERS

RTF

1. When asked by ATC or when operating under a procedural service
2. Aircraft identification, position, time, level, next position and ETA
3. Call sign, SID or Standard Departure Route Designator *(where appropriate)*, current or passing level PLUS initial climb level *(i.e. the first level at which the aircraft will level off unless otherwise cleared.)*
4. Ideally, Yes
5. 7600
6. AIP ENR 1-6, suitable IFR flight guide
7. Distress and Diversion on 121.500 or 243 MHz
8. VOLMET, Flight Information Station, Satellite weather if the aircraft is equipped

Aerodrome Operating Minima

1. 800 m or the published minima, whichever is the higher
2. 200 ft/550 m
3. No, Category 1 only
4. AIP, Approach plate, ATC
5. AFM
6. The UK AIP states:-

> *10.3 An aircraft may commence an instrument approach regardless of the reported RVR/Visibility but the approach shall not be continued below 1000 ft above the aerodrome if the relevant RVR/Visibility for that runway is at the time less than the specified minimum for landing.*

> *10.4 If, after passing 1000 ft in accordance with paragraph 10.3, the reported RVR/Visibility falls below the applicable minimum, the approach may be continued to DA/H or MDA/H.*

> *10.5 The approach may be continued below DA/H or MDA/H and the landing may be completed provided that the required visual reference is established at the DA/H or MDA/H and is maintained.*

7. If the visibility drops below the required minimum once you are within 1000 ft aal, the approach maybe continued to DA(H) or MDA/H.

Icing

1. It will be stated in the AFM
2. AFM, Operations Manual
3. It is stated on the F215, it can also be estimated by checking where the zero degree isotherm is on the F214
4. Inform ATC and change level
5. Yes, all equipment should be checked in accordance with the AFM and approved checklist. It is especially important to purge air out of a 'wet wing' anti-ice system
6. MEL
7. Anytime whilst operating in icing conditions and always in accordance with the AFM
8. The OAT gauge
9. NO! All wing, tail and propeller surfaces must be free of any ice, frost or contamination

Tolerances

1. +/- 3 mins
2. +/- 5°
3. Half scale deflection for both the localiser and glideslope
4. +10/-5 mins
5. +/- 100 ft
6. Standards Document 1

Typical Test Routes

The following typical test routes are given as a guide to the length and typical flight plan route that a candidate might expect to fly. They are not to be taken as official test routes as these do not exist. The examiner's choice on test destination and diversion is dependent on many factors. Candidates must not go into the briefing with any pre-conceived destinations based on previous candidates' experiences. As regional test centres have recently been withdrawn examiners may travel to the individual ATO location, which increases the number of new airfields and routings.

As a flight planning exercise; for each route consider what you would file in the route section of the ATC flight plan. Information regarding this can be found in the UK AIP-AD, ENR and SRD sections and a suitable airways chart and supplement booklet. You could also use flight planning software to find the information, which is far quicker, but you may find benefit in consulting the original documents!

Bournemouth (EGHH)

Alderney (EGJA)
Cardiff (EGFF)
Exeter (EGTE)
Yeovil (Westland) (EGHG)

Bristol (EGGD)

Cardiff (EGFF)
Exeter (EGTE)
Gloucestershire (EGBJ)
Yeovil (Westland) (EGHG)

Cranfield (EGTC)

Cambridge (EGSC)
East Midlands (EGNX)

Exeter (EGTE)

Alderney (EGJA)
Bristol (EGGD)
Cardiff (EGFF)

Gloucestershire (EGBJ)

Bristol (EGGD)
Cardiff (EGFF)
RAF Brize Norton (EGVN)

Chester (Hawarden)

Blackpool (EGNH)
Doncaster (EGCN)
East Midlands (EGNX)
Leeds Bradford (EGNM)
Manchester International (EGCC)

Leeds Bradford (EGNM)

Blackpool (EGNH)
Doncaster Sheffield (EGCN)
Durham Tees Valley (EGNV)

Liverpool (EGGP)

Blackpool (EGNH)
Hawarden (Chester) (EGNR)
Leeds Bradford (EGNM)

Oxford (Kidlington) (EGTK)

Bristol (EGGD)
Gloucester (EGBJ)
RAF Brize Norton (EGVN)

Perth (Scone) (EGPT)

Aberdeen (EGPD)
Prestwick (EGPK)

Shoreham (EGKA)

Bournemouth (EGHH)
Lydd (EGMD)

intentionally blank

8 - APPENDIX 2

Airfield Contact

THESE CONTACT DETAILS ARE SUBJECT TO CHANGE, ALWAYS CONSULT A SUITABLE FLIGHT GUIDE FOR THE LATEST NUMBERS

Details & ATIS Telephone Numbers

Most of the airfields mentioned require a training slot to be booked prior to departing. Submission of an ATC flight plan does not meet this requirement. Operations may well book the training slot for you, however, if they don't then these may well be useful:-

ALDERNEY ATC: 01481 822851

BENSON OPS (Civil): 01491 827017/827018, ATIS 01491 837766 Ext. 7524

BIRMINGHAM ATC: 0121 7800906, ATIS: 0121 7800910

BLACKPOOL: 08700 273777, ATIS: 01253 343 434 Ext. 8315

BOURNEMOUTH: 01202 364150, ATIS: 01202 364 151

BRISTOL: ATC: 01275 473712/473713, ATIS: 08448481022

CALAIS: 00 33 3 21 00 11 11

CAMBRIDGE ATC: 01223 293737

CARDIFF ATC: 01446 712 562, ATIS: 01446 729 319

CHESTER (Hawarden) ATC: 01244 522012

CRANFIELD ATC 01234 754761

DONCASTER Sheffield ATC: 01302 625642

DURHAM TEES VALLEY: 01325 332811

EAST MIDLANDS: 01871 9199000, ATIS: 01332 852852 Ext. 3201

EDINBURGH ATC Admin: 0131 3336216, ATIS: 0131 333 6216

EXETER OPS: 01392 367433

AIRFIELD CONTACT DETAILS

FARNBOROUGH Radar: 01252 526015

GLASGOW ATC: 0141 8408029, ATIS: 0141 8407449

GLOUCESTERSHIRE ATC: 01452 857700 Ext 223 (OPS/ATC)

GUERNSEY: 01481 237766, ATIS: 01481 238957

HUMBERSIDE ATC: 01652 682022, ATIS: 01652 682 020

JERSEY ATC: 01534 466086/466087

LE TOUQUET: 00 33 3 21 05 03 99, ATIS: 00 33 3 21 06 6284

LEEDS Bradford: 0844 4143282, ATIS 0113 250 9696 Ext.2489

LIVERPOOL ATC: 01519071541, ATIS: 0115 907 2000 Ext.5150

LYDD ATC: 01797 320881, ATIS: 01797 322422

OXFORD Kidlington ATC: 01865 290650

PERTH: 01738 551631

PRESTWICK ATC: 01292 511107

RAF BRIZE NORTON: 01993 842551

SHOREHAM ATC: 01273 467377/8, ATIS: 01273 467372

SOUTHAMPTON Admin: 0870 0400009

SOUTHEND ATC: 01702 608100

STAPLEFORD: 01708 688380

WYCOMBE Air Park Booker: 01494 529261

YEOVIL (Westland): 01935 455497/455498

Calculation of Aerodrome Operating Minima

INSTRUMENT-RATED MINIMA FOR A PRECISION APPROACH
e.g. 3D approach runway 28 at Blackpool

- Take the approach minima from the approach plate

  See Note 1

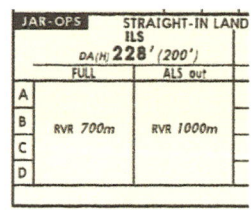

JAR-OPS	STRAIGHT-IN LAND
	ILS
	DA(H) **228'** *(200')*
	FULL / ALS out
A	
B	RVR *700m* / RVR *1000m*
C	
D	

↓

- Add PEC error to the DA e.g. 50 ft
- If no autopilot fitted, or not allowed for use; take 800 m or procedure minimum whichever is higher

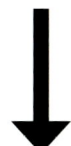

- 228 ft + 50 ft
- 700 or 800 m as applicable

↓

IR Minima

IRT Minima = 278 ft & 800 m

NOTE 1. *The comparison between OCA and System minima has been completed by the approach plate publisher.*

INSTRUMENT-RATED MINIMA FOR A 2D APPROACH
e.g. VOR/DME approach runway 05L at Manchester

- Take the approach minima from the approach plate

  See Note 1

ACFT	VOR+DME	Circling
A (EU OPS)	640 (428) 1300m	750 (493) 1.5km
B		820 (563) 1.6km
C		1110 (853) 2.4km
D		1110 (853) 3.6km

- If using the CDFA technique + increment of 50 ft unless exempt by the CAA
- If using the 'dive and drive' technique no increment required to the MDA but 200 m must be added for Cat A aeroplanes to the required RVR
- If no autopilot fitted, or not allowed for use; take 800 m or procedure RVR whichever is higher

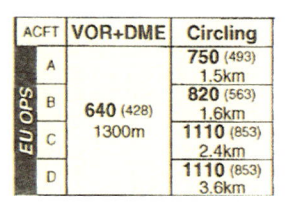

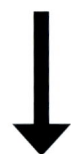

- 640 ft + 50 ft (CDFA)

- 640 ft + 200 m to RVR (Non CDFA)

- Procedure RVR is higher so use 1300m (CDFA) or 1500 m (Non CDFA) as appropriate

IR Minima

IRT Minima = 690 ft (CDFA)/1300 m
Or
640 ft/1500 m (Non CDFA)

NOTE 1. *The comparison between OCA and System minima has been completed by the approach plate publisher.*

Test Day Checklist

Make sure that you have checked or obtained the following before meeting the examiner:-

- ✔ Confirm examiner and test booking.
- ✔ Confirm all syllabus hours completed.
- ✔ Logbook up to date including any retraining *(if second attempt)*.
- ✔ Flight crew licence, radio licence *(or test completed)*, aircraft rating and medical all valid and appropriately signed.
- ✔ ATO certificate which certifies that you are ready for test *(this replaces the old UK CAA F170a)*. A course completion certificate is not required for ICAO IR conversions.
- ✔ Receipt of payment for the test *(unless free re-test)*.
- ✔ Relevant CAA correspondence *(letter of assessment, exemptions, etc.)*.
- ✔ Aircraft documents, Technical log checked and current.
- ✔ Fuel, Oil and Anti-ice fluid loaded as required.
- ✔ IF screens serviceable *(know how to fit them!)*.
- ✔ 2 checklists and 2 compatible headsets with one spare.
- ✔ NOTAMS, NANUs, and weather documents checked and prepared for the briefing.
- ✔ Confirm ATO weather and performance planning requirements are met.
- ✔ Compile all current departure, en-route, arrival and IAP plates for all possible destinations and alternate airfields.
- ✔ Review ATO Operations and Training manuals.
- ✔ Are you fit to fly?

intentionally blank

Part-FCL IR Skill Test

Below is Appendix 7 to Part-FCL from CAP 804. This can be downloaded from **www.caa.co.uk**

1. An applicant for an IR shall have received instruction on the same class or type of aircraft to be used in the test.

2. An applicant shall pass all the relevant sections of the skill test. If any item in a section is failed, that section is failed. Failure in more than one section will require the applicant to take the entire test again. An applicant failing only one section shall only repeat the failed section. Failure in any section of the retest, including those sections that have been passed on a previous attempt, will require the applicant to take the entire test again. All relevant sections of the skill test shall be completed within 6 months. Failure to achieve a pass in all relevant sections of the test in two attempts will require further training.

3. Further training may be required following a failed skill test. There is no limit to the number of skill tests that may be attempted.

CONDUCT OF THE TEST

4. The test is intended to simulate a practical flight. The route to be flown shall be chosen by the examiner. An essential element is the ability of the applicant to plan and conduct the flight from routine briefing material. The applicant shall undertake the flight planning and shall ensure that all equipment and documentation for the execution of the flight are on board. The duration of the flight shall be at least 1 hour.

5. Should the applicant choose to terminate a skill test for reasons considered inadequate by the examiner, the applicant shall retake the entire skill test. If the test is terminated for reasons considered adequate by the examiner, only those sections not completed shall be tested in a further flight.

6. At the discretion of the examiner, any manoeuvre or procedure of the test may be repeated once by the applicant. The examiner may stop the test at any stage if it is considered that the applicant's demonstration of flying skill requires a complete retest.

7. An applicant shall fly the aircraft from a position where the PIC functions can be performed and to carry out the test as if there is no other crew member. The examiner shall take no part in the operation of the aircraft, except when intervention is necessary in the interests of safety or to avoid unacceptable delay to other traffic. Responsibility for the flight shall be allocated in accordance with national regulations.

8. Decision heights/altitude, minimum descent heights/altitudes and missed approach point shall be determined by the applicant and agreed by the examiner.

9. An applicant for an IR shall indicate to the examiner the checks and duties carried out, including the identification of radio facilities. Checks shall be completed in accordance with the authorised checklist for the aircraft on which the test is being taken. During pre-flight preparation for the test the applicant is required to determine power settings and speeds. Performance data for take-off, approach and landing shall be calculated by the applicant in compliance with the operations manual or flight manual for the aircraft used.

FLIGHT TEST TOLERANCES

10. The applicant shall demonstrate the ability to:-
    - *operate the aircraft within its limitations;*
    - *complete all manoeuvres with smoothness and accuracy;*
    - *exercise good judgment and airmanship;*
    - *apply aeronautical knowledge; and*
    - *maintain control of the aircraft at all times in such a manner that the successful outcome of a procedure or manoeuvre is never seriously in doubt.*

8 - APPENDIX 5

11. The following limits shall apply, corrected to make allowance for turbulent conditions and the handling qualities and performance of the aircraft used.

Height
  Generally ±100 feet
  Starting a go-around at decision height/altitude +50 feet/–0 feet
  Minimum descent height/MAP/altitude +50 feet/–0 feet

Tracking
  On radio aids ±5°
  Precision approach half scale deflection, azimuth and glide path

Heading
  All engines operating ±5°
  With simulated engine failure ±10°

Speed
  All engines operating ±5 knots
  With Simulated Engine Failure +10 Knots/–5 Knots

	SECTION 1 — PRE-FLIGHT OPERATIONS AND DEPARTURE Use of checklist, airmanship, anti-icing/de-icing procedures, etc., apply in all sections
a	Use of flight manual (or equivalent) especially a/c performance calculation, mass and balance
b	Use of Air Traffic Services document, weather document
c	Preparation of ATC flight plan, IFR flight plan/log
d	Pre-flight inspection
e	Weather Minima
f	Taxiing
g	Pre-take-off briefing, Take-off
h(°)	Transition to instrument flight
i(°)	Instrument departure procedures, altimeter setting
j(°)	ATC liaison - compliance, R/T procedures
	SECTION 2 — GENERAL HANDLING°
a	Control of the aeroplane by reference solely to instruments, including: level flight at various speeds, trim
b	Climbing and descending turns with sustained Rate 1 turn
c	Recoveries from unusual attitudes, including sustained 45° bank turns and steep descending turns
d(*)	Recovery from approach to stall in level flight, climbing/descending turns and in landing configuration — only applicable to aeroplanes
e	Limited panel: stabilised climb or descent, level turns at Rate 1 onto given headings, recovery from unusual attitudes — only applicable to aeroplanes

PART-FCL IR SKILL TEST

	SECTION 3 — EN-ROUTE IFR PROCEDURES°
a	Tracking, including interception, e.g. NDB, VOR, RNAV
b	Use of radio aids
c	Level flight, control of heading, altitude and airspeed, power setting, trim technique
d	Altimeter settings
e	Timing and revision of ETAs (en-route hold, if required)
f	Monitoring of flight progress, flight log, fuel usage, systems' management
g	Ice protection procedures, simulated if necessary
h	ATC liaison - compliance, R/T procedures
	SECTION 4 — PRECISION APPROACH PROCEDURES°
a	Setting and checking of navigational aids, identification of facilities
b	Arrival procedures, altimeter checks
c	Approach and landing briefing, including descent/approach/landing checks
d(+)	Holding procedure
e	Compliance with published approach procedure
f	Approach timing
g	Altitude, speed heading control (stabilised approach)
h(+)	Go-around action
i(+)	Missed approach procedure/landing
j	ATC liaison – compliance, R/T procedures
	SECTION 5 — NON-PRECISION APPROACH PROCEDURES°
a	Setting and checking of navigational aids, identification of facilities
b	Arrival procedures, altimeter settings
c	Approach and landing briefing, including descent/approach/landing checks
d(+)	Holding procedure
e	Compliance with published approach procedure
f	Approach timing
g	Altitude, speed, heading control (stabilised approach)
h(+)	Go-around action
i(+)	Missed approach procedure/landing
j	ATC liaison – compliance, R/T procedures
	SECTION 6 — FLIGHT WITH ONE ENGINE INOPERATIVE (multi-engine aeroplanes only)°
a	Simulated engine failure after take-off or on go-around
b	Approach, go-around and procedural missed approach with one engine inoperative
c	Approach and landing with one engine inoperative
d	ATC liaison – compliance, R/T procedures

(*) May be performed in an FFS, FTD 2/3 or FNPT II.
(+) May be performed in either section 4 or section 5.
(°) Must be performed by sole reference to instruments.

Common Errors and Omissions

The following are common mistakes that candidates make during the test which can lead to failure:-

- Incorrect altimeter setting procedures
- Failure to check radio navigation equipment on the ground, where possible
- Incorrect pre-flight inspection of anti/de-icing equipment
- Incorrect or lack of use of a checklist
- Poor understanding of Air Law in relation to instrument flight
- Not operating the aircraft in accordance with the AFM
- Failure to check gyroscopic instruments during taxi
- Incorrect use of GNSS equipment including checks before commencing an approach
- Failure to identify radio navigations aids once airborne and failure to monitor them once in use
- Not achieving ETAs within ± 3 minutes
- Poor situational awareness including incorrect MSA calculation
- Poor knowledge of airspace
- Failure to obtain an appropriate ATC clearance
- Poor RTF
- Failure to check the aircraft documents and technical log
- Poor pre-flight planning
- Failure to update the flight log
- Exceeding test tolerances
- Unstabilised approaches

- Incorrect hold entry and subsequent timing
- Exceeding test tolerances in regard to instrument minima
- Incorrect AOM calculation
- Failure to comply with the missed approach procedure
- Failure to fly the instrument approach within test tolerances
- Ignoring aircraft warning and caution systems
- Failure to file an ATC flight plan
- Missing a CTOT
- Failure to sufficiently control the aircraft following a simulated engine failure after take-off
- Failure to correctly trim the aircraft
- Missing ATC instructions and including incorrect read back
- Failure to maintain the correct vertical and horizontal profile of an instrument approach procedure

Skill Test Tolerances

The following is an extract from the Flight Examiners Handbook. Tables for CPL and IR Skill Tests are included for comparison.

(Figures in italics are National Requirements where no JAR guidance is given)

Profile	PPL Skill Test	CPL Skill Test	IR Skill Test & All Revalidations & Renewals
Altitude or Height			
Normal Flight	± 150ft	± 100ft	± 100ft
with Simulated Engine Failure	± 200ft	± 150ft	± 100ft
Limited or Partial Panel		± 200ft	± 200ft
Starting Go-Around at decision Altitude/Height			+ 50ft/- 0ft (SE + 100ft/- 0ft)
Minimum Descent Altitude/Height			+ 50ft/- 0ft (SE + 100ft/- 0ft)
Circling Minima			+ 100ft/- 0ft (SE + 100ft/- 0ft)
Tracking			
All except Precision Approach	± 10°	± 5°	± 5°
Precision Approach			half scale deflection azimuth & glidepath
Heading			
All Engines Operating	± 10°	± 10°	± 5°
With Simulated Engine Failure	± 15°	± 15°	± 10°
Limited or Partial Panel		± 15°	± 15°
Speed			
Take-Off/Vr	+ 10/- 5kt	+5/- 0kt	+ 5/- 0kt
Climb and Approach	± 15kt	± 10kt	± 5kt
Vat/Vref	+ 15/- 5kt	+ 5kt/- 0kt	+ 5kt/- 0kt
Cruise	± 15kt	± 10kt	± 5 kt
Limited or Partial Panel	N/A	± 10kt	± 10kt
With Simulated Engine Failure	+ 15/- 5kt	± 10/- 5kt	± 10/- 5kt
Blue Line Speed or Vyse/V_2	± 5kt	± 5 kt	± 5kt
Maximum Airspeed Error at any time	± 15kt	± 10kt	± 10kt

TABLE FOR CPL & IR SKILL TESTS

intentionally blank

Power & Attitude Settings Table

You may find it useful to enter the appropriate power and attitude values for the various manouvres you will need to fly during the test. These will vary between different aircraft in the training fleet and atmospheric conditions on the day, however, use them as rough settings which can then be refined.

	T/O	CLIMB	DES	CRUISE	INITIAL APP	FINAL APP	G/A
2 ENG PWR & ATT							
1 ENG PWR & ATT							

intentionally blank

8 - ABBREVIATIONS

A

aal	Above Aerodrome Level
ACA(H)	Asymmetric Committal Altitude (Height)
ADF	Automatic Direction Finding
AFIS	Aerodrome Flight Information Service
AFM	Aircraft Flight Manual
AFPEX	Assisted Flight Plan Exchange
AFTN	Aeronautical Fixed Telecommunication Network
AI	Attitude Indicator
AIC	Aeronautical Information Circular
AIP	Aeronautical Information Publication
AIRMET	Airmen's Meteorological Information
AIS	Aeronautical Information Service
ALT	Altimeter
AMC	Acceptable Means of Compliance
ANO	Air Navigation Order
AOC	Air Operators Certificate
AOM	Aerodrome Operating Minima
AOM	Airfield Operating Minima
APV	Approach Procedure with Vertical guidance
ARTE	Above Runway Threshold Elevation
ASDA	Accelerate Stop Distance Available
ASI	Airspeed Indicator
ASI	Airspeed Indicator
ATA	Actual Time of Arrival
ATC	Air Traffic Control
ATO	Approved Training Organisation
ATPL	Airline Transport Pilots Licence
ATS	Air Traffic Service
ATS	Air Traffic Service
ATSU	Air Traffic Service Unit

ABBREVIATIONS

A

ATSU	Air Traffic Service Unit
ATZ	Aerodrome Traffic Zone

B

BECMG	Becoming

C

CAA	Civil Aviation Authority
CAP 413	Civil Aviation Publication 413
CAP 774	Civil Aviation Publication 774
CAP 804	Civil Aviation Publication 804
CAT	Commercial Air Transport
CAVOK	Cloud and Visibility Okay
CDA	Constant Descent Approach
CDFA	Constant Descent Final Approach
CDI	Course Deviation Indicator
COM	Commercial
COM	Communication
CPL	Commercial Pilot's Licence
CRE	Class Rating Examiner
CRI	Class Rating Instructor
CRS	Certificate of Release to Service
CSU	Constant Speed Unit
CTA	Control Area
CTOT	Calculated Take-Off Time
CTR	Control Zone

D

DCT	Direct
DI	Direction Indicator
DME	Distance-Measuring Equipment
DOC	Designated Operational Coverage/Document
DOF	Date of Flight

ABBREVIATIONS A-D

ABBREVIATIONS

E

EASA	European Aviation Safety Agency
EAT	Expected Approach Time
EET	Estimated Elapsed Time
EFATO	Engine Failure After Take Off
ENR	En-Route
EOBT	Estimated Off Blocks Time
EST	Estimated
ETA	Estimated Time of Arrival
ETOPS	Extended Twin Operations
EU-OPS	European Union-Operations
EVS	Enhanced Vision System
EXM	Exam

F

FADEC	Fully Automated Digital Engine Control
FALS	Final Approach Lighting System
FAT	Final Approach Track
FCL	Flight Crew Licensing
FE	Flight Examiner
FI	Flight Instructor
FIC	Flight Instructor Course
FL	Flight Level
FM	From
FMS	Flight Management System
FNPT	Flight and Navigation Procedures Trainer
FOD	Foreign Object Debris
FPL	Flight Plan
FT	Feet
FTO	Flight Training Organisation

ABBREVIATIONS

G

G/S	Ground Speed
GEN	General
GMT	Greenwich Mean Time
GND	Ground Control
GNSS	Global Navigation Satellite System
GPS	Global Positioning System

H

HDG	Heading
HSI	Horizontal Situation Indicator
HUDLS	Head Up Display Landing System

I

IAS	Indicated Airspeed
ICAO	International Civil Aviation Organisation
IFPS	Initial Flight Plan Processing System
IFR	Instrument Flight Rules
ILS	Instrument Landing System
ILS	Instrument Landing System
IMC	Instrument Meteorological Conditions
IR	Instrument Rating
IR'S	Implementing Rules
IRT	Instrument Rating Test
ISA	International Standard Atmosphere

K-L

KT	Knots
LASORS	Licensing and Standards
LDA	Landing Distance Available
LDR	Landing Distance Required
LLZ	Localiser
LVP	Low Visibility Procedures

ABBREVIATIONS G-L

ABBREVIATIONS

M

MAG	Magnetic
MATZ	Military Aerodrome Traffic Zone
MDA(H)	Minimum Descent Altitude(Height)
MEA	Minimum En-route Altitude
MEF	Maximum Elevation Figure
MEL	Minimum Equipment List
MEP	Multi-Engine Piston Rating
METAR	Meteorological Actual Report
MIN	Minute
MLS	Microwave Landing System
MOCA	Minimum Obstacle Clearance Altitude
MOR	Mandatory Occurrence Report
MORA	Minimum Off Route Altitude
MSA	Minimum Safe Altitude

N

NADP	Noise Abatement Departure Procedure
NANUS	Notice Advisories to NAVSTAR Users
NAP	Noise Abatement Procedure
NAV	Navigation
NDB	Non-Directional Beacon
NM	Nautical mile
NOTAM	Notice to Airmen
NPA	Non-Precision Approach

O

OAT	Outside Air Temperature
OBS	Omni Bearing Selector
OCH	Obstacle Clearance Height
OPR	Operator
OPS	Operations

ABBREVIATIONS

P

P2	Co-pilot
PAPI	Precision Approach Path Indicator
PEC	Precision Error Correction
PIC u/s	Pilot-in-Command under supervision
PIC	Pilot-in-Command
PLOG	Pilot's Log
POB	Persons On Board
POH	Pilots Operating Handbook
PPL	Private Pilot's Licence
PPR	Prior Permission Required

Q

QDM	Magnetic bearing to facility
QDR	Magnetic bearing from facility
QFE	Height above airport elevation
QNE	Altimeter setting 1013.2 hPa or 29.92" Hg
QNH	Altitude above sea level based on local pressure
QTE	True bearing from facility

R

RAIM	Receiver autonomous integrity monitoring
R/T, RTF	Radiotelephony
RBI	Radio Bearing Indicator
RCLL	Runway Centreline Lighting
REG	Registration
RMI	Radio Magnetic Indicator
RMK	Remark
RNAV	Area Navigation
ROD	Rate Of Descent
RPS	Regional Pressure Setting
RTZL	Runway Touchdown Zone Lighting

ABBREVIATIONS

R

RVR	Runway Visual Range	
RWY	Runway	

S

SEP	Single Engine Piston	
SID	Standard Instrument Departure	
SPA	Special Approval	
SPS	Standard Pressure Setting	
SRD	Standard Route Document	

T

TA	Transition Altitude	
TAF	Terminal Area Forecast	
TAS	True Air Speed	
TCAS	Traffic Collision Avoidance System	
TEMPO	Temporarily	
TMA	Terminal Manoeuvring Area	
TODA	Take off Distance Available	
TODR	Take off Distance Required	
TORA	Take off Run Available	
TRA	Temporary Restricted Area	
TWR	Tower	
TWY	Taxiway	

U-V

UTC	Coordinated Universal Time	

VDF	VHF Direction Finding	
VFE	Velocity Flap Extension	
VFR	Visual Flight Rules	
VHF	Very High Frequency	
VLO	Velocity Landing Gear Operation	
VLR	Velocity Landing Gear Retraction	

ABBREVIATIONS

V

VMC	Visual Meteorological Conditions
VMCA	Velocity Minimum Control Airspeed
VOLMET	Meteorological information for aircraft in flight
VOR	Very High Frequency Omnidirectional Range
VREF	Velocity Reference
VRP	Visual Reporting Point
VSI	Vertical Speed Indicator
VX	Velocity Best Angle of Climb
VXSE	Velocity Best Angle of Climb Single Engine
VY	Velocity Best Rate of Climb
VYSE	Velocity Best Rate of Climb Single Engine

W

W/V	Wind Velocity
WX	Weather

Z

Z	Zulu Time/Universal Coordinated Time

Index

A

Abbreviations 193
Abnormal operations 161
Aerodrome Operating Minima (AOM) 26, 27, 166, 171
Aeronautical Fixed Telecommunication Network (AFTN) 14
AFPEx 14
After take off checks 39
AIC 106/2004 60
AIP 26, 28
AIP ENR1.1 157
Aircraft 2, 5
Aircraft category 138
Aircraft Flight Manual (AFM) 10
Airfield Contact 177
Airframe Icing 60
AIRMET 60
Airport marking and signals 33
Air Traffic Services document and Weather document 11
Airway charts 11, 48, 49
Altimeter Setting Procedures 54
Altimetry 163, 169
Altitude Correction Table 73
Anti-icing and de-icing procedures 37, 59
Approach and landing briefing 119
Approach ban 28
Approach briefing 71, 74
Approach checks 69, 124
Approach timing 77, 142
Approvals 2
Arrival procedures 64, 118
Asymmetric approach 156
Asymmetric approach and full stop landing 155
Asymmetric approach and landing 155
Asymmetric approach and procedural go-around 154
Asymmetric Committal Altitude (ACA) 155
Asymmetric go-around 154
ATC 54
ATC abnormal procedures 156

ATC clearance 35
ATC flight plan 14
ATC instructions and clearances 137
ATC Liaison 81, 146, 156
ATC Service Principles Outside Controlled Airspace 66
ATC speed restrictions 78
ATIS Frequencies 52
ATO - Approved Training Organisation 2
ATSU 66
Autopilot 52, 53
Auto-tune facility 52

B

Barometric altimeter errors 71
Base Turn 134
Basic Area Navigation (B-RNAV) 50
Basic Service 66
Briefing 6, 23
B-RNAV Basic Area Navigation 50

C

CA48 ATC Flight Plan 17
CAA Document 31 2
Calculated Take Off Time (CTOT) 31
Calculating timed turns 106
Calculation of Aerodrome Operating Minima 179
CAP 413 61, 71
CAP 694 14
CAP 773 116
CDFA technique 121, 123
Choosing an Approved Training Organisation (ATO) 2
Circling Approach Profile 137, 141
Circling manoeuvre 155
Circling Procedure 139
Clearance limit 64
Climb checks 45
Clockcode 37
Cold weather altimeter corrections 71, 72
Common Errors and Omissions 187

Compass & OBS/ADF 106
Conduct of the Test 183
Constant Descent Final Approach (CDFA) 28
Continuous Descent Approach (CDA) 69
Course Structure 4
Crosswind 36

D

Dead reckoning 51
Deconfliction Service 67, 68, 83
De-icing truck 21
Departure 9
Departure Plates 41
Designated Operational Coverage (DOC) 51
Destination Alternate 29
Destination Minima 27
Direct routing 50, 51
Documentation 23

E

EAFTO checklist 154
EAT 125
EFIS 47, 91
Electronic planning software 48
Engine Failure after Take Off 153
En-route planning minima 29
Estimated Off Blocks Time (EOBT) 17, 31
ETA 56
EU-OPS 1.295 (b) 27
EU-OPS 1.430 121
EUROCONTROL 31, 48
Examiner Briefing 6
Expected Approach Time (EAT) 124

F

Facilities 2
FCL.620 IR(A) Skill Test 5
FCL.625.A IR (A) Revalidation 5
FCL.625 IR(A) Validity, Revalidation & Renewal 4
Flight log 11

Index

Flight plan 11
Flight planned route 17
Flight Planning 164, 170
Flights Joining Airways 43
Flight Test Tolerances 184
FMS 50
Fuel check 57
Fuel gauges 57
Fuel Required 18

G

Gate position 131
General Handling 83
GNSS approach plate 116
Go-around 78
Go-around/landing 146
GPS 32, 50, 51, 115, 116
GPS 'GOTO' function 50
Grid MORA 55

H

HASELL check 90
HELL 90
Hold en-route 57
Holding pattern 124
Holding procedures 74, 124
Holding speed 125
Holdover time 22

I

IAF 63
Ice accretion rate 59
Ice accumulation 61
Ice check 45
Ice inspection lights 46
Ice precautions 45
Ice protection equipment 21
Ice protection procedures 59
Icing 166, 172
Icing conditions 37, 60
IFR diversion 63

ILS Approach Profile 76
ILS Frequency 63
Initial Briefing 6
Instructors 2
Instrument approach plates 11
Instrument departure procedure 40
Instrument Flight Rules 19
Instrument flying screens 38
Instrument-rated minima for
 a 2D approach 180
Instrument-rated minima for
 a 3D approach 179
Interception procedures 158
IRT profiles 146
IRT Skill Test Profile 6

J

Joining a Holding Pattern 125
Joining an airway from controlled
 airspace via a SID 42
Joining an airway from uncontrolled
 airspace 43

L

Landing performance 19
Level bust 54
Level flight control 53
Limited Panel 91
Low Visibility Procedures (LVPs) 33, 34

M

Mandatory Occurrence Report (MOR) 54
MAYDAY 156
MEA - The Minimum En-route Altitude 55
MEL - Minimum Equipment List 10, 24
Minimum rate of climb/descent 54
Missed approach 63, 81
Missed approach altitude 80
Missed approach procedure/landing 80
MOCA - Minimum Obstacle Clearance
 Altitude 55

MORA - Minimum Off Route Altitude 55, 118
Morse Identifier 63
MSA - the Minimum Sector Altitude 54, 55, 56, 118

N

NAP - 2D Approach (NPA) 120
Navigation Aids 42, 63, 115
Navigation Log 13, 48, 56
Noise Routing 42
NOTAMs/TRAs 11
NPA -2D Approach 28, 63

O

Operations Manual 9, 10
Oral Questioning 163

P

PAN 156
Passenger briefing 36
PEC - Precision Error Correction 28, 71, 122
Performance 18
Pilots Log or PLOG 13
Pneumatic boot de-icing system 21
Position report 58
Power & Attitude Settings Table 191
Pre-Course Experience 3
Pre-Course Revision 1
Pre-flight Briefing 7
Pre-flight Inspection 20, 21
Preparation 1
Pre-planned diversion 83
Pre take-off briefing 36
Privileges 4
Procedural approach 124
Procedural Service 58, 68
Procedure Turns 132, 133
Promulgated range 51
Protected area 128
Published approach procedure 74, 136
Published holds 132

Index

Q

Quadrantal Rule 83

R

Racetrack Pattern 134
Radar vectoring chart 68
Radar vectors 63
Radio failure 125, 156, 157
Radio navigation position fix 118
RAIM 117
Range checks 143
Reputation 2
Revalidation 4, 5
RNAV 57, 66, 115
RNAV/GPS waypoints 132
Route briefing 7
RTF 165, 171
RTF procedures 61
Runway incursion hotspots 34

S

Sector 1 Entry 125
Sector 2 Entry 126
Sector 3 Entry 126
SE ILS 63
Signals Initiated by Intercepting Aircraft 159, 160
Simulated Asymmetric Flight 153, 163
Simulated engine failure 63
Simulated engine failure after take-off 153
Single needle tracking 47, 115
Single pilot operations 122
Situational awareness 70, 83, 118
Skill Test Tolerances 42, 189
Stable approach 77
Stall in level flight 90
Standard Route Document 48
Standard routings 48
Standards Document 1 8
Standby conventional instruments 92
STAR - Standard Instrument Arrival 63, 64

Steep Descending Turns 88, 89
Steep Level Turn 84, 85, 87

T

Take-off alternate 26
Take-off technique 39
Taxi chart 34
Taxying 31
Technical Log 10, 23
Test Day Checklist 181
Timings & ETAs 56
Tolerances 53, 74, 167, 172
Touch drills 154
Tracking 47
Track miles 70
Traffic separation 68
Traffic Service 67
Training location 2
Training Manual 10
Transition altitude 55, 83
Transition to instrument flight 39
Transponder code 66
Turning point 57
Typical 2D Approach Procedure 120
Typical Test Routes 173

U

UK AIP 51
UK SRD 48
Unusual attitudes 84, 91, 107
Use of radio aids 51

V

Validity 4
Vectors to Final 70
Vyse 155

W

Weather documents 11
Weather minima 26
Weather radar 44
Weeping wing ice protection system 21
Wind correction 128
Wind in the hold 129

Z

Zero thrust 154